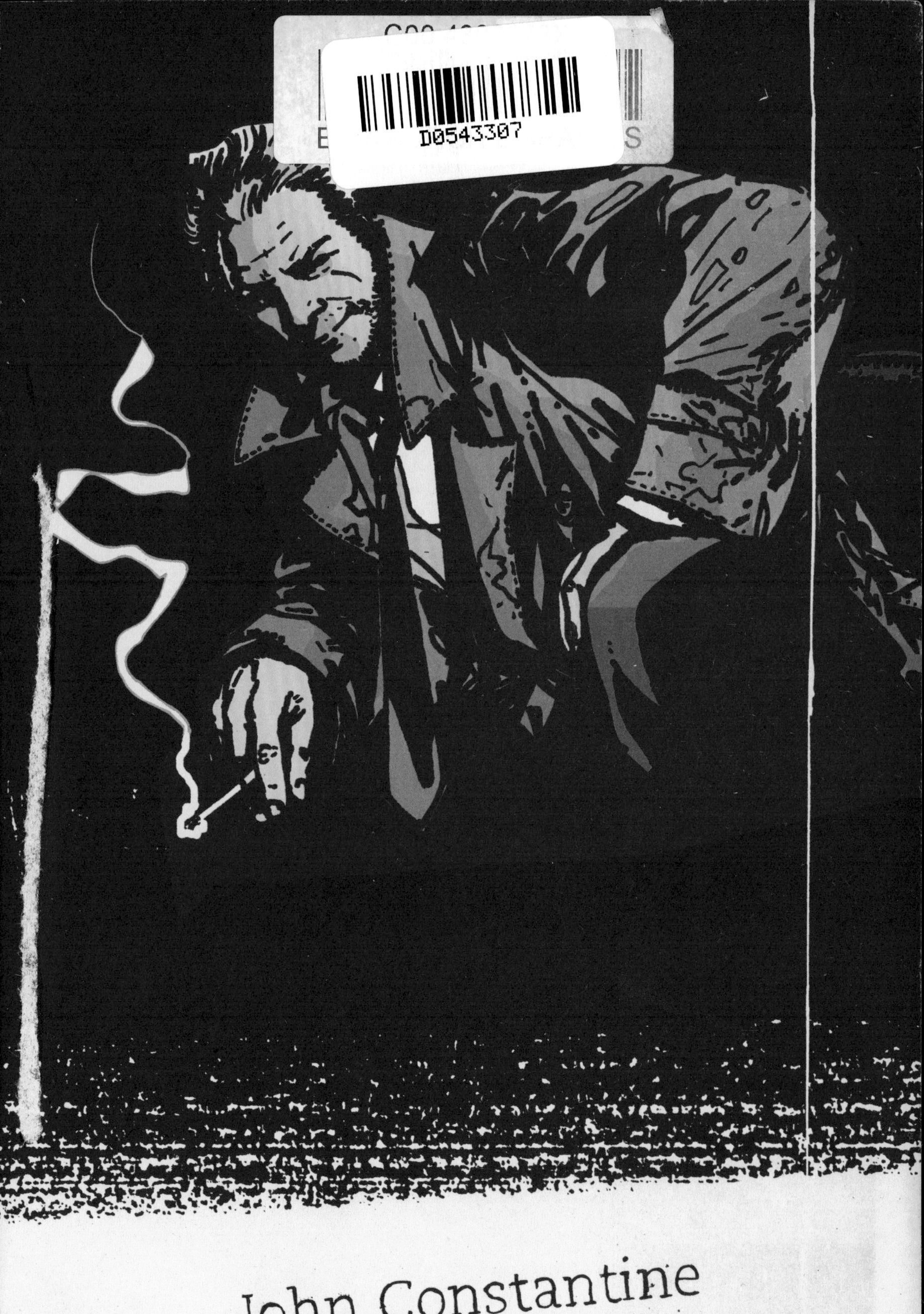

John Constantine

HELLBLAZER

The Red Right Hand

John Constantine
HELLBL
The Red Right Hand

Denise Mina-writer

Leonardo Manco-The Red Right Hand
Cristiano Cucina-The Season of The Zealot
Artists

Lee Loughridge-colorist
Jared K. Fletcher-letterer
Lee Bermejo-Original Series Covers

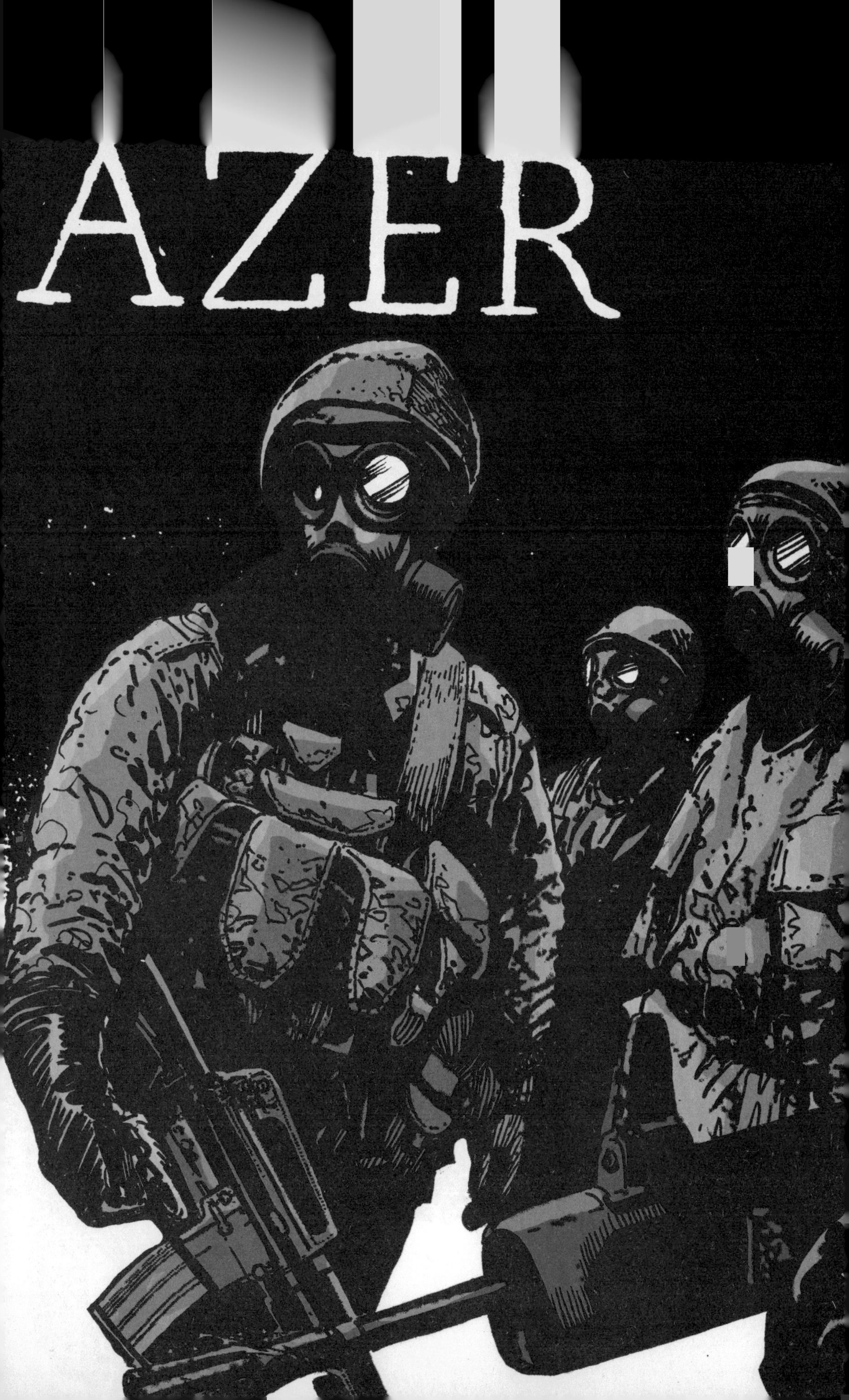
AZER

Karen Berger, Senior VP-Executive Editor

Jonathan Vankin, Editor-original series

Casey Seijas, Assistant Editor-original series

Bob Harras, Editor-collected edition

Robbin Brosterman, Senior Art Director

Paul Levitz, President & Publisher

Georg Brewer, VP-Design & DC Direct Creative

Richard Bruning, Senior VP-Creative Director

Patrick Caldon, Executive VP-Finance & Operations

Chris Caramalis, VP-Finance

John Cunningham, VP-Marketing

Terri Cunningham, VP-Managing Editor

Alison Gill, VP-Manufacturing

Hank Kanalz, VP-General Manager, WildStorm

Jim Lee, Editorial Director-WildStorm

Paula Lowitt, Senior VP-Business & Legal Affairs

MaryEllen McLaughlin, VP-Advertising & Custom Publishing

John Nee, VP-Business Development

Gregory Noveck, Senior VP-Creative Affairs

Sue Pohja, VP-Book Trade Sales

Cheryl Rubin, Senior VP-Brand Management

Jeff Trojan, VP-Business Development, DC Direct

Bob Wayne, VP-Sales

Cover illustration by Lee Bermejo.

JOHN CONSTANTINE: HELLBLAZER: THE RED RIGHT HAND
Published by DC Comics. Cover and compilation copyright ©
2007 DC Comics. All Rights Reserved. Originally published in
single magazine form as HELLBLAZER 223-228 Copyright ©
2006, 2007 DC Comics. All Rights Reserved. VERTIGO and all
characters, their distinctive likenesses and related elements
featured in this publication are trademarks of DC Comics. The
stories, characters and incidents featured in this publication
are entirely fictional. DC Comics does not read or accept
unsolicited submissions of ideas, stories or artwork.
DC Comics, 1700 Broadway, New York, NY 10019. A Warner
Bros. Entertainment Company. Printed in Canada.
First Printing. ISBN:1-4012-1342-1. ISBN 13: 978-1-4012-1342-8

THE SEASON OF THE ZEALOT

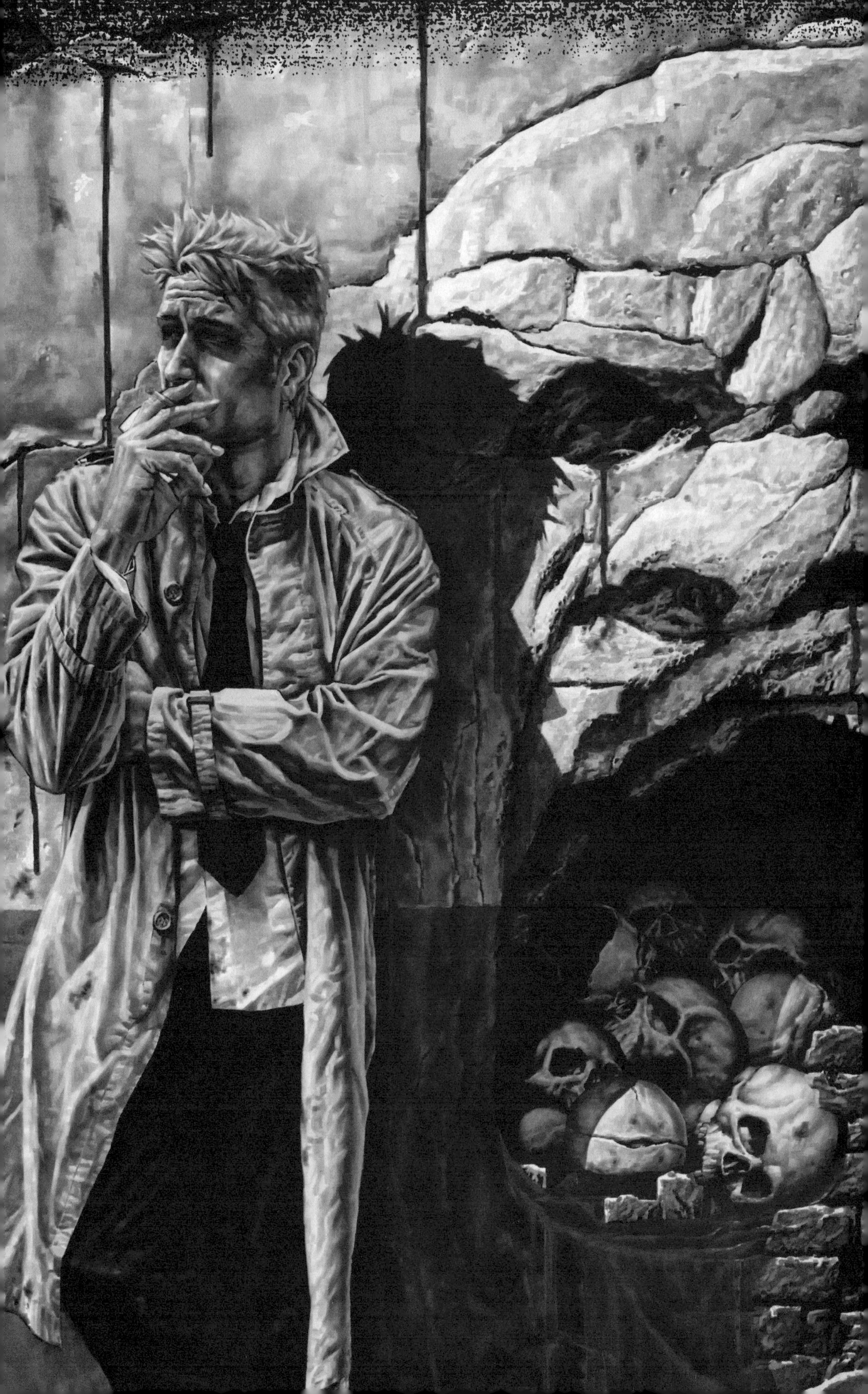

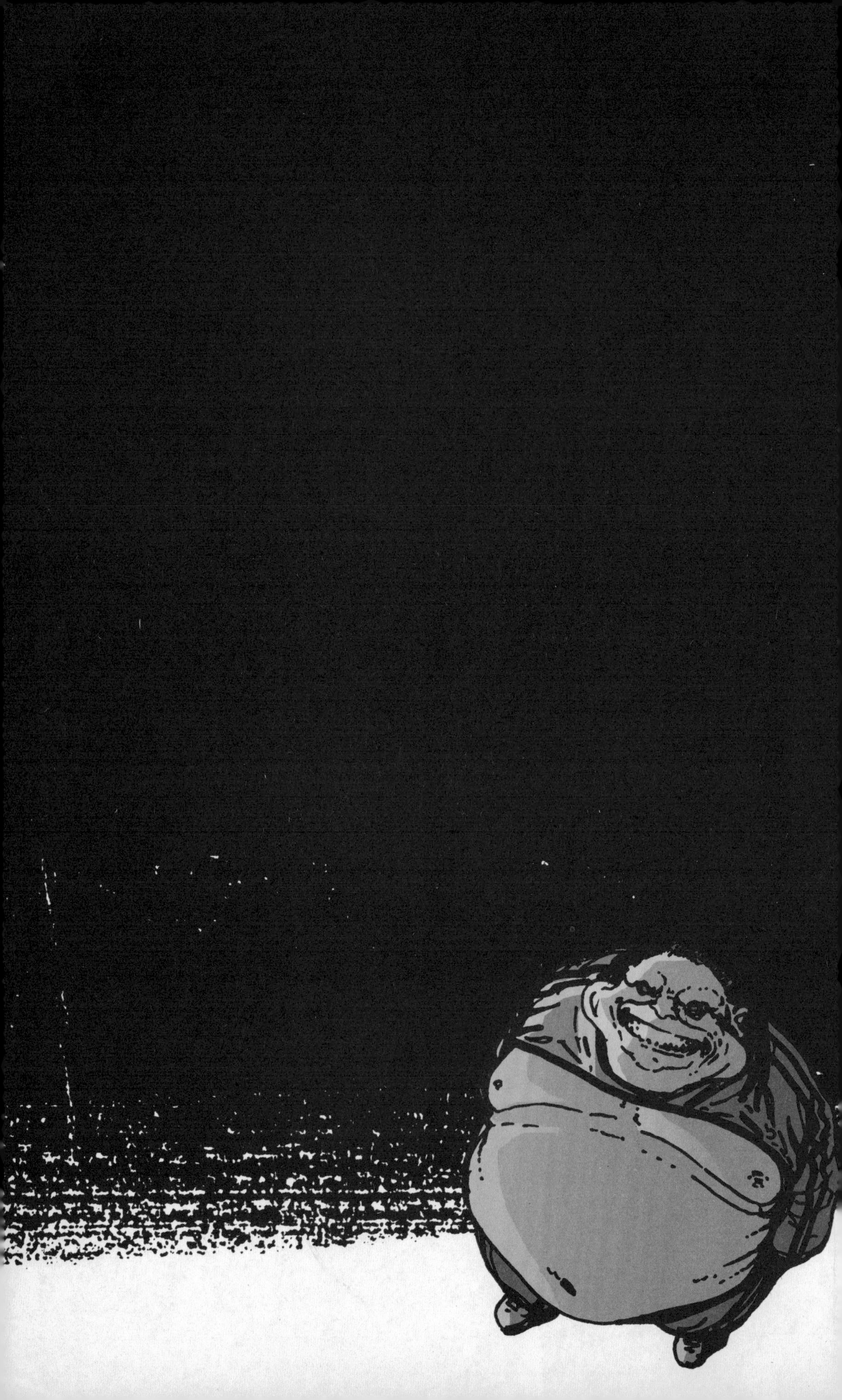

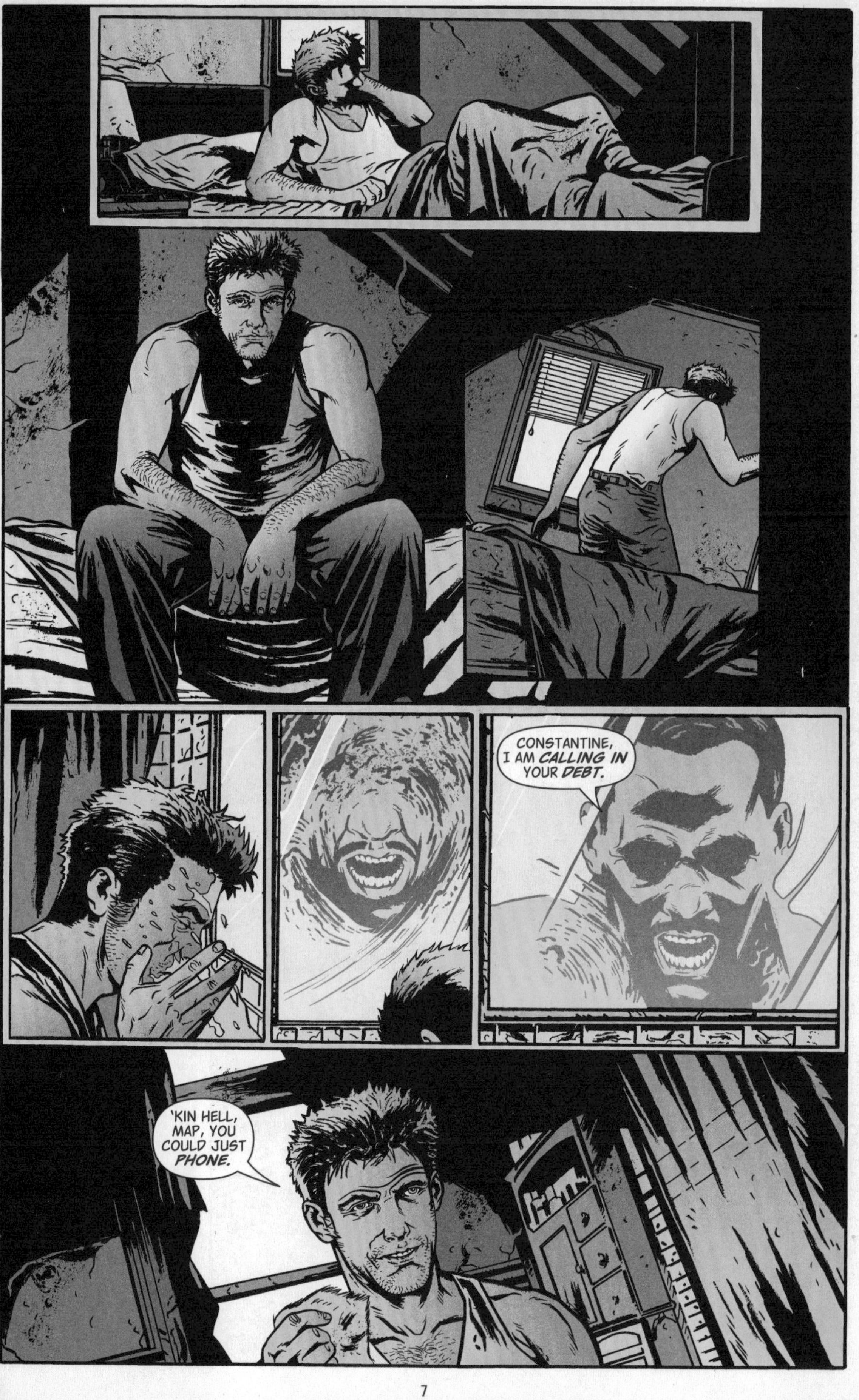
CONSTANTINE, I AM *CALLING IN* YOUR *DEBT*.
'KIN HELL, MAP, YOU COULD JUST *PHONE*.

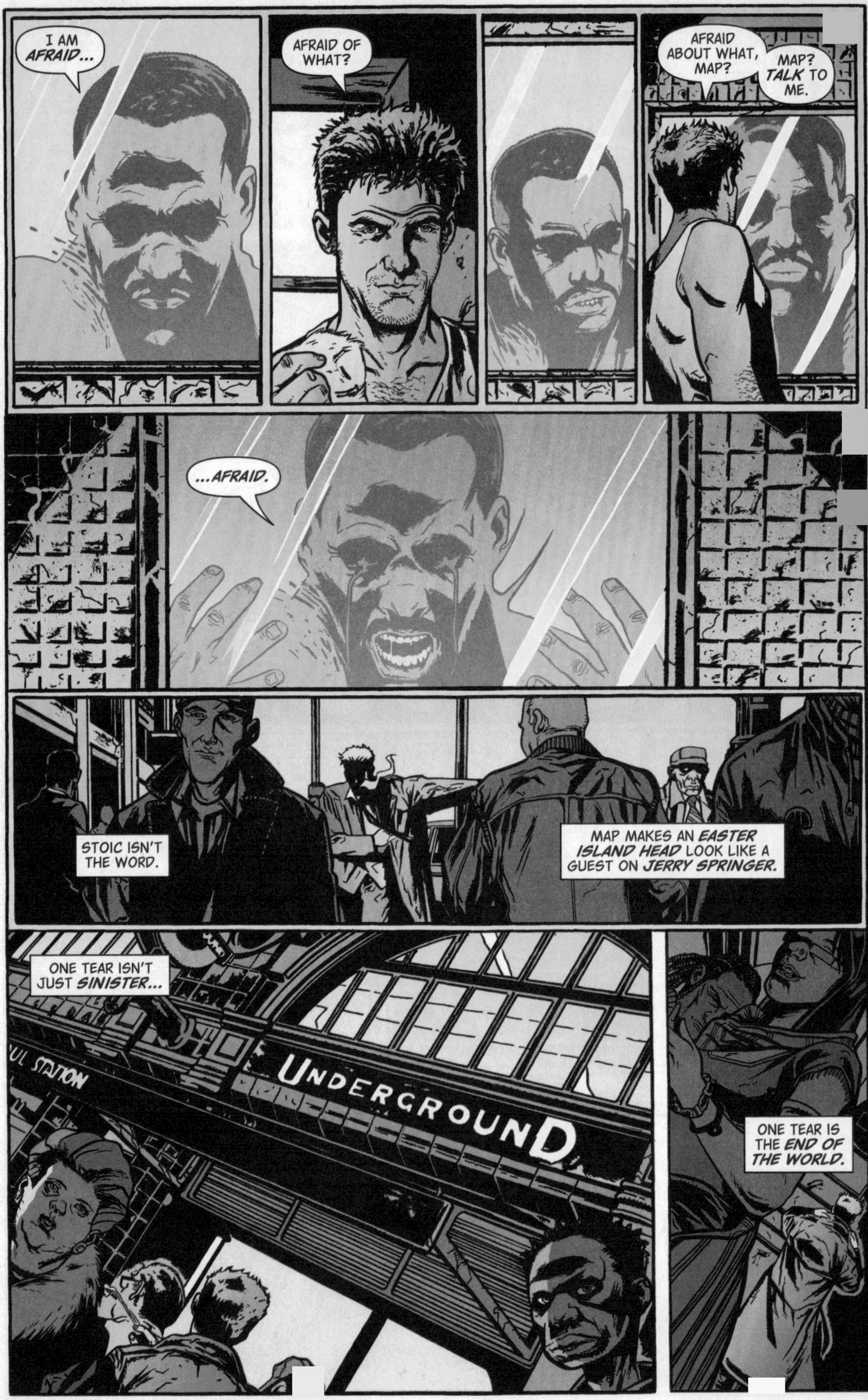
I AM AFRAID...
AFRAID OF WHAT?
AFRAID ABOUT WHAT, MAP?
MAP? TALK TO ME.
...AFRAID.
STOIC ISN'T THE WORD.
MAP MAKES AN EASTER ISLAND HEAD LOOK LIKE A GUEST ON JERRY SPRINGER.
ONE TEAR ISN'T JUST SINISTER...
UNDERGROUND
ONE TEAR IS THE END OF THE WORLD.

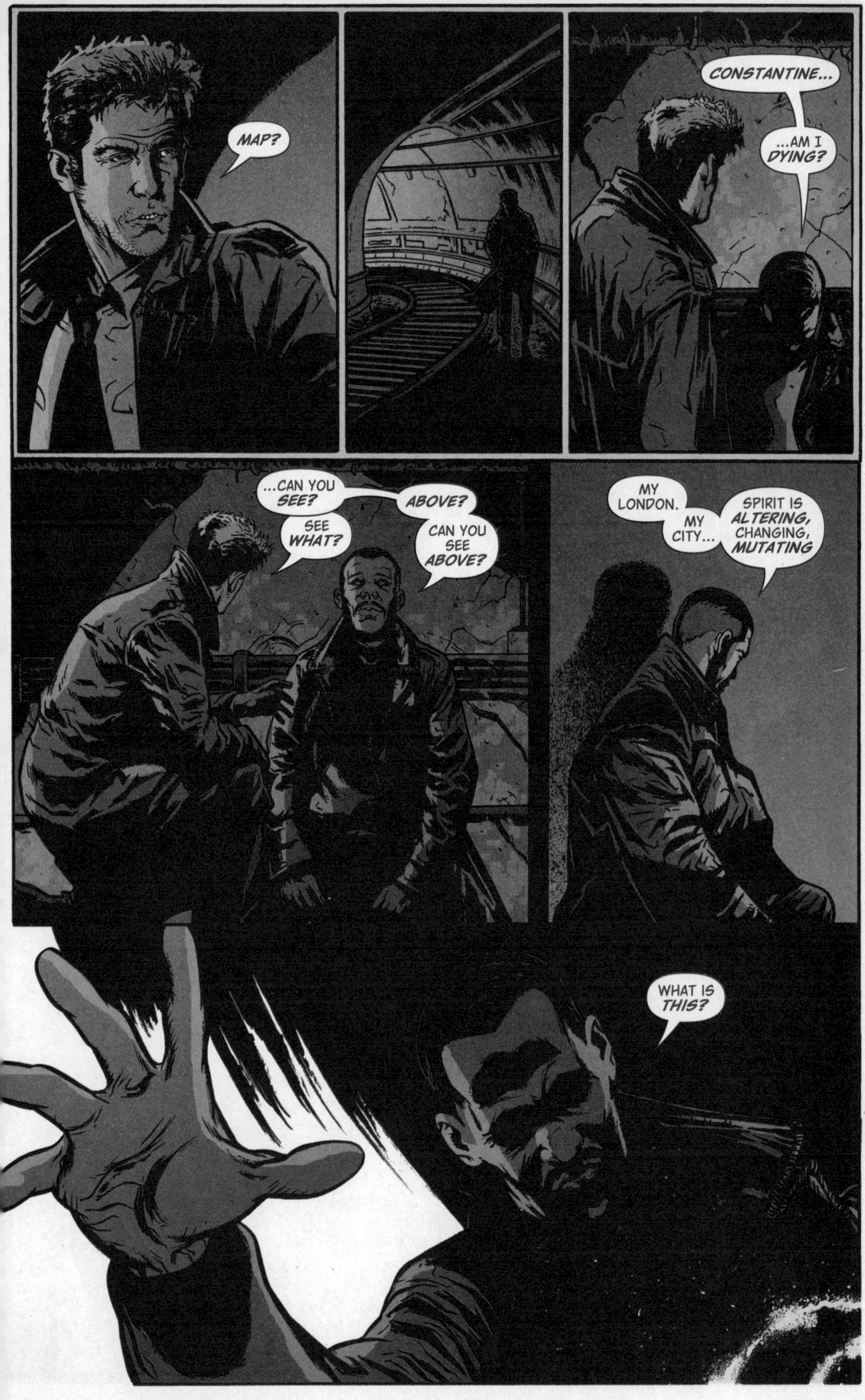
MAP?
CONSTANTINE...
...AM I DYING?
...CAN YOU SEE?
SEE WHAT?
ABOVE?
CAN YOU SEE ABOVE?
MY LONDON.
MY CITY...
SPIRIT IS ALTERING, CHANGING, MUTATING
WHAT IS THIS?

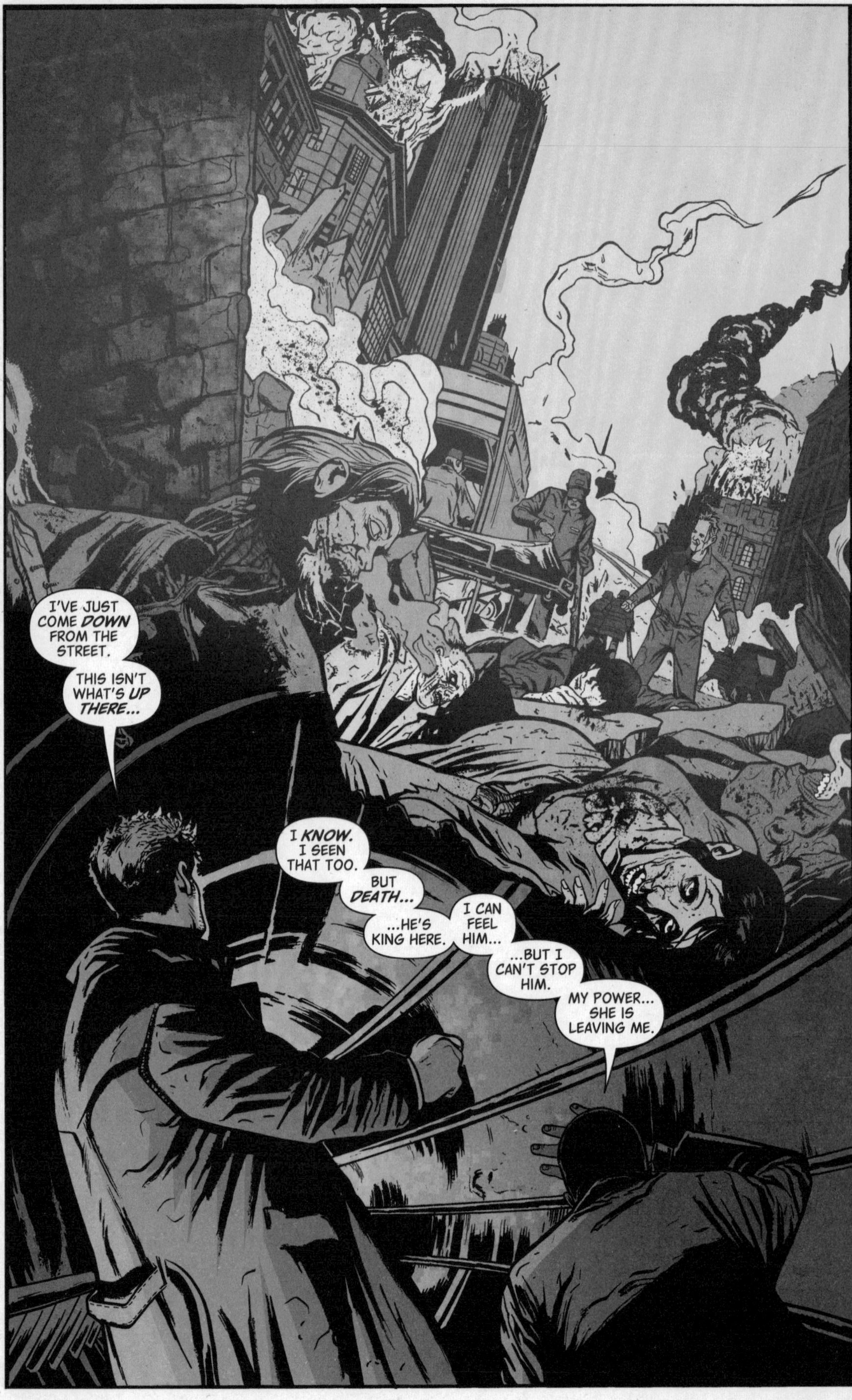

I'VE JUST COME DOWN FROM THE STREET.
THIS ISN'T WHAT'S UP THERE...
I KNOW. I SEEN THAT TOO.
BUT DEATH...
...HE'S KING HERE.
I CAN FEEL HIM...
...BUT I CAN'T STOP HIM.
MY POWER... SHE IS LEAVING ME.

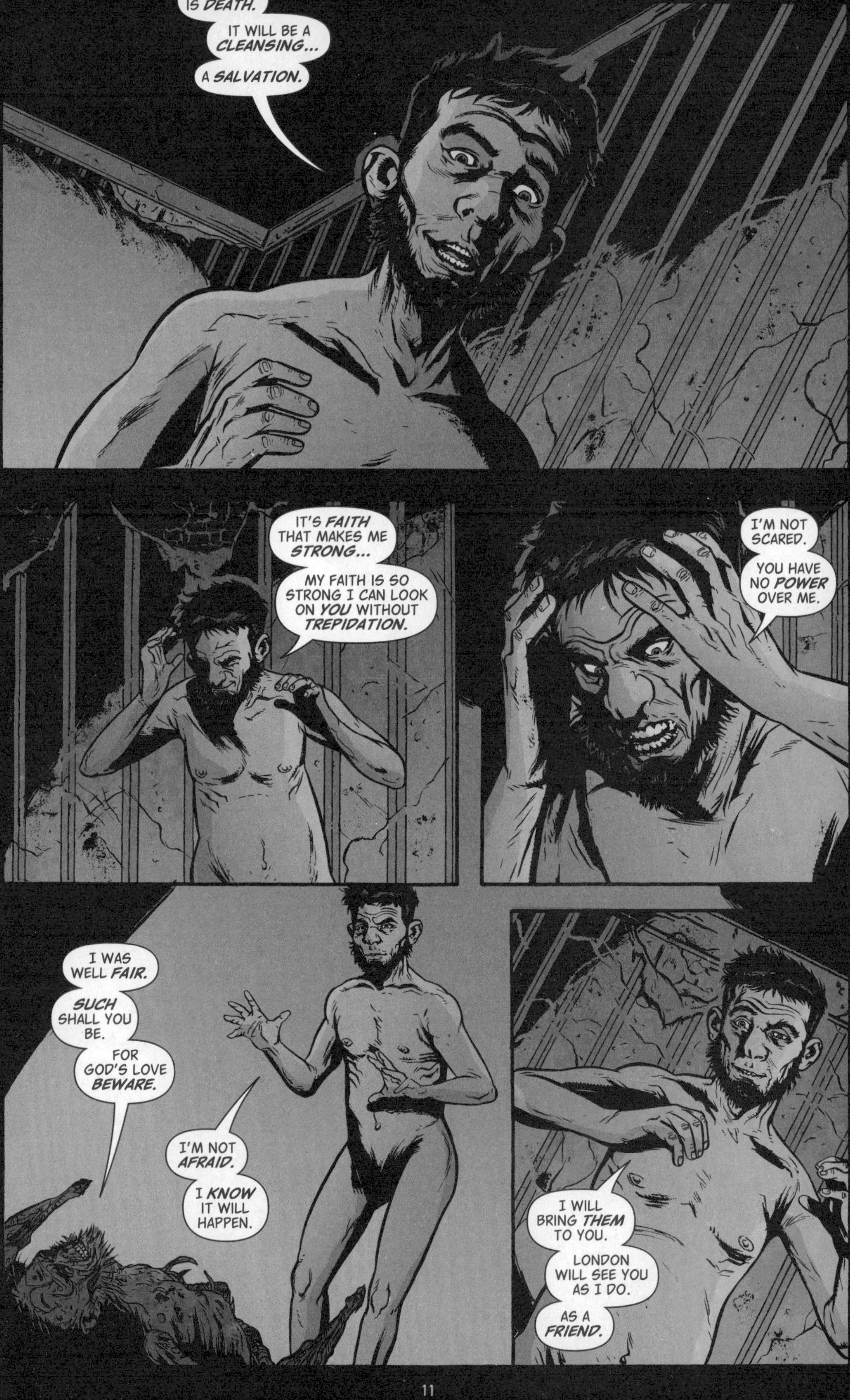
MY GIFT IS DEATH.
IT WILL BE A CLEANSING...
A SALVATION.
IT'S FAITH THAT MAKES ME STRONG...
MY FAITH IS SO STRONG I CAN LOOK ON YOU WITHOUT TREPIDATION.
I'M NOT SCARED.
YOU HAVE NO POWER OVER ME.
I WAS WELL FAIR.
SUCH SHALL YOU BE.
FOR GOD'S LOVE BEWARE.
I'M NOT AFRAID.
I KNOW IT WILL HAPPEN.
I WILL BRING THEM TO YOU.
LONDON WILL SEE YOU AS I DO.
AS A FRIEND.

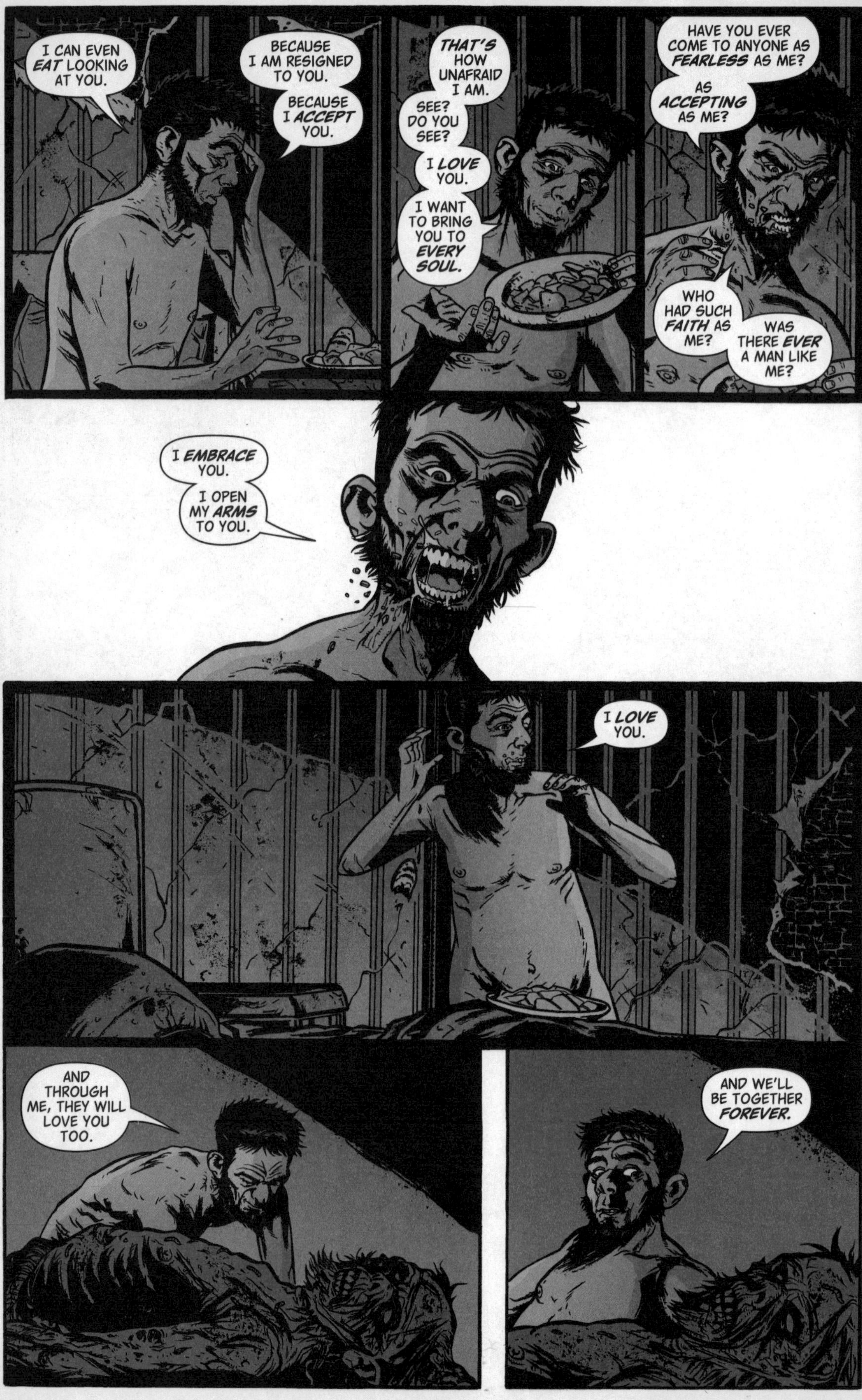
I CAN EVEN EAT LOOKING AT YOU.
BECAUSE I AM RESIGNED TO YOU.
BECAUSE I ACCEPT YOU.
THAT'S HOW UNAFRAID I AM.
SEE? DO YOU SEE?
I LOVE YOU.
I WANT TO BRING YOU TO EVERY SOUL.
HAVE YOU EVER COME TO ANYONE AS FEARLESS AS ME?
AS ACCEPTING AS ME?
WHO HAD SUCH FAITH AS ME?
WAS THERE EVER A MAN LIKE ME?
I EMBRACE YOU.
I OPEN MY ARMS TO YOU.
I LOVE YOU.
AND THROUGH ME, THEY WILL LOVE YOU TOO.
AND WE'LL BE TOGETHER FOREVER.

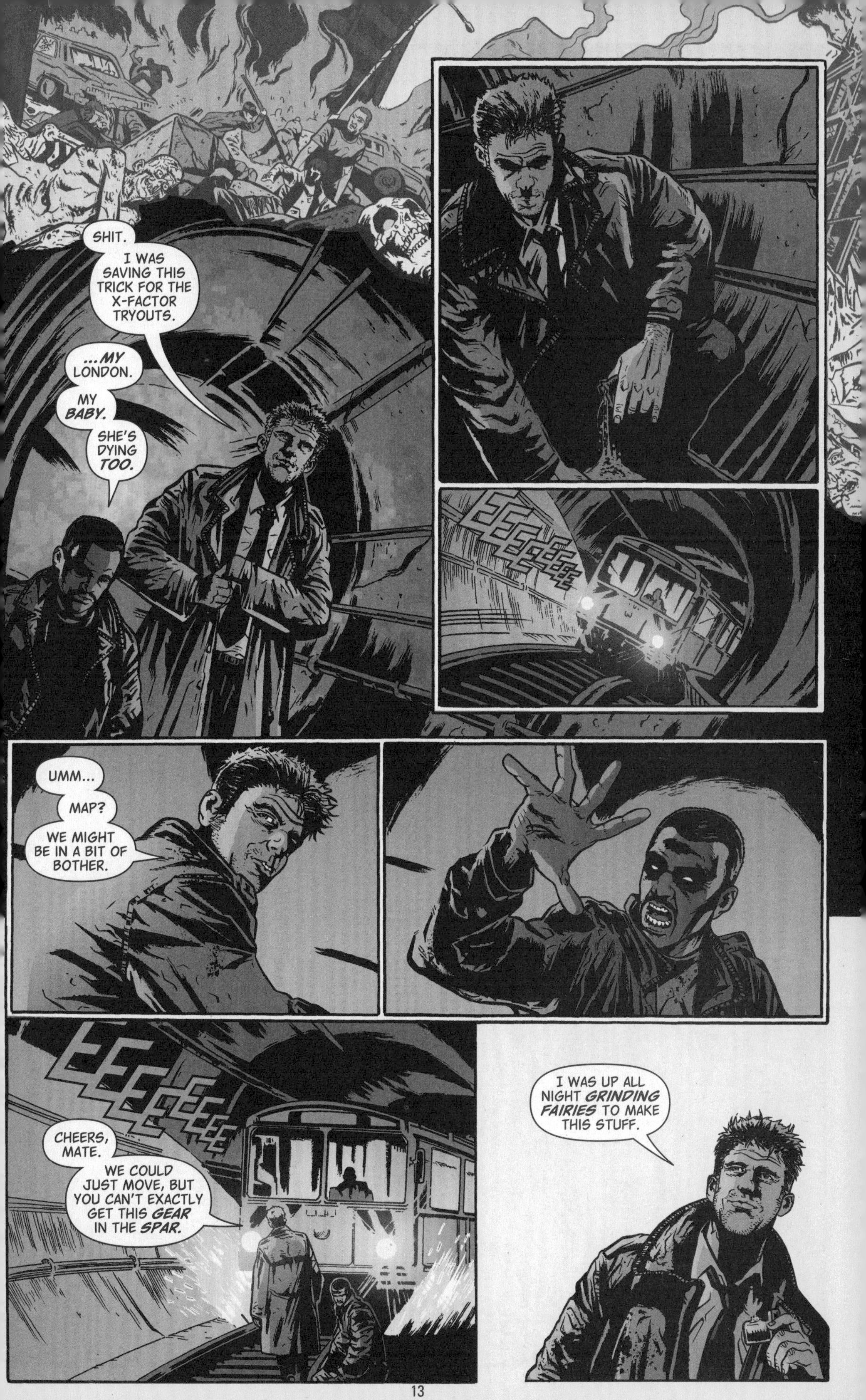

SHIT.
I WAS SAVING THIS TRICK FOR THE X-FACTOR TRYOUTS.
...MY LONDON.
MY BABY.
SHE'S DYING TOO.
UMM...
MAP?
WE MIGHT BE IN A BIT OF BOTHER.
CHEERS, MATE.
WE COULD JUST MOVE, BUT YOU CAN'T EXACTLY GET THIS GEAR IN THE SPAR.
I WAS UP ALL NIGHT GRINDING FAIRIES TO MAKE THIS STUFF.

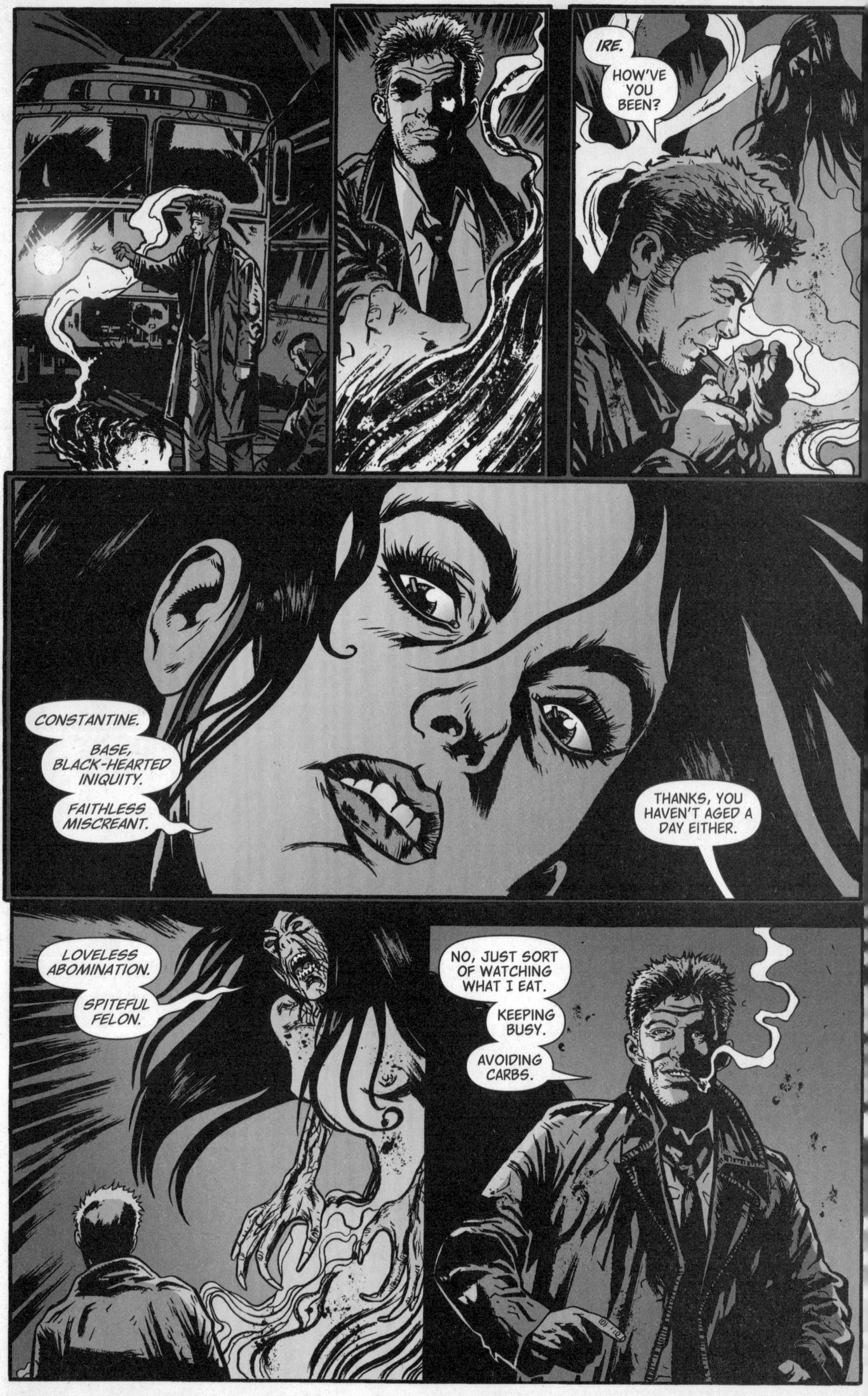
IRE.
HOW'VE YOU BEEN?
CONSTANTINE.
BASE, BLACK-HEARTED INIQUITY.
FAITHLESS MISCREANT.
THANKS, YOU HAVEN'T AGED A DAY EITHER.
LOVELESS ABOMINATION.
SPITEFUL FELON.
NO, JUST SORT OF WATCHING WHAT I EAT.
KEEPING BUSY.
AVOIDING CARBS.

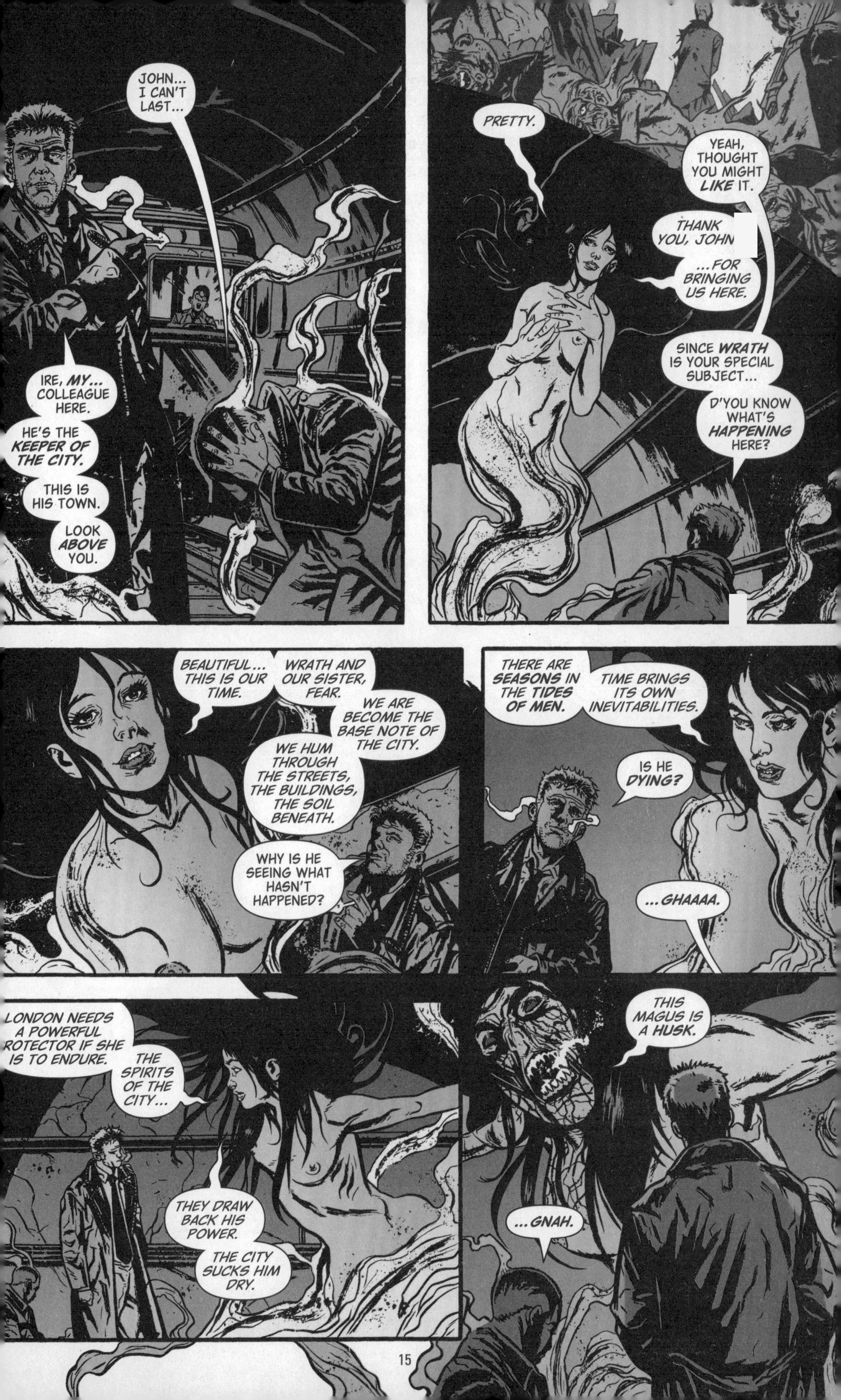
JOHN... I CAN'T LAST...
IRE, MY... COLLEAGUE HERE.
HE'S THE KEEPER OF THE CITY.
THIS IS HIS TOWN.
LOOK ABOVE YOU.
PRETTY.
YEAH, THOUGHT YOU MIGHT LIKE IT.
THANK YOU, JOHN
...FOR BRINGING US HERE.
SINCE WRATH IS YOUR SPECIAL SUBJECT...
D'YOU KNOW WHAT'S HAPPENING HERE?
BEAUTIFUL... THIS IS OUR TIME.
WRATH AND OUR SISTER, FEAR.
WE ARE BECOME THE BASE NOTE OF THE CITY.
WE HUM THROUGH THE STREETS, THE BUILDINGS, THE SOIL BENEATH.
WHY IS HE SEEING WHAT HASN'T HAPPENED?
THERE ARE SEASONS IN THE TIDES OF MEN.
TIME BRINGS ITS OWN INEVITABILITIES.
IS HE DYING?
...GHAAAA.
LONDON NEEDS A POWERFUL ROTECTOR IF SHE IS TO ENDURE.
THE SPIRITS OF THE CITY...
THEY DRAW BACK HIS POWER.
THE CITY SUCKS HIM DRY.
THIS MAGUS IS A HUSK.
...GNAH.

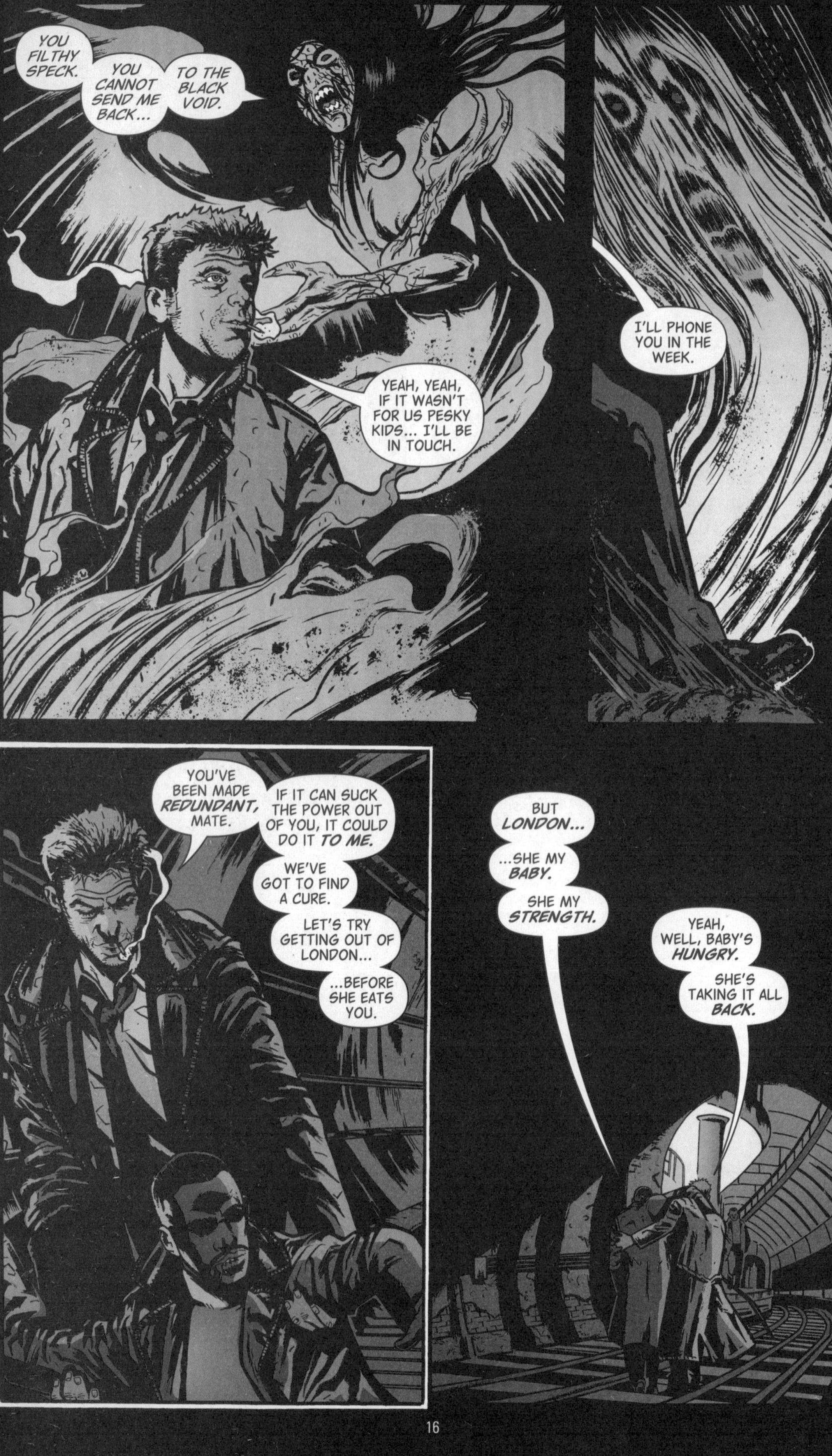
YOU FILTHY SPECK.
YOU CANNOT SEND ME BACK...
TO THE BLACK VOID.
YEAH, YEAH, IF IT WASN'T FOR US PESKY KIDS... I'LL BE IN TOUCH.
I'LL PHONE YOU IN THE WEEK.
YOU'VE BEEN MADE REDUNDANT, MATE.
IF IT CAN SUCK THE POWER OUT OF YOU, IT COULD DO IT TO ME.
WE'VE GOT TO FIND A CURE.
LET'S TRY GETTING OUT OF LONDON...
...BEFORE SHE EATS YOU.
BUT LONDON...
...SHE MY BABY.
SHE MY STRENGTH.
YEAH, WELL, BABY'S HUNGRY.
SHE'S TAKING IT ALL BACK.

YOU WEIGH A FUCKING TON.

I'S DYING.

THAT'S NO EXCUSE.

TAXI!

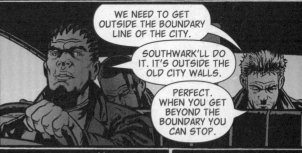

WE NEED TO GET OUTSIDE THE BOUNDARY LINE OF THE CITY.

SOUTHWARK'LL DO IT. IT'S OUTSIDE THE OLD CITY WALLS.

PERFECT. WHEN YOU GET BEYOND THE BOUNDARY YOU CAN STOP.

HOSPITAL?

SOUTH, MATE, FAST AS YOU CAN.

SURE YOU DON'T WANT A HOSPITAL?

THE OLD FATHER LOOKS IN A BAD WAY.

JUST KEEP DRIVING.

WHAT'S WRONG WITH HIM?

DEAD DRUNK.

JUST LOST HIS JOB.

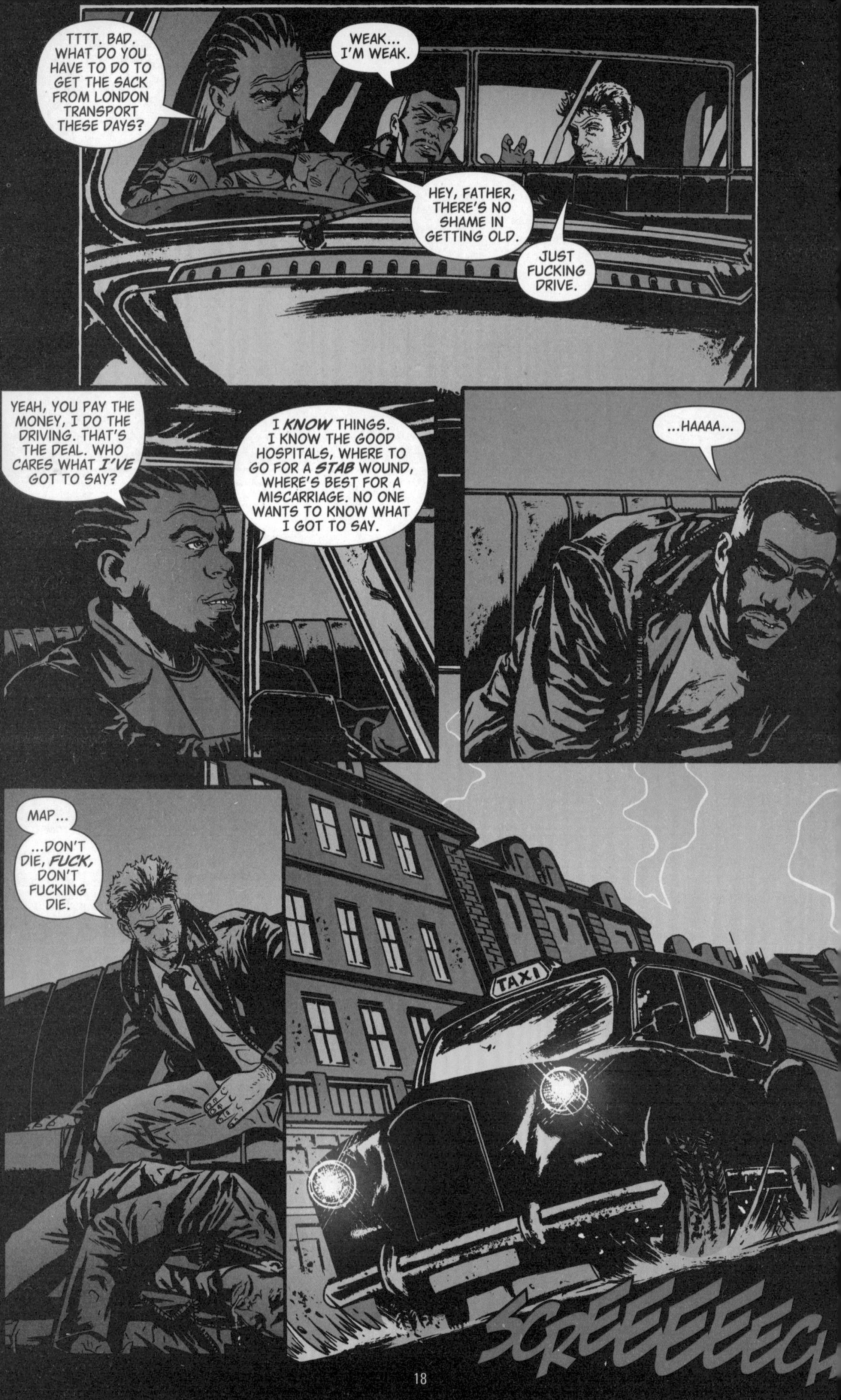
TTTT. BAD. WHAT DO YOU HAVE TO DO TO GET THE SACK FROM LONDON TRANSPORT THESE DAYS?
WEAK... I'M WEAK.
HEY, FATHER, THERE'S NO SHAME IN GETTING OLD.
JUST FUCKING DRIVE.
YEAH, YOU PAY THE MONEY, I DO THE DRIVING. THAT'S THE DEAL. WHO CARES WHAT I'VE GOT TO SAY?
I KNOW THINGS. I KNOW THE GOOD HOSPITALS, WHERE TO GO FOR A STAB WOUND, WHERE'S BEST FOR A MISCARRIAGE. NO ONE WANTS TO KNOW WHAT I GOT TO SAY.
...HAAAA...
MAP...
...DON'T DIE, FUCK, DON'T FUCKING DIE.
TAXI
SCREEEEECH

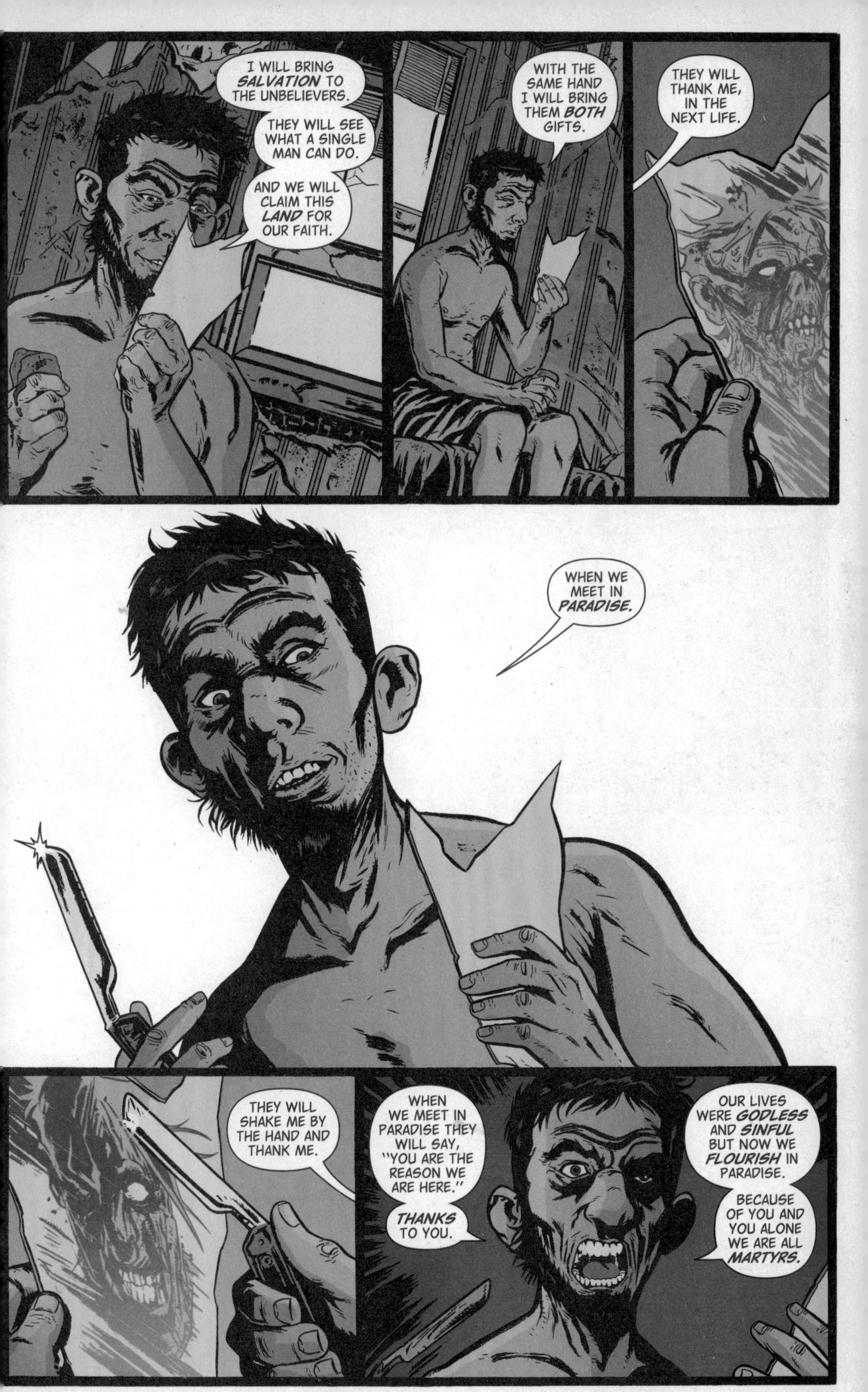
I WILL BRING SALVATION TO THE UNBELIEVERS.
THEY WILL SEE WHAT A SINGLE MAN CAN DO.
AND WE WILL CLAIM THIS LAND FOR OUR FAITH.
WITH THE SAME HAND I WILL BRING THEM BOTH GIFTS.
THEY WILL THANK ME, IN THE NEXT LIFE.
WHEN WE MEET IN PARADISE.
THEY WILL SHAKE ME BY THE HAND AND THANK ME.
WHEN WE MEET IN PARADISE THEY WILL SAY, "YOU ARE THE REASON WE ARE HERE."
THANKS TO YOU.
OUR LIVES WERE GODLESS AND SINFUL BUT NOW WE FLOURISH IN PARADISE.
BECAUSE OF YOU AND YOU ALONE WE ARE ALL MARTYRS.

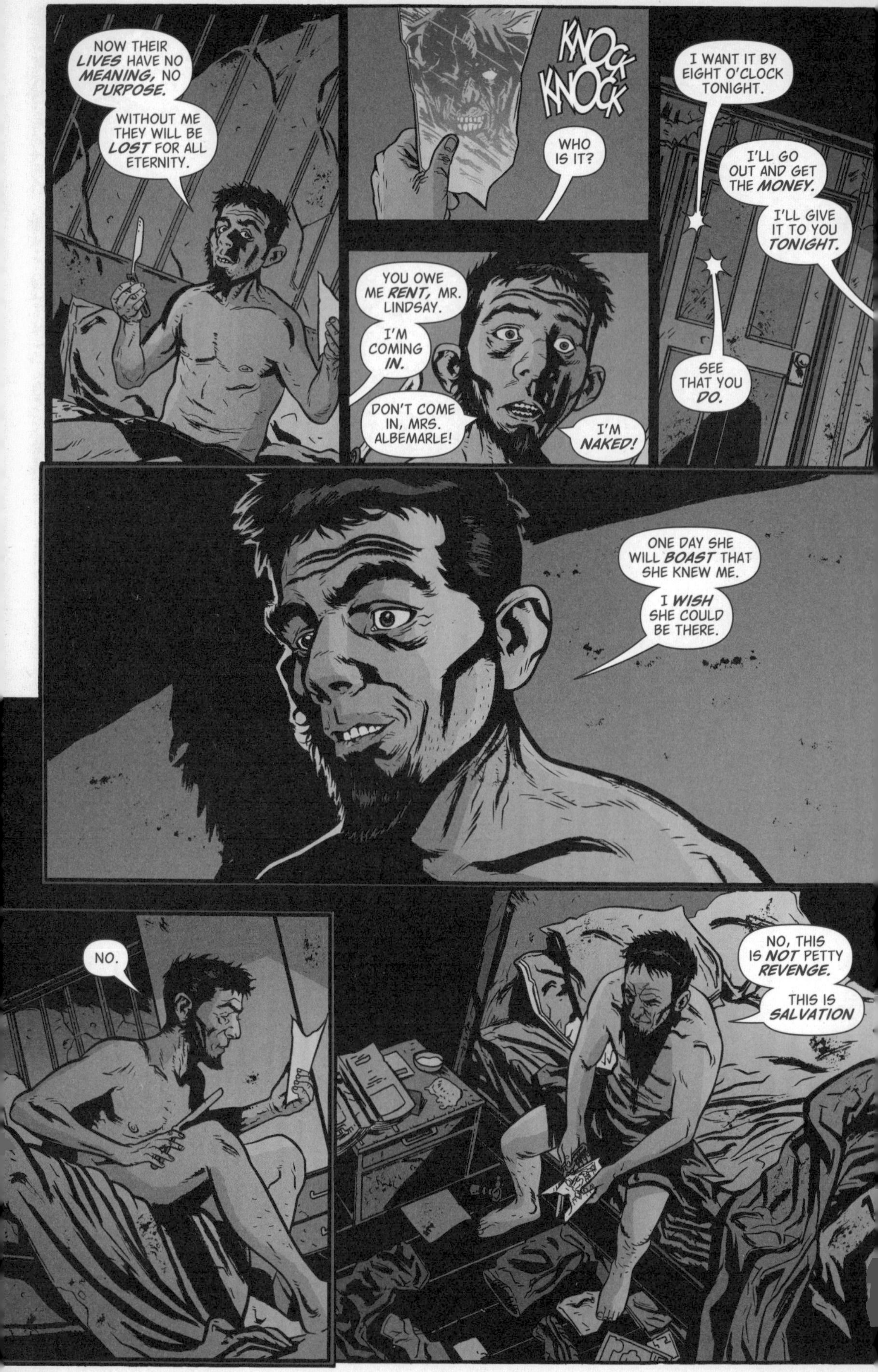
NOW THEIR LIVES HAVE NO MEANING, NO PURPOSE.
WITHOUT ME THEY WILL BE LOST FOR ALL ETERNITY.
KNOCK KNOCK
WHO IS IT?
I WANT IT BY EIGHT O'CLOCK TONIGHT.
I'LL GO OUT AND GET THE MONEY.
I'LL GIVE IT TO YOU TONIGHT.
SEE THAT YOU DO.
YOU OWE ME RENT, MR. LINDSAY.
I'M COMING IN.
DON'T COME IN, MRS. ALBEMARLE!
I'M NAKED!
ONE DAY SHE WILL BOAST THAT SHE KNEW ME.
I WISH SHE COULD BE THERE.
NO.
NO, THIS IS NOT PETTY REVENGE.
THIS IS SALVATION

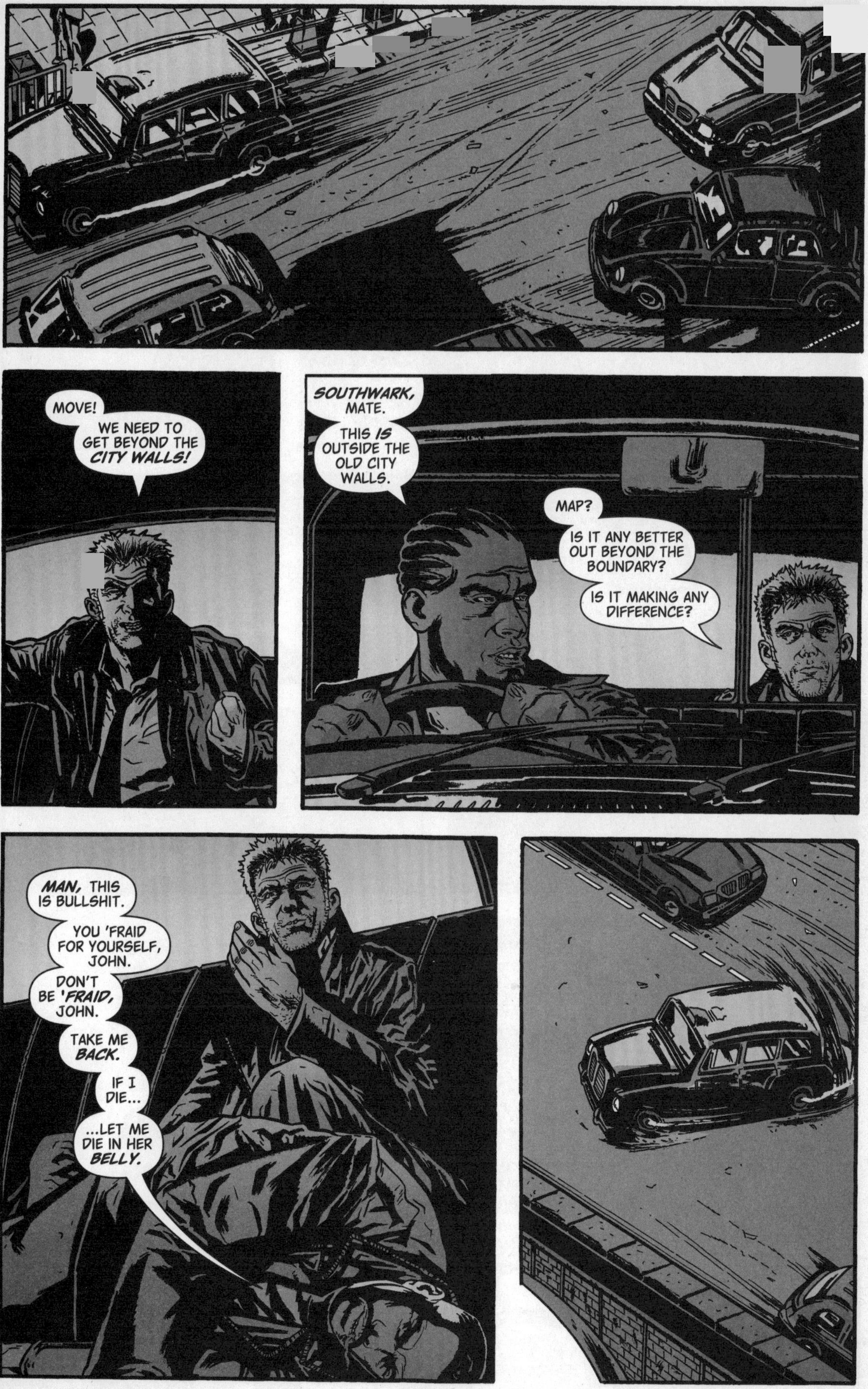
MOVE!
WE NEED TO GET BEYOND THE CITY WALLS!
SOUTHWARK, MATE.
THIS IS OUTSIDE THE OLD CITY WALLS.
MAP?
IS IT ANY BETTER OUT BEYOND THE BOUNDARY?
IS IT MAKING ANY DIFFERENCE?
MAN, THIS IS BULLSHIT.
YOU 'FRAID FOR YOURSELF, JOHN.
DON'T BE 'FRAID, JOHN.
TAKE ME BACK.
IF I DIE...
...LET ME DIE IN HER BELLY.

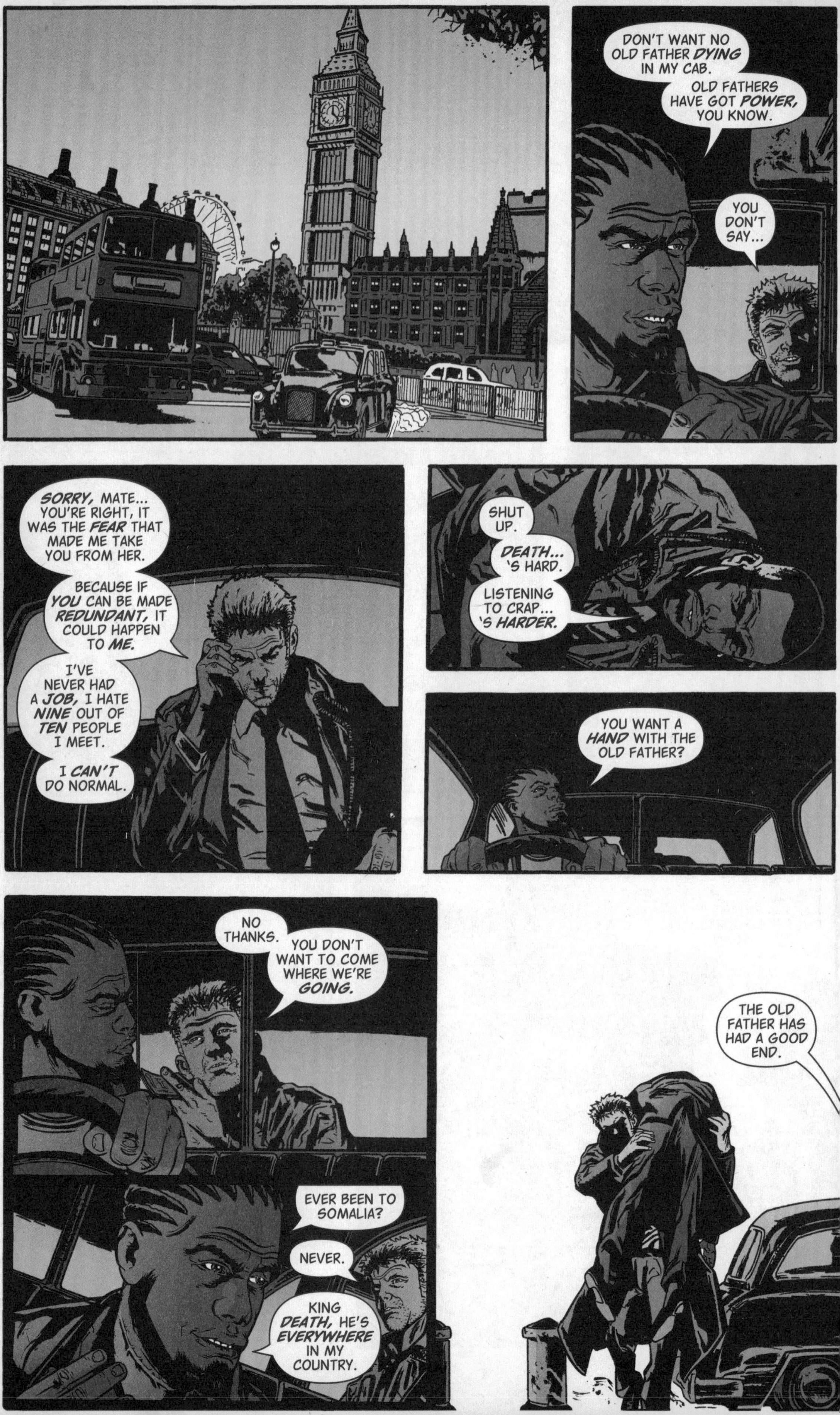
DON'T WANT NO OLD FATHER DYING IN MY CAB.
OLD FATHERS HAVE GOT POWER, YOU KNOW.
YOU DON'T SAY...
SORRY, MATE... YOU'RE RIGHT, IT WAS THE FEAR THAT MADE ME TAKE YOU FROM HER.
BECAUSE IF YOU CAN BE MADE REDUNDANT, IT COULD HAPPEN TO ME.
I'VE NEVER HAD A JOB, I HATE NINE OUT OF TEN PEOPLE I MEET.
I CAN'T DO NORMAL.
SHUT UP.
DEATH... 'S HARD.
LISTENING TO CRAP... 'S HARDER.
YOU WANT A HAND WITH THE OLD FATHER?
NO THANKS.
YOU DON'T WANT TO COME WHERE WE'RE GOING.
EVER BEEN TO SOMALIA?
NEVER.
KING DEATH, HE'S EVERYWHERE IN MY COUNTRY.
THE OLD FATHER HAS HAD A GOOD END.

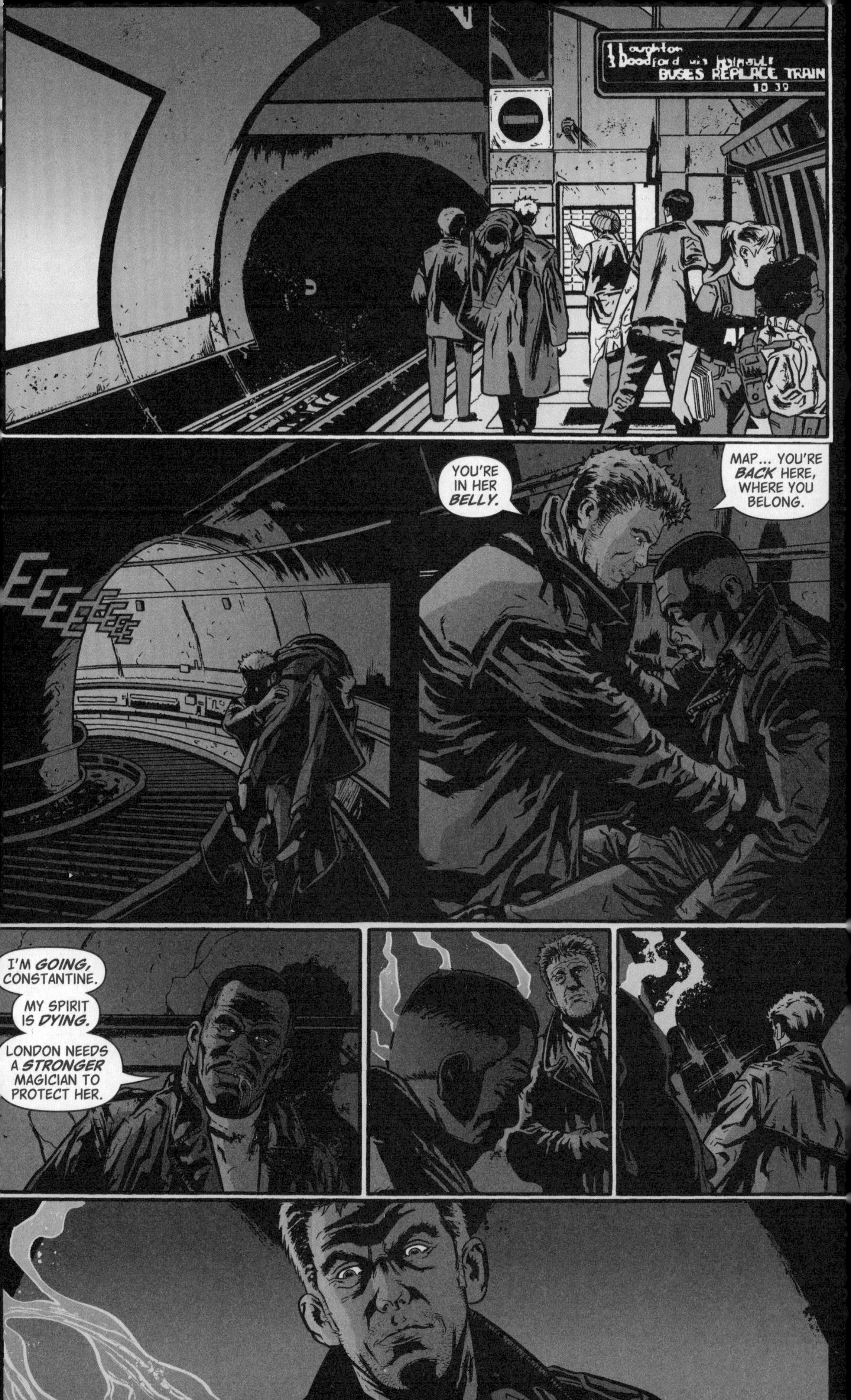
BUSES REPLACE TRAIN
YOU'RE IN HER BELLY.
MAP... YOU'RE BACK HERE, WHERE YOU BELONG.
I'M GOING, CONSTANTINE.
MY SPIRIT IS DYING.
LONDON NEEDS A STRONGER MAGICIAN TO PROTECT HER.

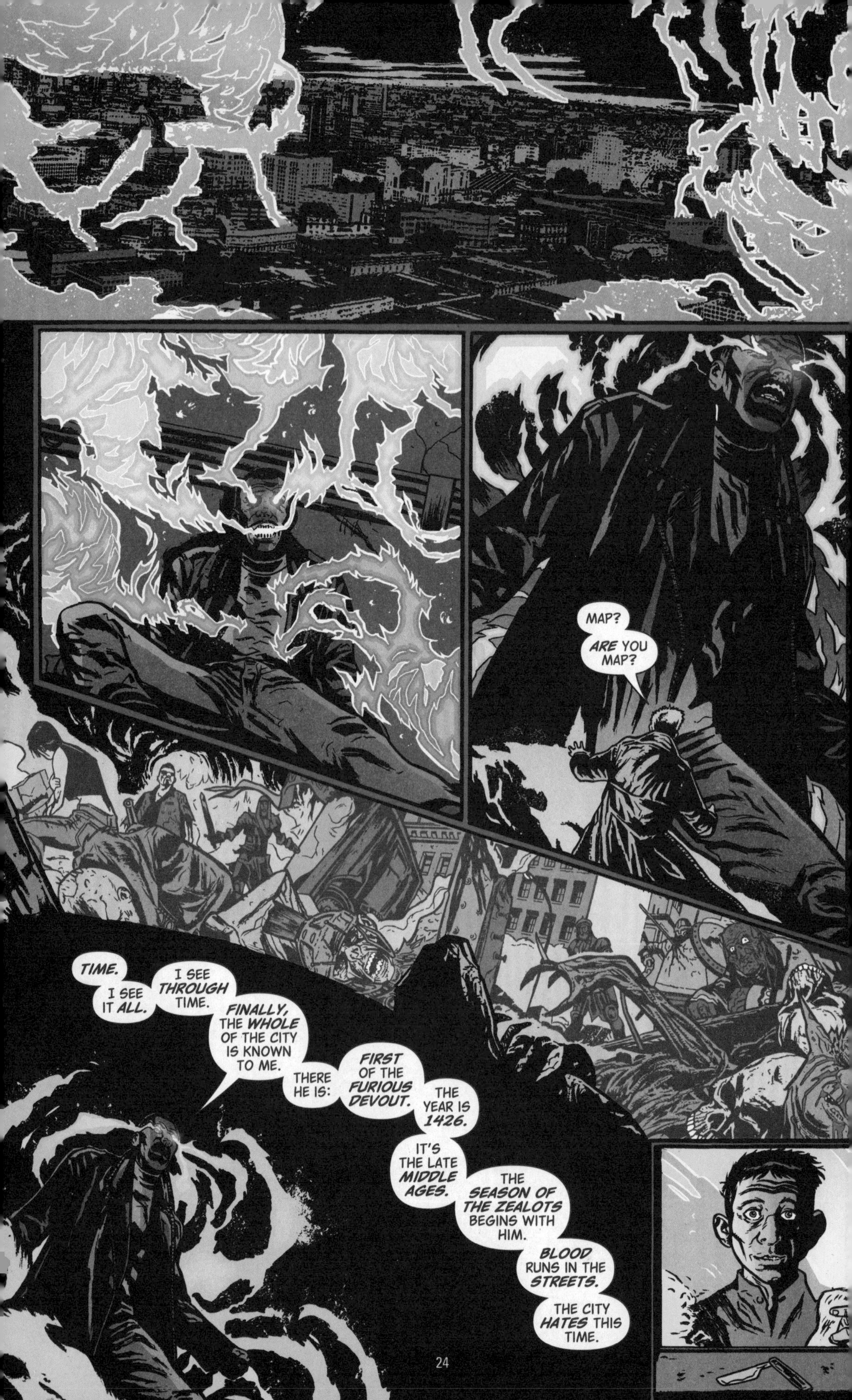
MAP?
ARE YOU MAP?
TIME.
I SEE IT ALL.
I SEE THROUGH TIME.
FINALLY, THE WHOLE OF THE CITY IS KNOWN TO ME.
THERE HE IS:
FIRST OF THE FURIOUS DEVOUT.
THE YEAR IS 1426.
IT'S THE LATE MIDDLE AGES.
THE SEASON OF THE ZEALOTS BEGINS WITH HIM.
BLOOD RUNS IN THE STREETS.
THE CITY HATES THIS TIME.

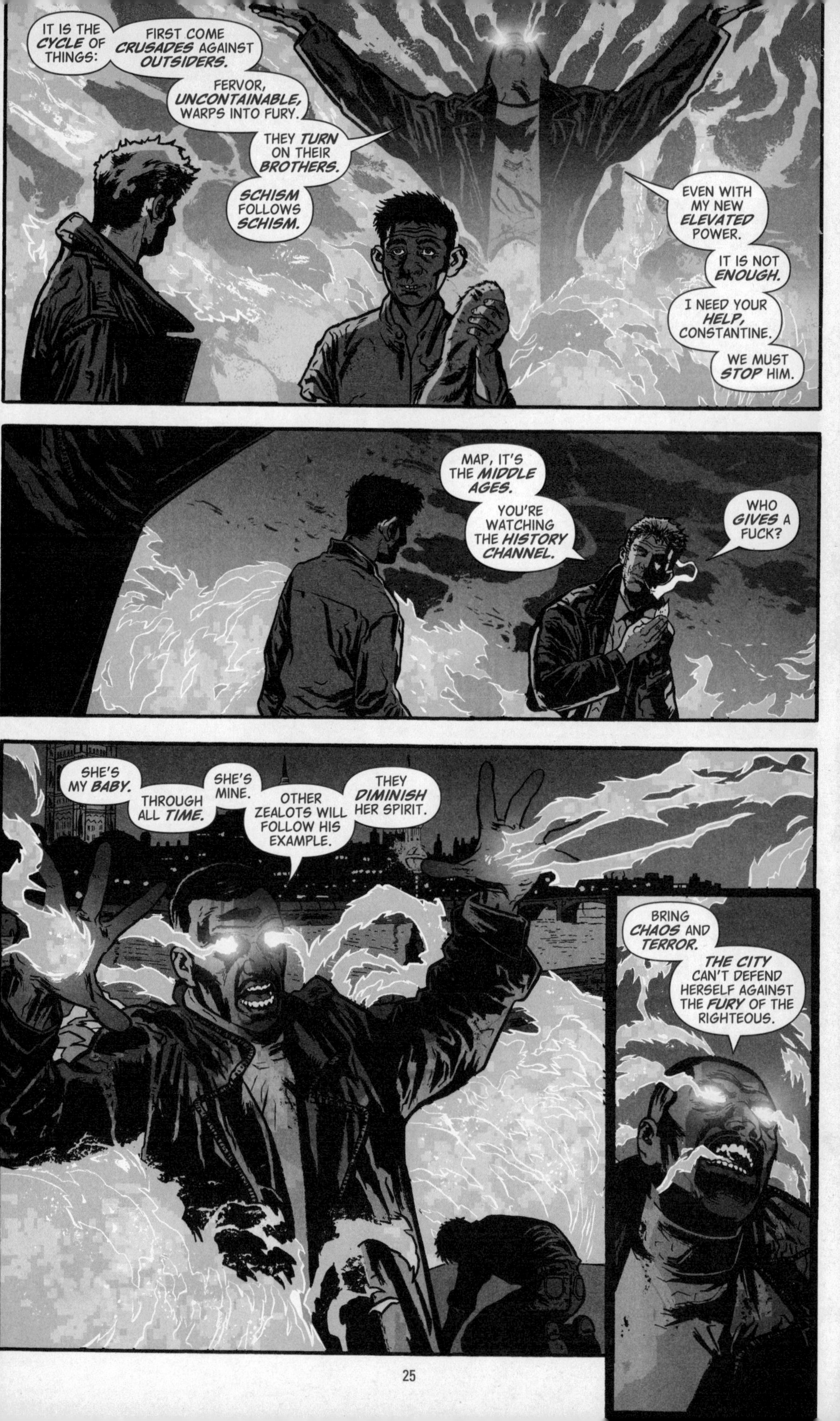
IT IS THE CYCLE OF THINGS:
FIRST COME CRUSADES AGAINST OUTSIDERS.
FERVOR, UNCONTAINABLE, WARPS INTO FURY.
THEY TURN ON THEIR BROTHERS.
SCHISM FOLLOWS SCHISM.
EVEN WITH MY NEW ELEVATED POWER.
IT IS NOT ENOUGH.
I NEED YOUR HELP, CONSTANTINE.
WE MUST STOP HIM.
MAP, IT'S THE MIDDLE AGES.
YOU'RE WATCHING THE HISTORY CHANNEL.
WHO GIVES A FUCK?
SHE'S MY BABY.
THROUGH ALL TIME.
SHE'S MINE.
OTHER ZEALOTS WILL FOLLOW HIS EXAMPLE.
THEY DIMINISH HER SPIRIT.
BRING CHAOS AND TERROR.
THE CITY CAN'T DEFEND HERSELF AGAINST THE FURY OF THE RIGHTEOUS.

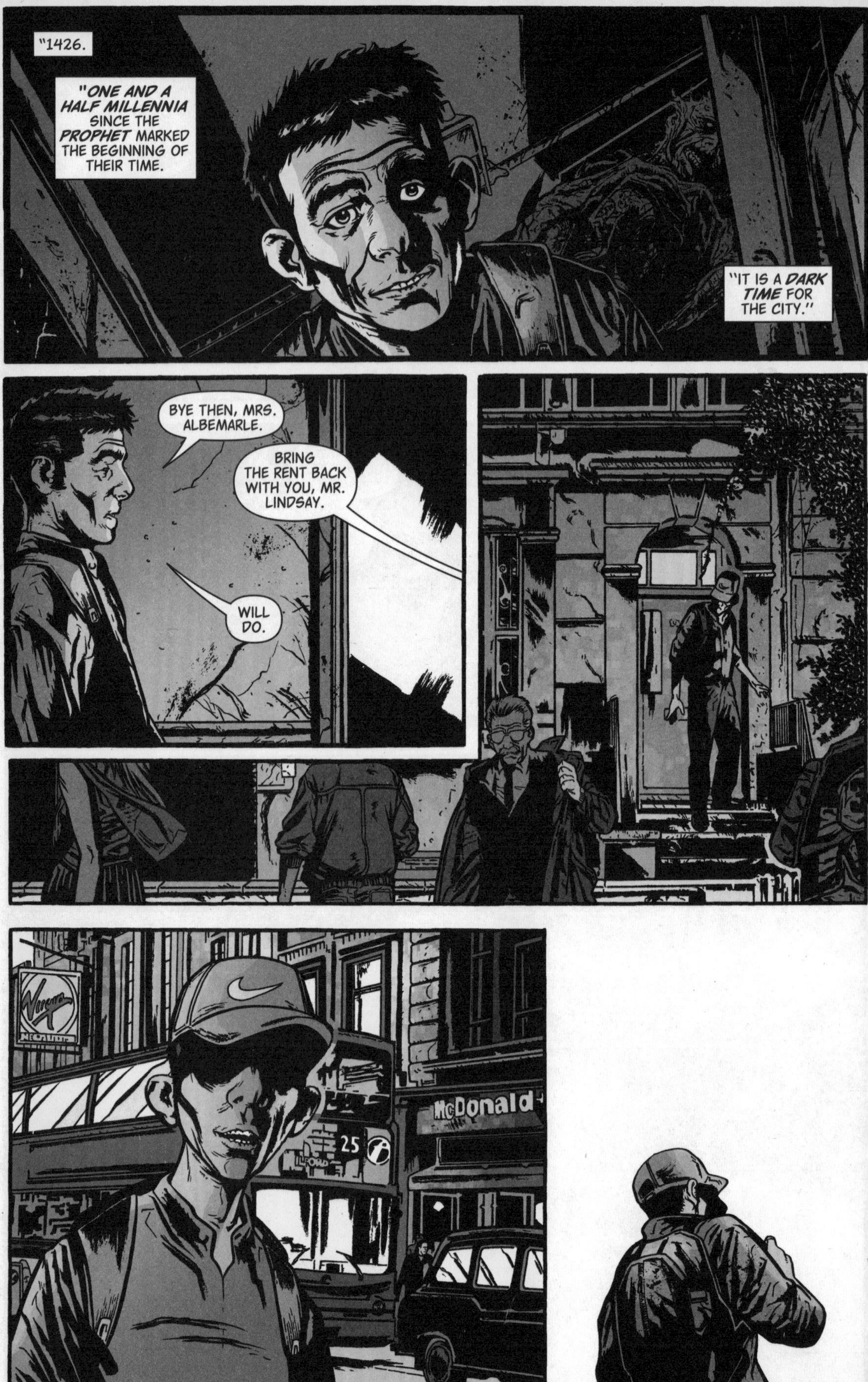
"1426.
"ONE AND A HALF MILLENNIA SINCE THE PROPHET MARKED THE BEGINNING OF THEIR TIME.
"IT IS A DARK TIME FOR THE CITY."
BYE THEN, MRS. ALBEMARLE.
BRING THE RENT BACK WITH YOU, MR. LINDSAY.
WILL DO.
McDonald
25

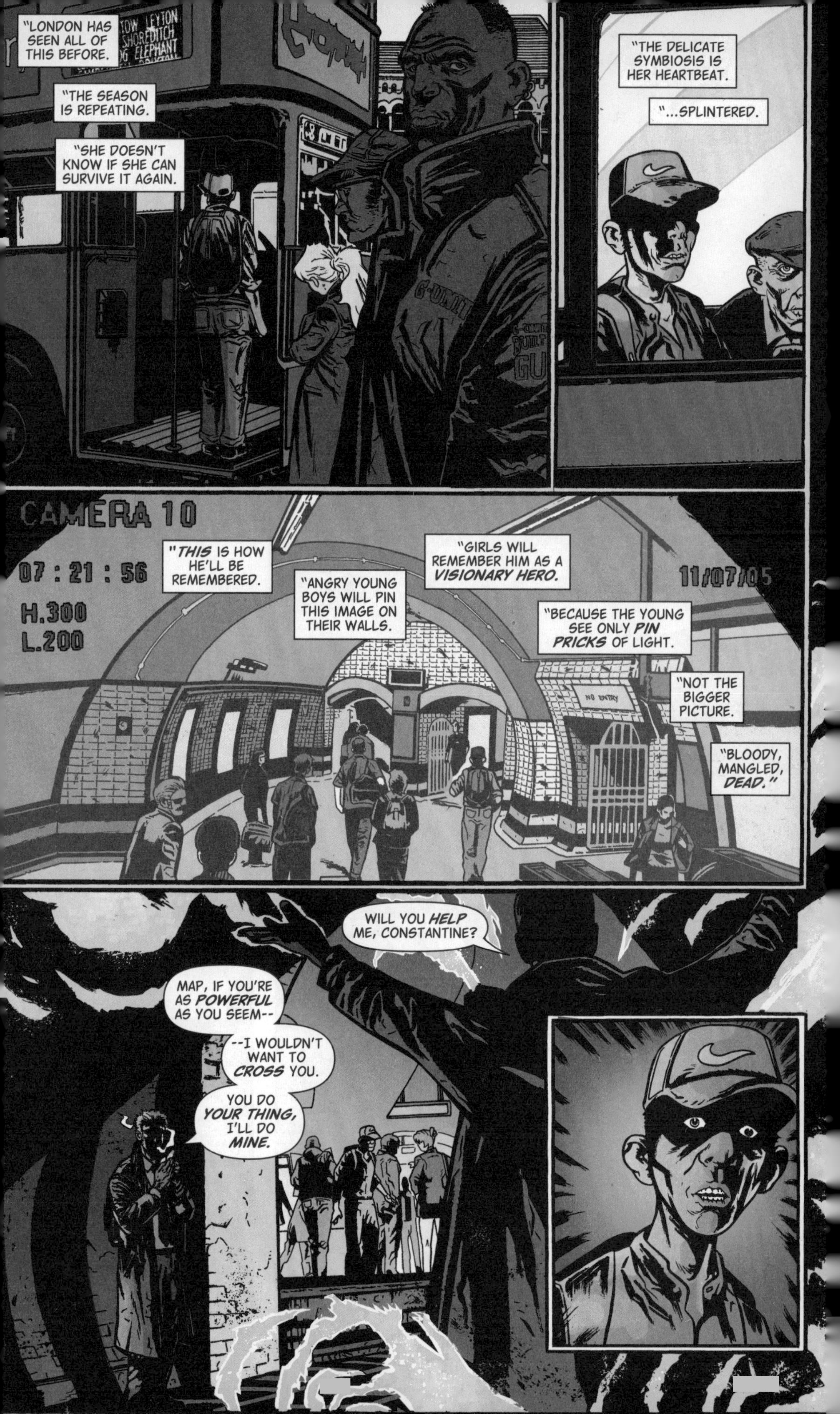
"LONDON HAS SEEN ALL OF THIS BEFORE.
"THE SEASON IS REPEATING.
"SHE DOESN'T KNOW IF SHE CAN SURVIVE IT AGAIN.
"THE DELICATE SYMBIOSIS IS HER HEARTBEAT.
"...SPLINTERED.
CAMERA 10
07 : 21 : 56
H.300
L.200
11/07/05
"THIS IS HOW HE'LL BE REMEMBERED.
"ANGRY YOUNG BOYS WILL PIN THIS IMAGE ON THEIR WALLS.
"GIRLS WILL REMEMBER HIM AS A VISIONARY HERO.
"BECAUSE THE YOUNG SEE ONLY PIN PRICKS OF LIGHT.
"NOT THE BIGGER PICTURE.
"BLOODY, MANGLED, DEAD."
NO ENTRY
WILL YOU HELP ME, CONSTANTINE?
MAP, IF YOU'RE AS POWERFUL AS YOU SEEM--
--I WOULDN'T WANT TO CROSS YOU.
YOU DO YOUR THING, I'LL DO MINE.

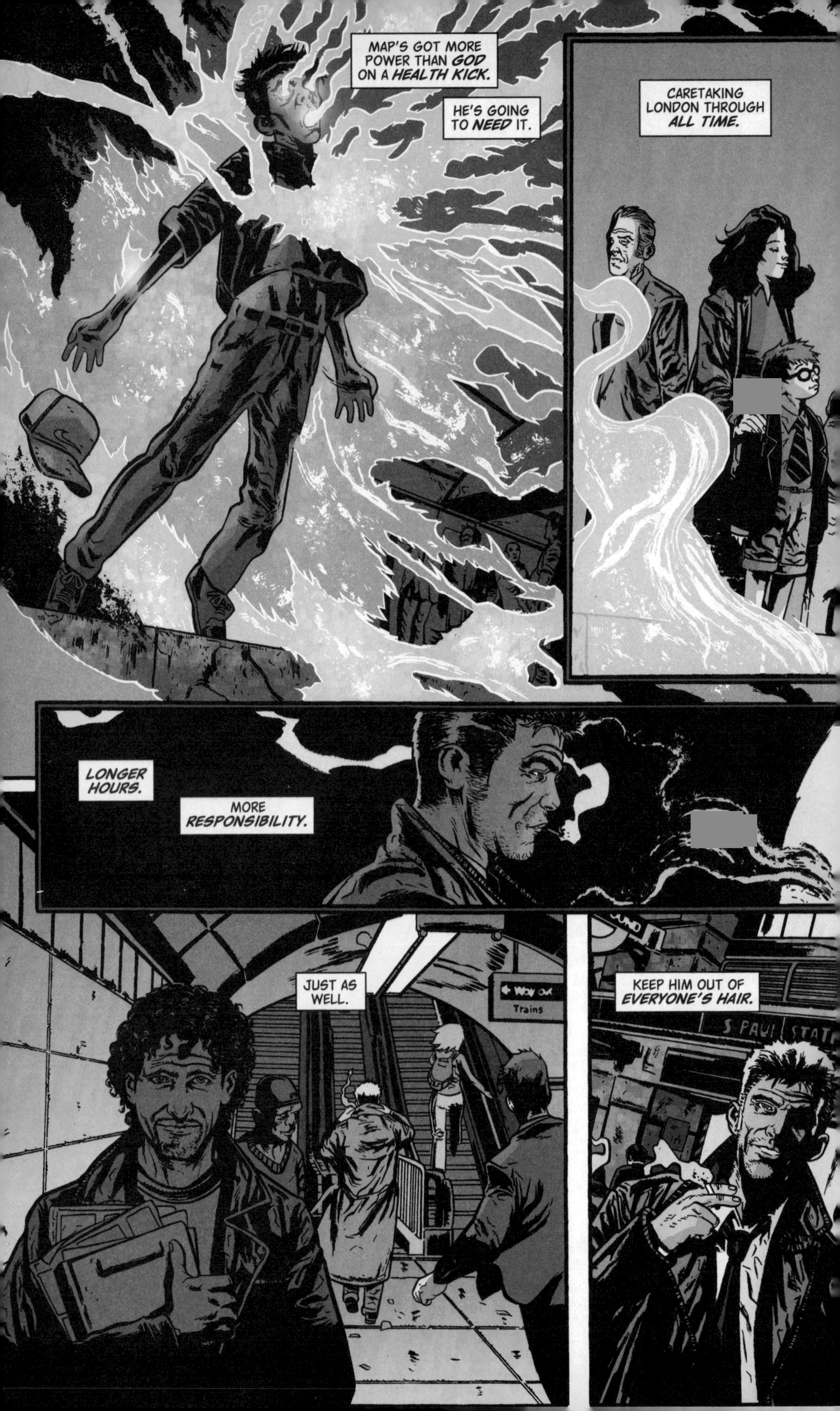
MAP'S GOT MORE POWER THAN GOD ON A HEALTH KICK.
HE'S GOING TO NEED IT.
CARETAKING LONDON THROUGH ALL TIME.
LONGER HOURS.
MORE RESPONSIBILITY.
JUST AS WELL.
Way out
Trains
KEEP HIM OUT OF EVERYONE'S HAIR.

THE RED RIGHT HAND Chapter 1

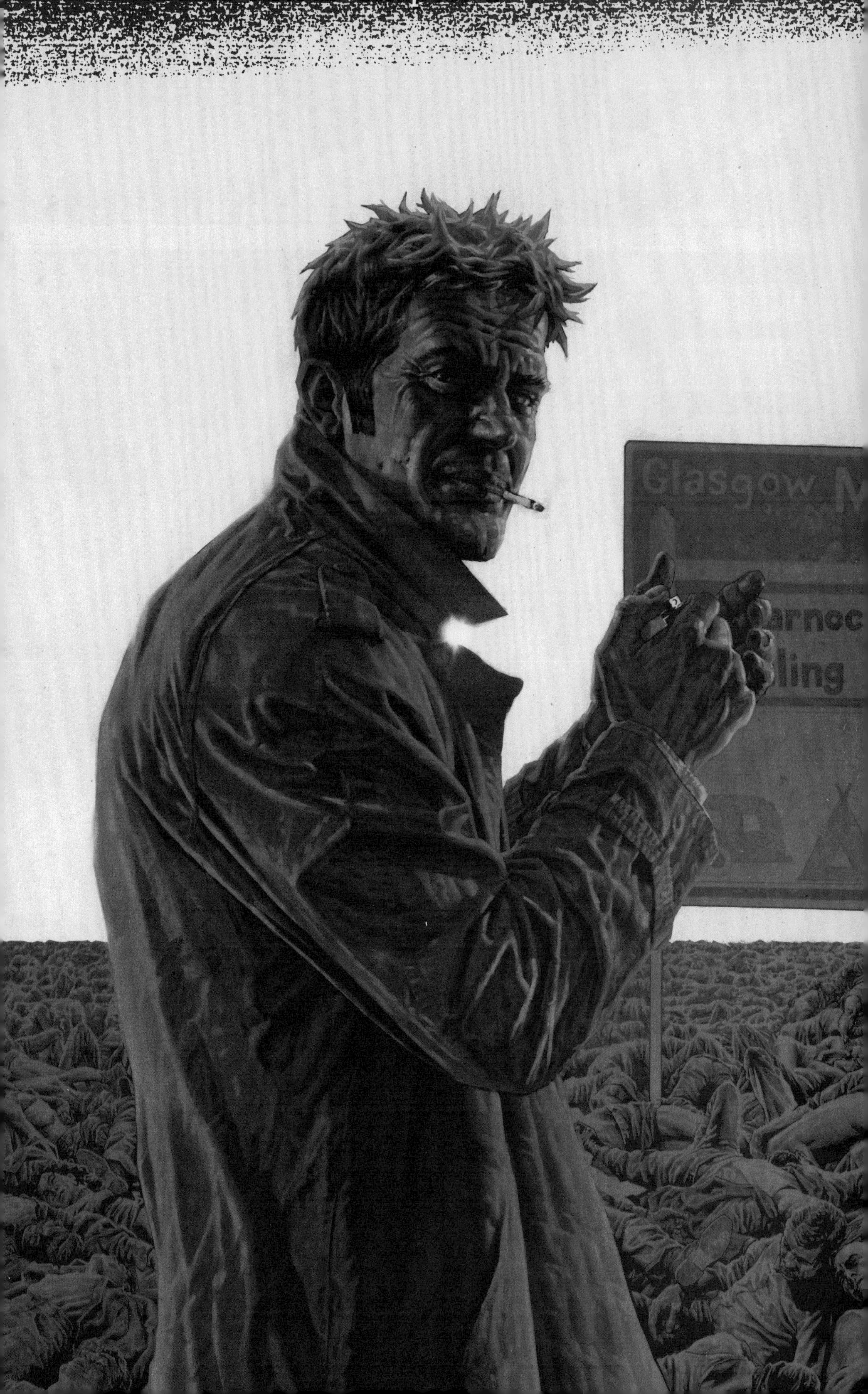
Glasgow

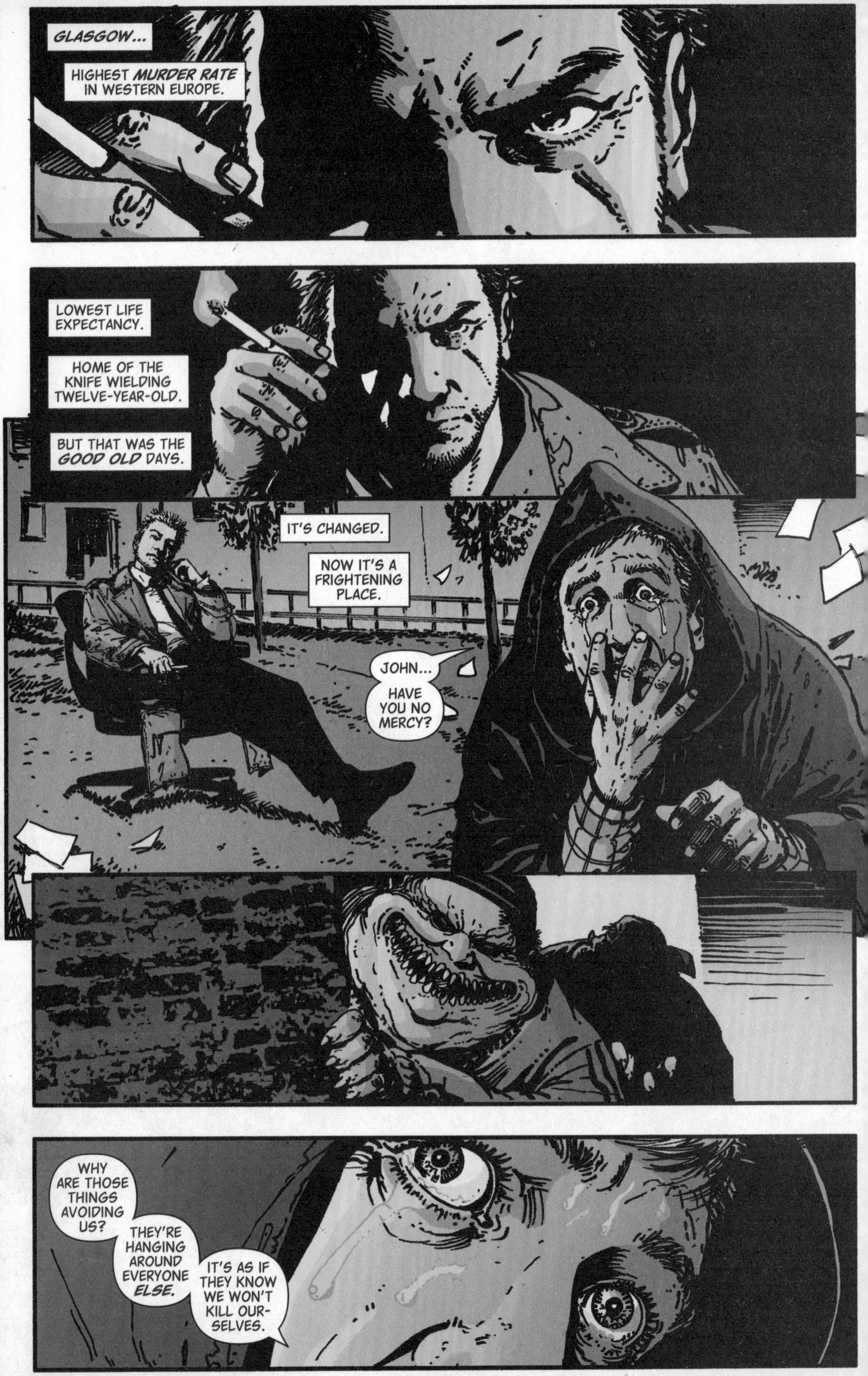
GLASGOW...
HIGHEST MURDER RATE IN WESTERN EUROPE.
LOWEST LIFE EXPECTANCY.
HOME OF THE KNIFE WIELDING TWELVE-YEAR-OLD.
BUT THAT WAS THE GOOD OLD DAYS.
IT'S CHANGED.
NOW IT'S A FRIGHTENING PLACE.
JOHN...
HAVE YOU NO MERCY?
WHY ARE THOSE THINGS AVOIDING US?
THEY'RE HANGING AROUND EVERYONE ELSE.
IT'S AS IF THEY KNOW WE WON'T KILL OUR-SELVES.

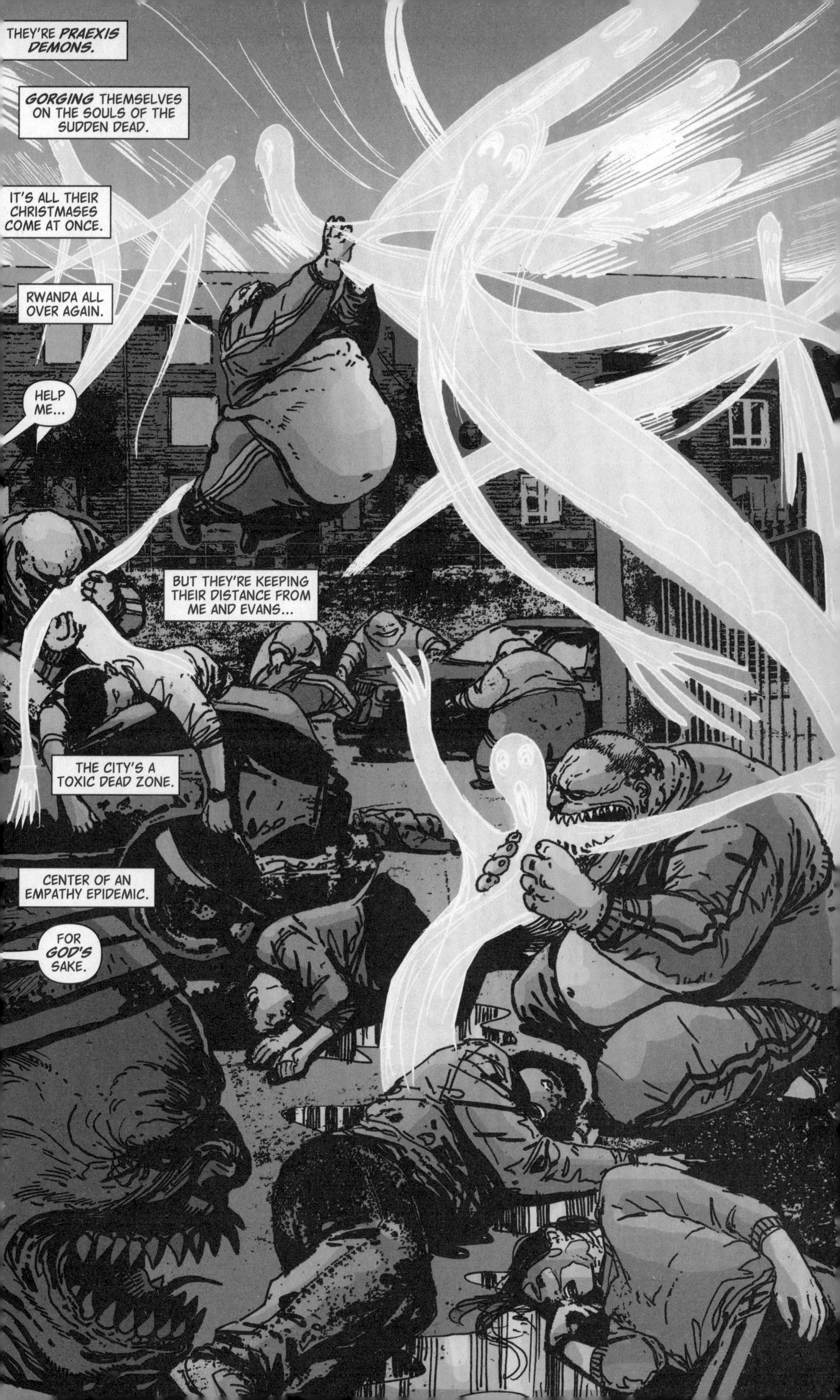
THEY'RE *PRAEXIS DEMONS.*
GORGING THEMSELVES ON THE SOULS OF THE SUDDEN DEAD.
IT'S ALL THEIR CHRISTMASES COME AT ONCE.
RWANDA ALL OVER AGAIN.
HELP ME...
BUT THEY'RE KEEPING THEIR DISTANCE FROM ME AND EVANS...
THE CITY'S A TOXIC DEAD ZONE.
CENTER OF AN EMPATHY EPIDEMIC.
FOR *GOD'S* SAKE.

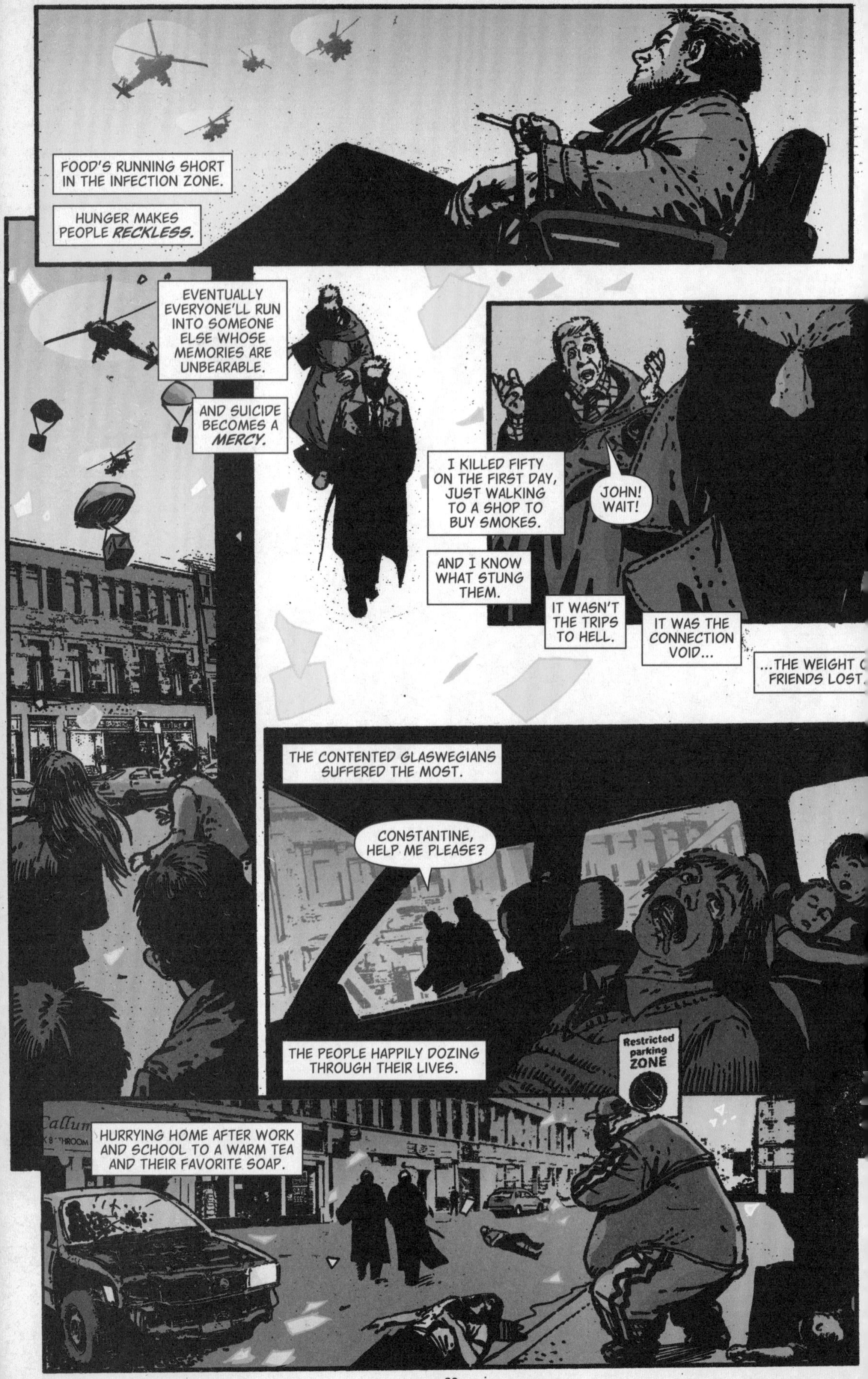
FOOD'S RUNNING SHORT IN THE INFECTION ZONE.
HUNGER MAKES PEOPLE RECKLESS.
EVENTUALLY EVERYONE'LL RUN INTO SOMEONE ELSE WHOSE MEMORIES ARE UNBEARABLE.
AND SUICIDE BECOMES A MERCY.
I KILLED FIFTY ON THE FIRST DAY, JUST WALKING TO A SHOP TO BUY SMOKES.
JOHN! WAIT!
AND I KNOW WHAT STUNG THEM.
IT WASN'T THE TRIPS TO HELL.
IT WAS THE CONNECTION VOID...
...THE WEIGHT OF FRIENDS LOST.
THE CONTENTED GLASWEGIANS SUFFERED THE MOST.
CONSTANTINE, HELP ME PLEASE?
THE PEOPLE HAPPILY DOZING THROUGH THEIR LIVES.
Restricted parking ZONE
HURRYING HOME AFTER WORK AND SCHOOL TO A WARM TEA AND THEIR FAVORITE SOAP.

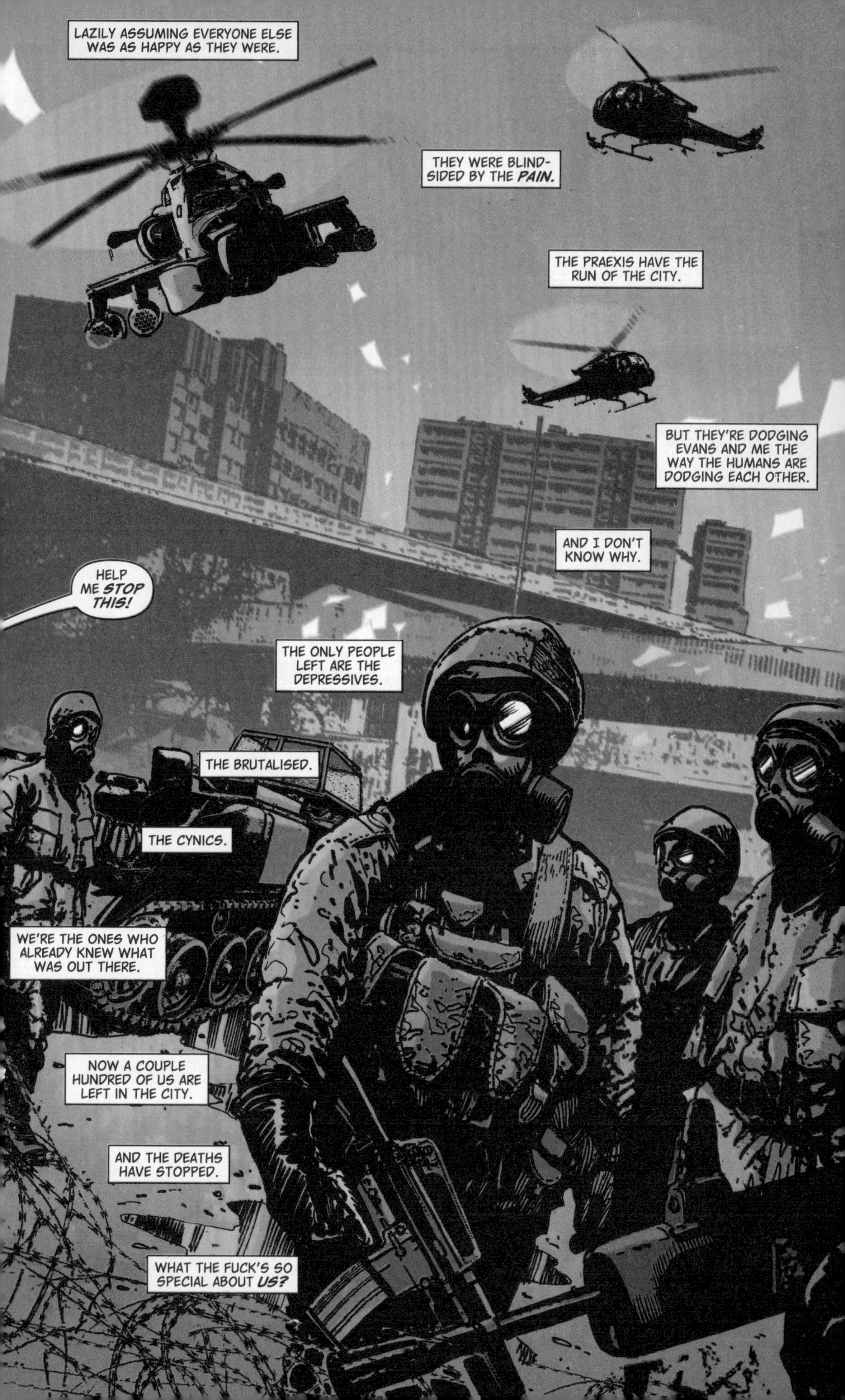
LAZILY ASSUMING EVERYONE ELSE WAS AS HAPPY AS THEY WERE.
THEY WERE BLIND-SIDED BY THE *PAIN.*
THE PRAEXIS HAVE THE RUN OF THE CITY.
BUT THEY'RE DODGING EVANS AND ME THE WAY THE HUMANS ARE DODGING EACH OTHER.
AND I DON'T KNOW WHY.
HELP ME *STOP THIS!*
THE ONLY PEOPLE LEFT ARE THE DEPRESSIVES.
THE BRUTALISED.
THE CYNICS.
WE'RE THE ONES WHO ALREADY KNEW WHAT WAS OUT THERE.
NOW A COUPLE HUNDRED OF US ARE LEFT IN THE CITY.
AND THE DEATHS HAVE STOPPED.
WHAT THE FUCK'S SO SPECIAL ABOUT *US?*

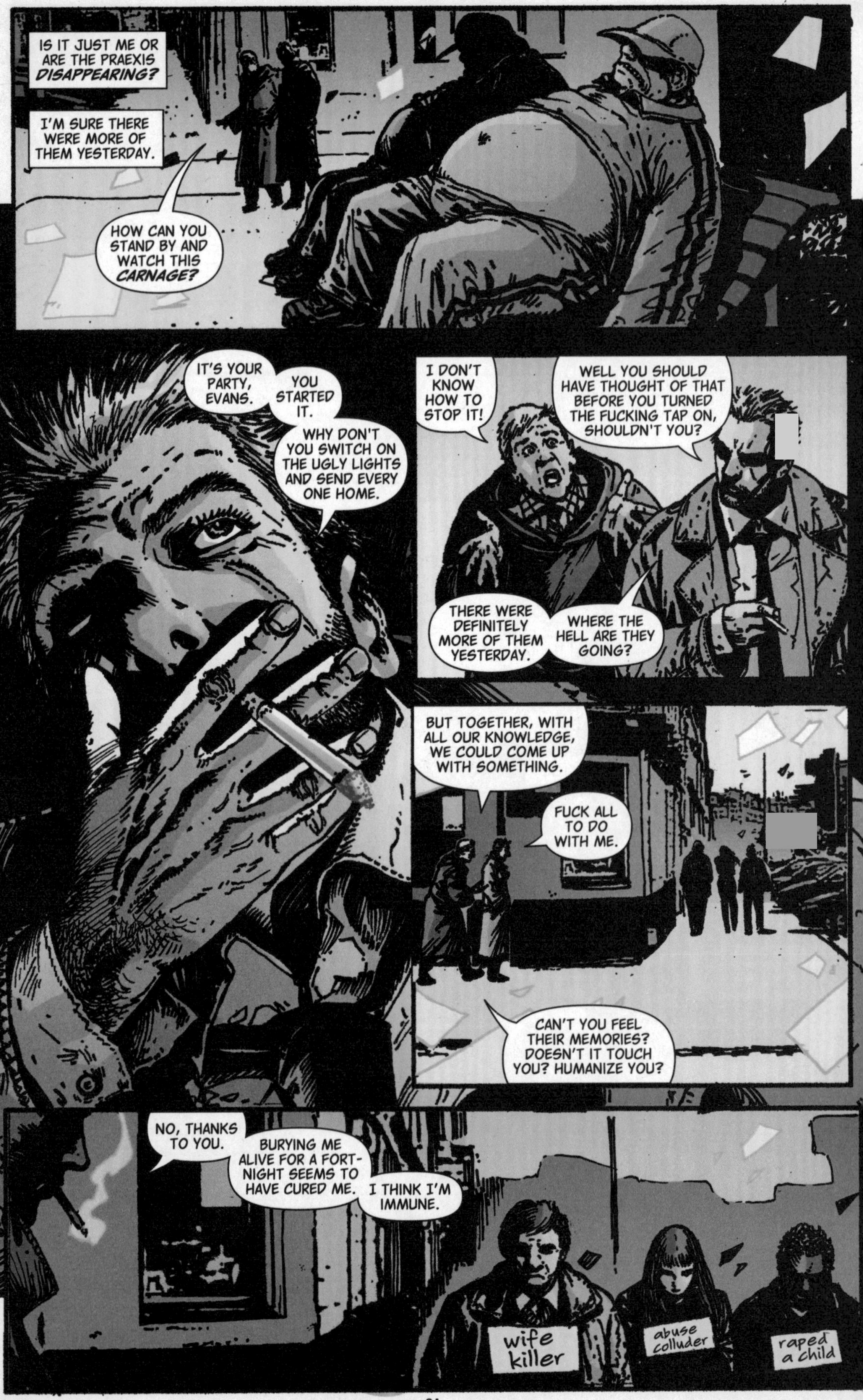
IS IT JUST ME OR ARE THE PRAEXIS DISAPPEARING?
I'M SURE THERE WERE MORE OF THEM YESTERDAY.
HOW CAN YOU STAND BY AND WATCH THIS CARNAGE?
IT'S YOUR PARTY, EVANS.
YOU STARTED IT.
WHY DON'T YOU SWITCH ON THE UGLY LIGHTS AND SEND EVERY ONE HOME.
I DON'T KNOW HOW TO STOP IT!
WELL YOU SHOULD HAVE THOUGHT OF THAT BEFORE YOU TURNED THE FUCKING TAP ON, SHOULDN'T YOU?
THERE WERE DEFINITELY MORE OF THEM YESTERDAY.
WHERE THE HELL ARE THEY GOING?
BUT TOGETHER, WITH ALL OUR KNOWLEDGE, WE COULD COME UP WITH SOMETHING.
FUCK ALL TO DO WITH ME.
CAN'T YOU FEEL THEIR MEMORIES? DOESN'T IT TOUCH YOU? HUMANIZE YOU?
NO, THANKS TO YOU.
BURYING ME ALIVE FOR A FORTNIGHT SEEMS TO HAVE CURED ME.
I THINK I'M IMMUNE.
wife killer
abuse colluder
raped a child

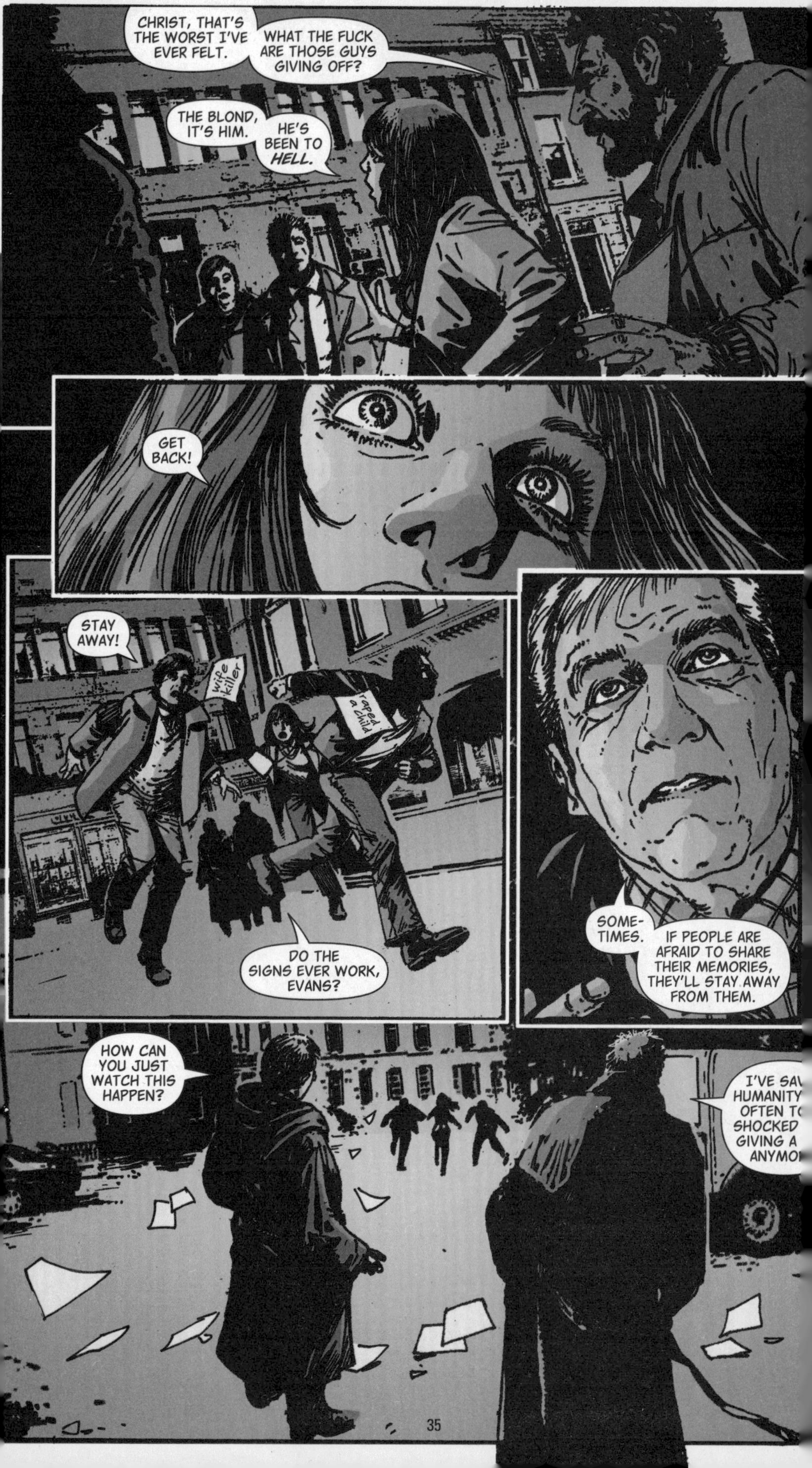

CHRIST, THAT'S THE WORST I'VE EVER FELT.
WHAT THE FUCK ARE THOSE GUYS GIVING OFF?
THE BLOND, IT'S HIM.
HE'S BEEN TO HELL.
GET BACK!
STAY AWAY!
wife killer
raped a child
DO THE SIGNS EVER WORK, EVANS?
SOME-TIMES.
IF PEOPLE ARE AFRAID TO SHARE THEIR MEMORIES, THEY'LL STAY AWAY FROM THEM.
HOW CAN YOU JUST WATCH THIS HAPPEN?
I'VE SAV
HUMANITY
OFTEN TO
SHOCKED
GIVING A
ANYMO

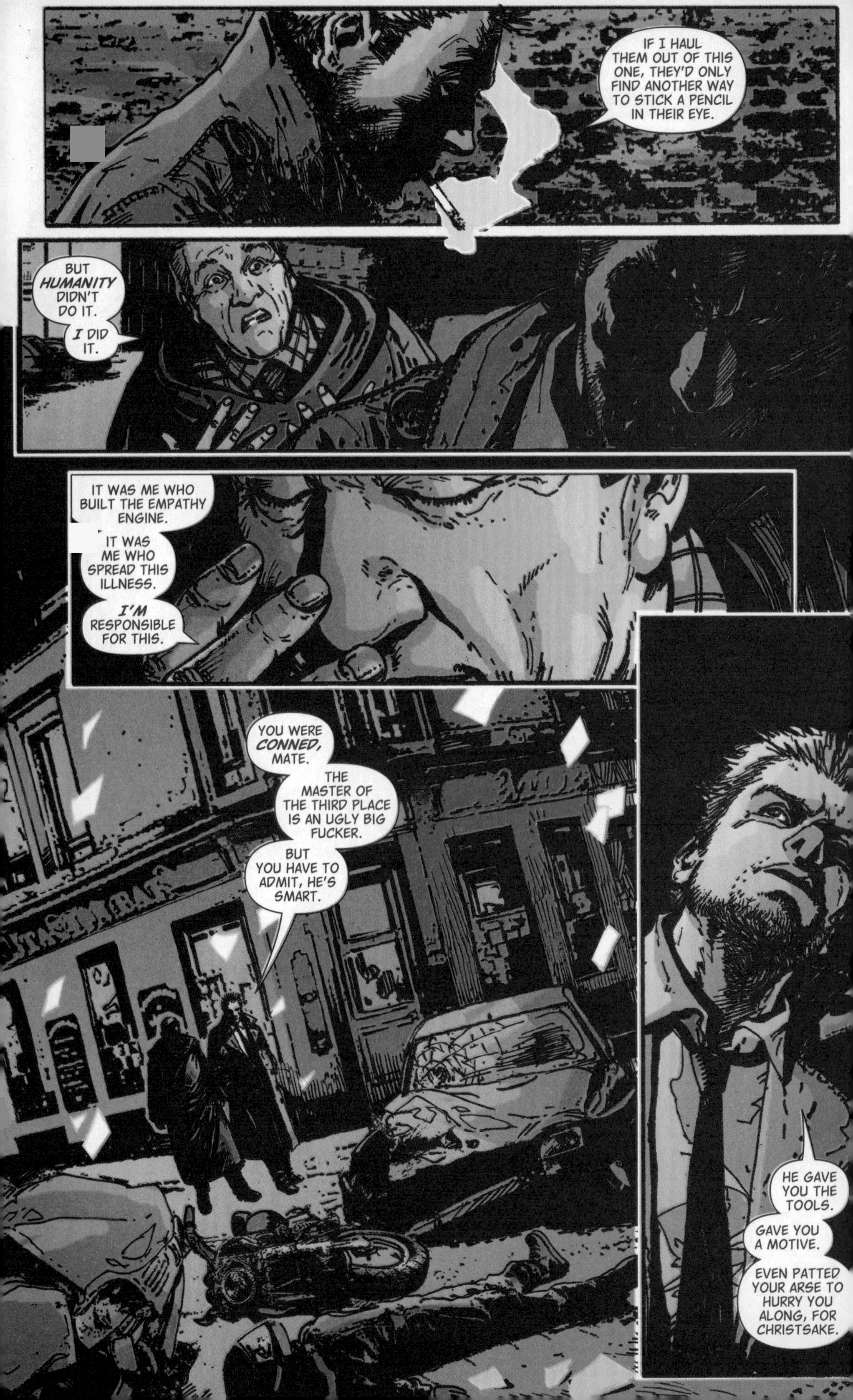
IF I HAUL THEM OUT OF THIS ONE, THEY'D ONLY FIND ANOTHER WAY TO STICK A PENCIL IN THEIR EYE.
BUT *HUMANITY* DIDN'T DO IT.
I DID IT.
IT WAS ME WHO BUILT THE EMPATHY ENGINE.
IT WAS ME WHO SPREAD THIS ILLNESS.
I'M RESPONSIBLE FOR THIS.
YOU WERE *CONNED,* MATE.
THE MASTER OF THE THIRD PLACE IS AN UGLY BIG FUCKER.
BUT YOU HAVE TO ADMIT, HE'S SMART.
HE GAVE YOU THE TOOLS.
GAVE YOU A MOTIVE.
EVEN PATTED YOUR ARSE TO HURRY YOU ALONG, FOR CHRISTSAKE.

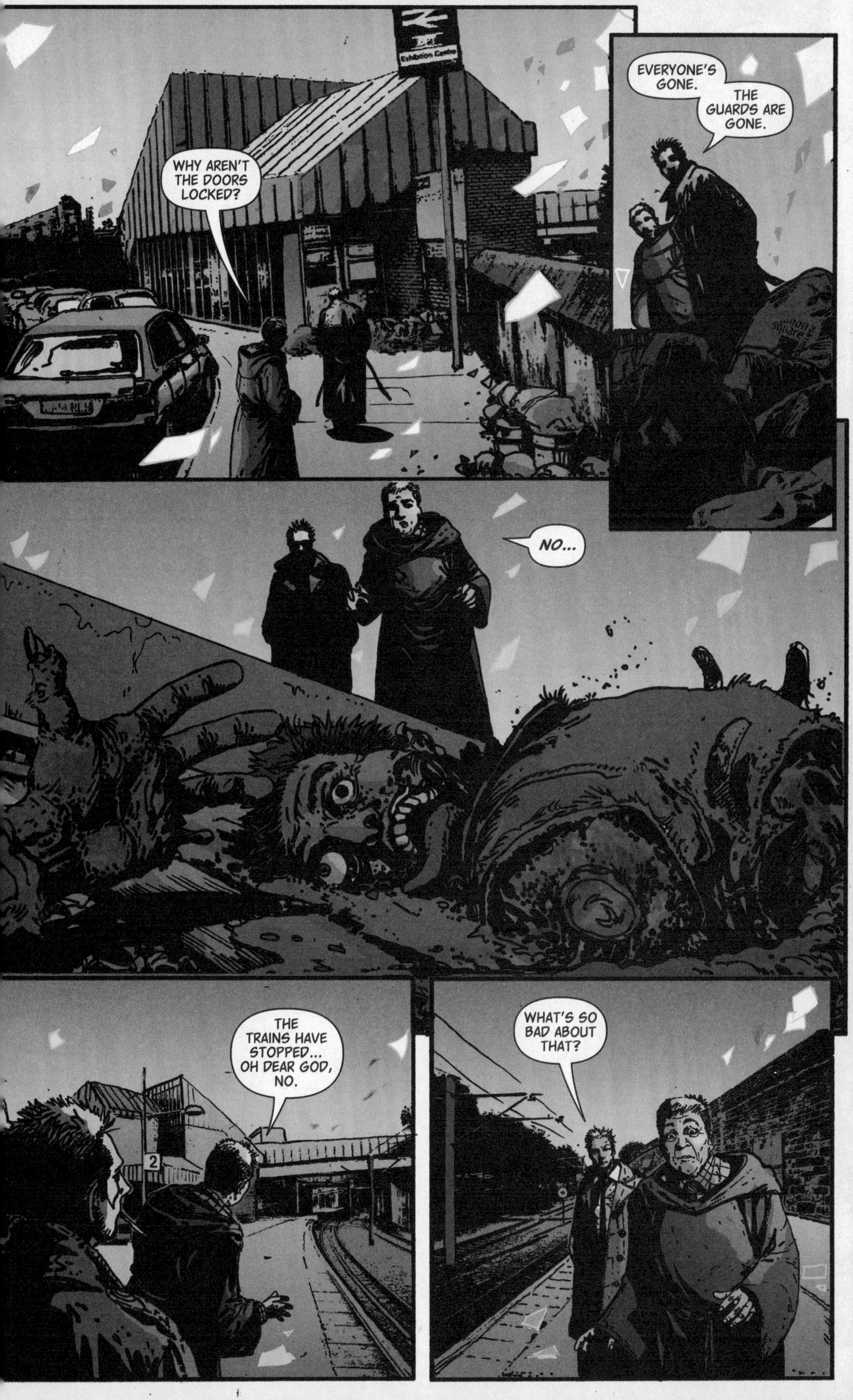
Exhibition Centre
WHY AREN'T THE DOORS LOCKED?
EVERYONE'S GONE.
THE GUARDS ARE GONE.
NO...
THE TRAINS HAVE STOPPED... OH DEAR GOD, NO.
WHAT'S SO BAD ABOUT THAT?

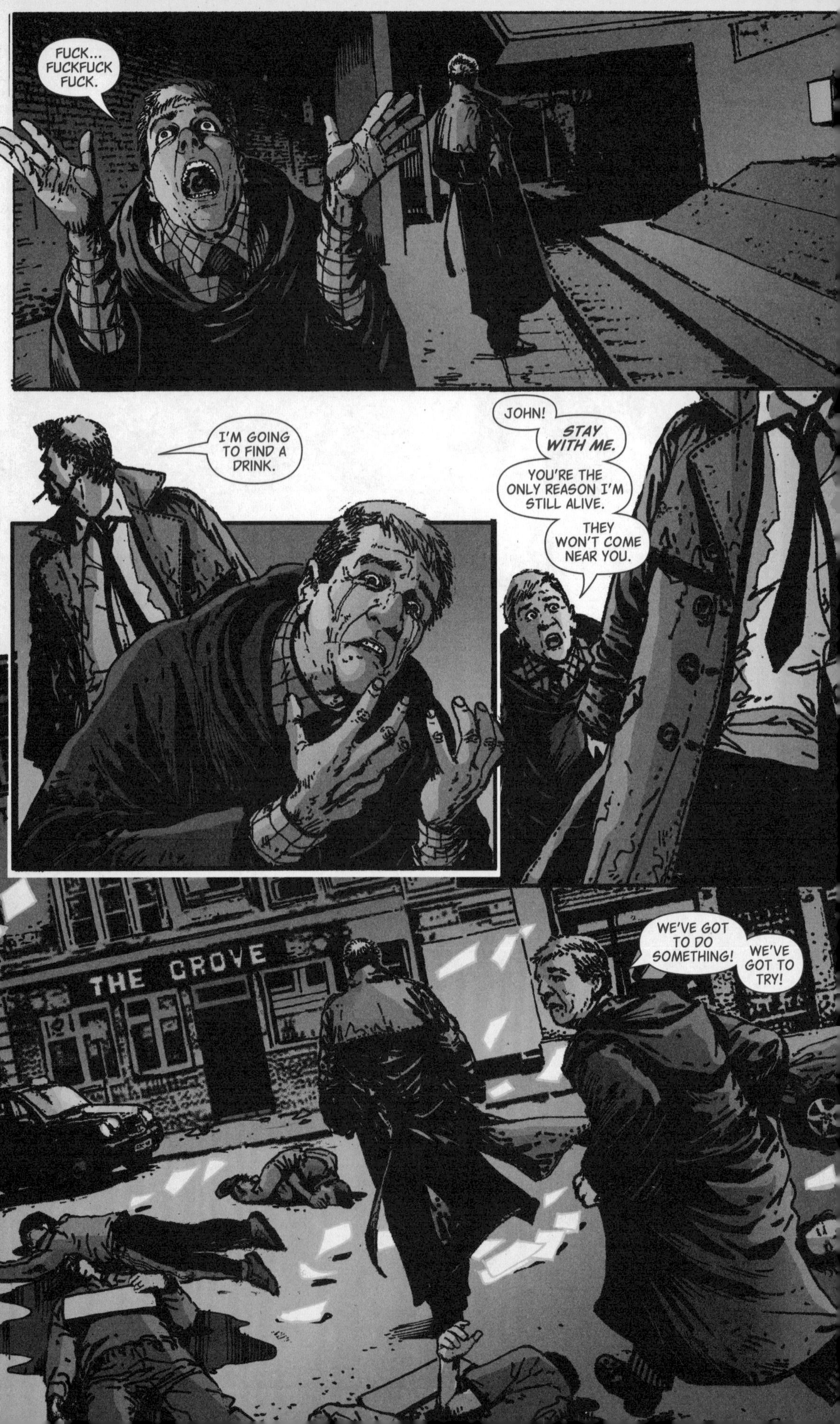
FUCK... FUCKFUCK FUCK.
I'M GOING TO FIND A DRINK.
JOHN! STAY WITH ME.
YOU'RE THE ONLY REASON I'M STILL ALIVE.
THEY WON'T COME NEAR YOU.
THE CROVE
WE'VE GOT TO DO SOMETHING!
WE'VE GOT TO TRY!

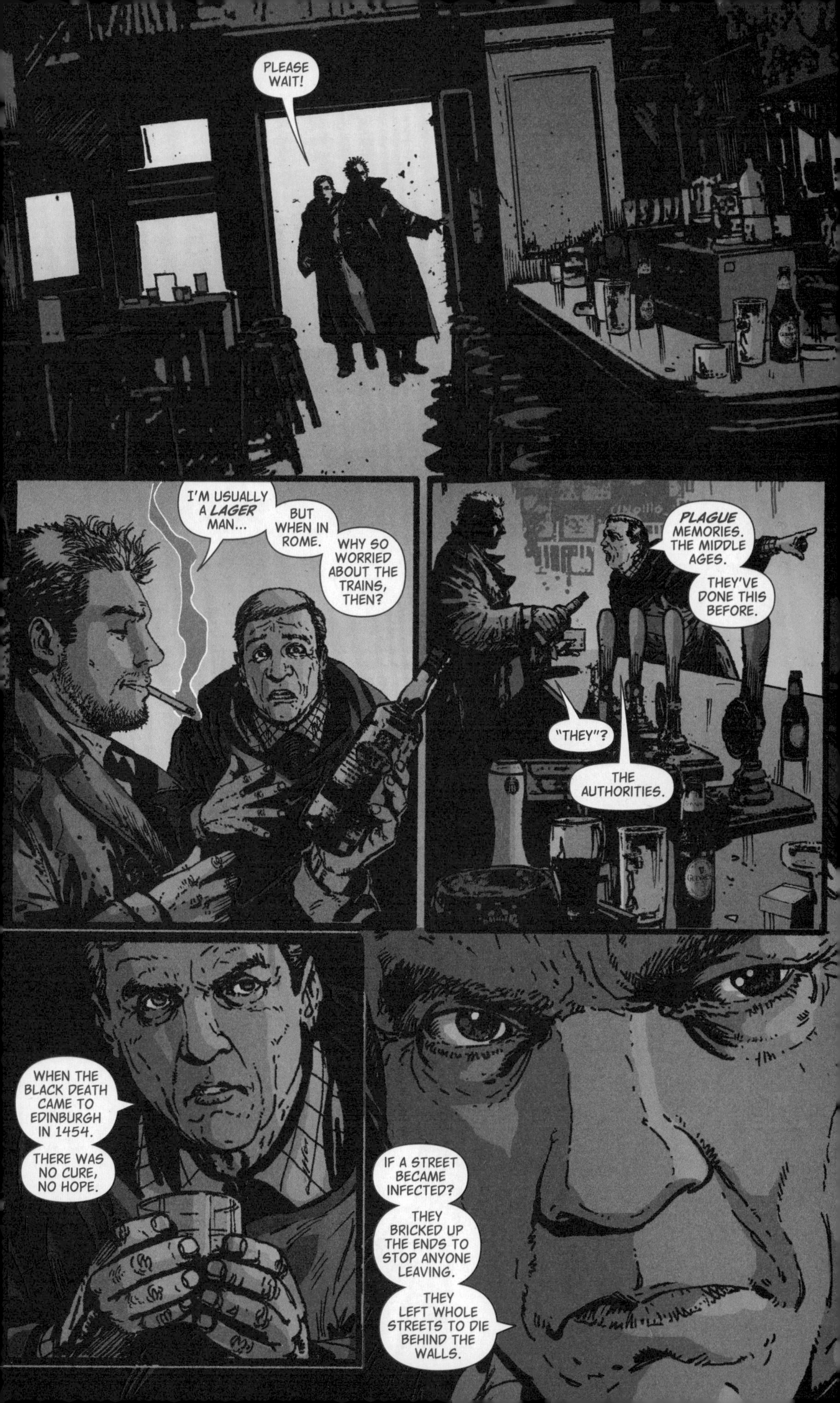
PLEASE WAIT!
I'M USUALLY A *LAGER* MAN...
BUT WHEN IN ROME.
WHY SO WORRIED ABOUT THE TRAINS, THEN?
PLAGUE MEMORIES. THE MIDDLE AGES.
THEY'VE DONE THIS BEFORE.
"THEY"?
THE AUTHORITIES.
WHEN THE BLACK DEATH CAME TO EDINBURGH IN 1454.
THERE WAS NO CURE, NO HOPE.
IF A STREET BECAME INFECTED?
THEY BRICKED UP THE ENDS TO STOP ANYONE LEAVING.
THEY LEFT WHOLE STREETS TO DIE BEHIND THE WALLS.

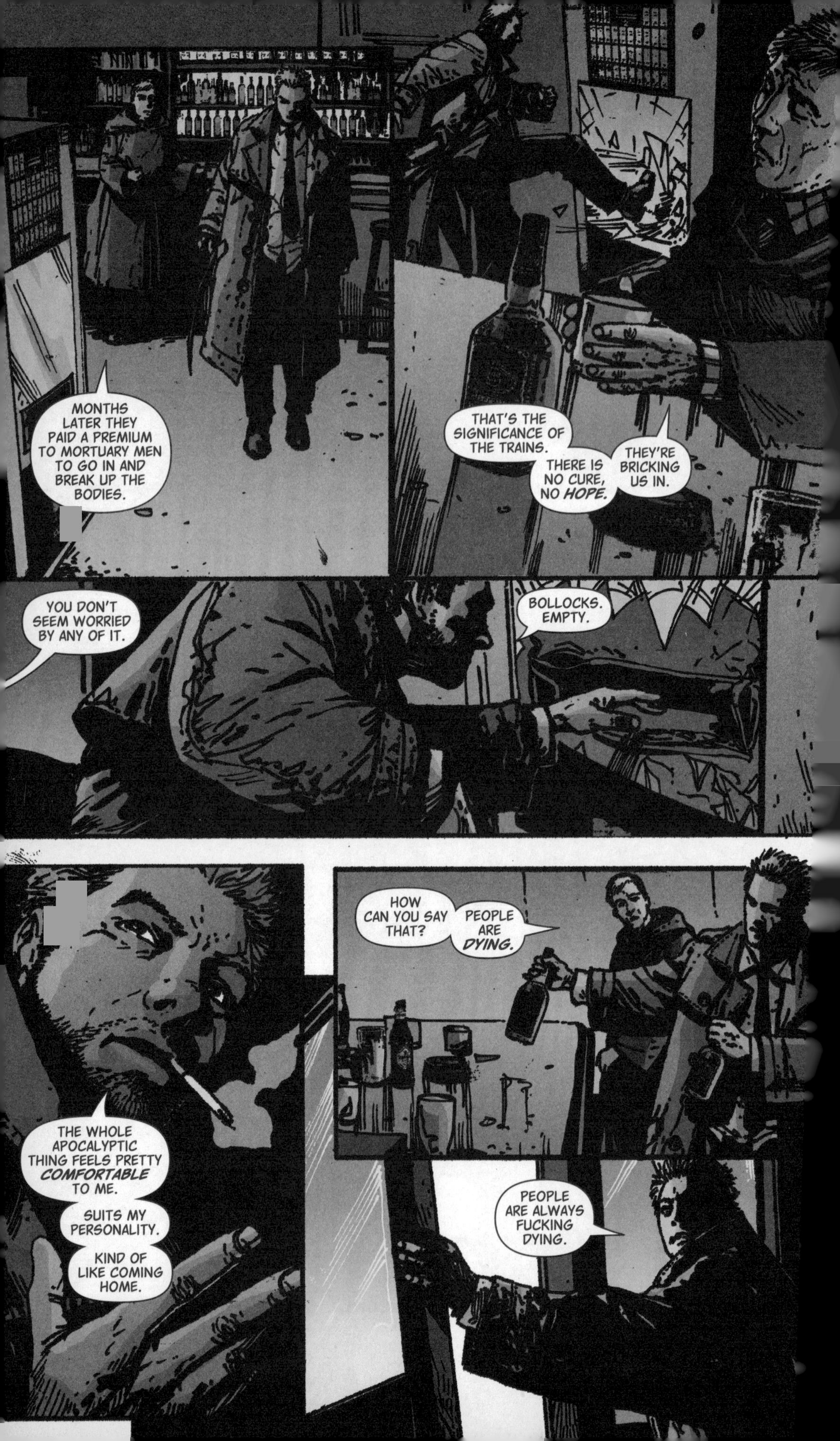
MONTHS LATER THEY PAID A PREMIUM TO MORTUARY MEN TO GO IN AND BREAK UP THE BODIES.
THAT'S THE SIGNIFICANCE OF THE TRAINS.
THERE IS NO CURE, NO *HOPE.*
THEY'RE BRICKING US IN.
YOU DON'T SEEM WORRIED BY ANY OF IT.
BOLLOCKS. EMPTY.
THE WHOLE APOCALYPTIC THING FEELS PRETTY *COMFORTABLE* TO ME.
SUITS MY PERSONALITY.
KIND OF LIKE COMING HOME.
HOW CAN YOU SAY THAT?
PEOPLE ARE *DYING.*
PEOPLE ARE ALWAYS FUCKING DYING.

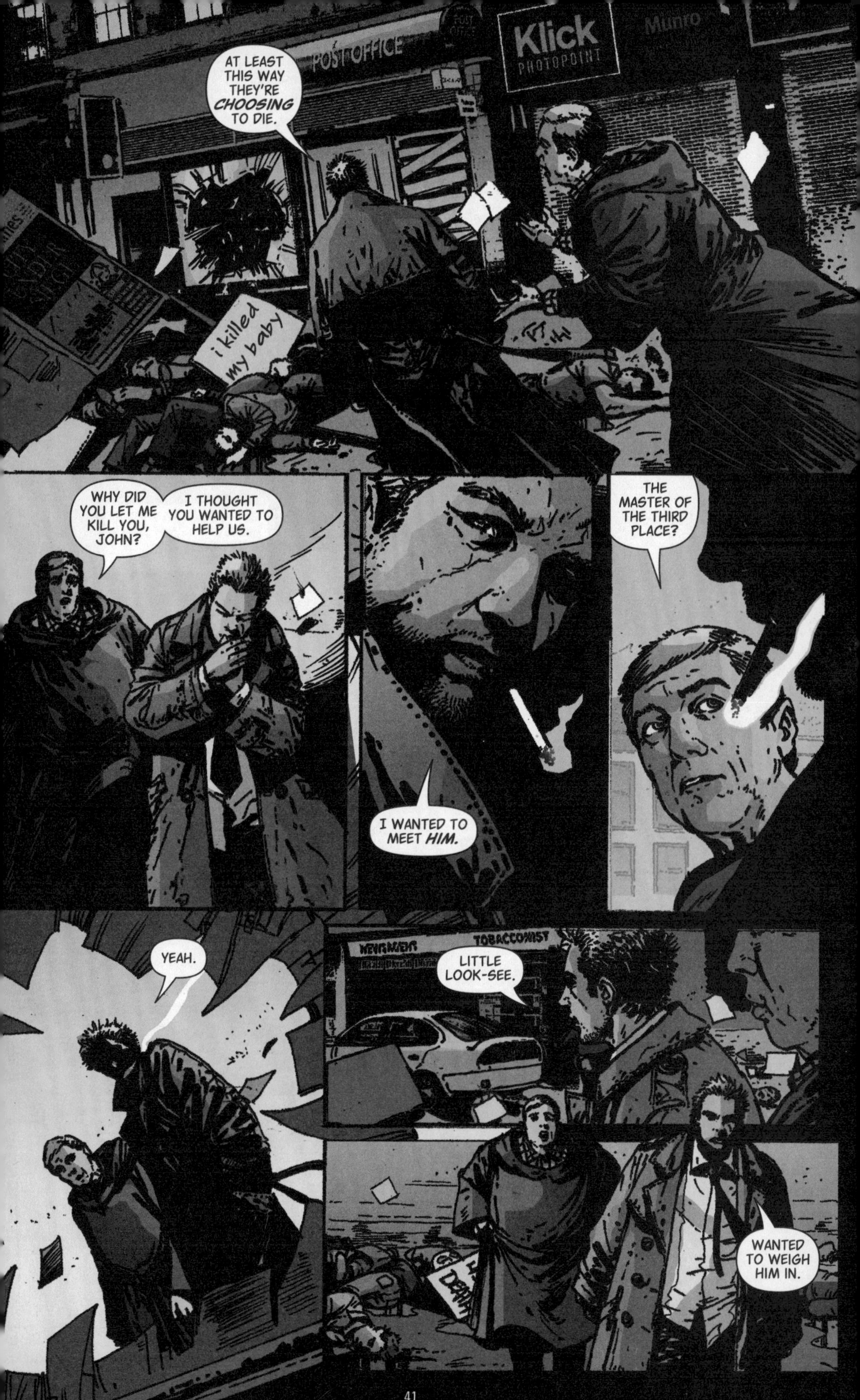

POST OFFICE
Klick
PHOTOPOINT
Munro
AT LEAST THIS WAY THEY'RE *CHOOSING* TO DIE.
i killed my baby
WHY DID YOU LET ME KILL YOU, JOHN?
I THOUGHT YOU WANTED TO HELP US.
I WANTED TO MEET *HIM.*
THE MASTER OF THE THIRD PLACE?
YEAH.
TOBACCONIST
LITTLE LOOK-SEE.
WANTED TO WEIGH HIM IN.

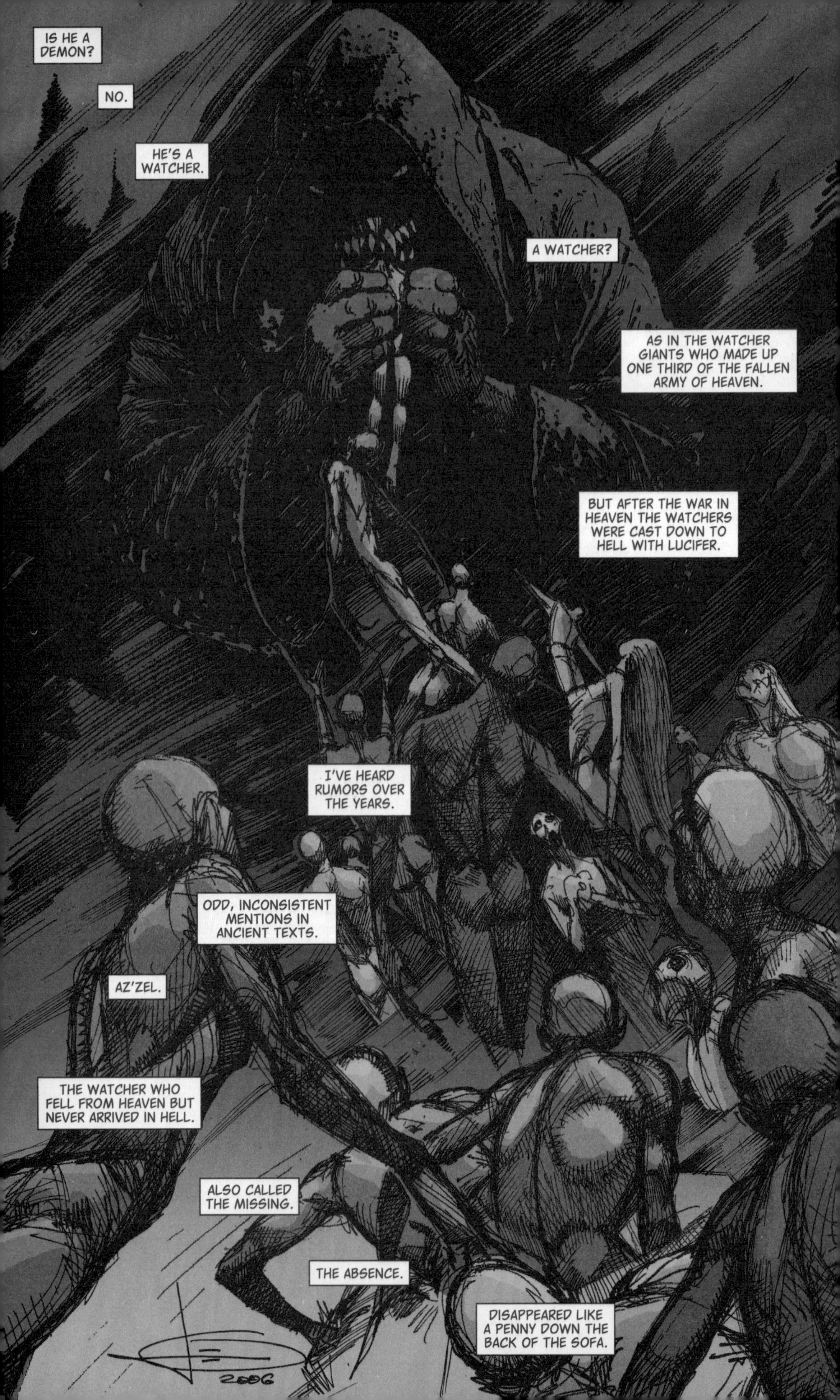
IS HE A DEMON?
NO.
HE'S A WATCHER.
A WATCHER?
AS IN THE WATCHER GIANTS WHO MADE UP ONE THIRD OF THE FALLEN ARMY OF HEAVEN.
BUT AFTER THE WAR IN HEAVEN THE WATCHERS WERE CAST DOWN TO HELL WITH LUCIFER.
I'VE HEARD RUMORS OVER THE YEARS.
ODD, INCONSISTENT MENTIONS IN ANCIENT TEXTS.
AZ'ZEL.
THE WATCHER WHO FELL FROM HEAVEN BUT NEVER ARRIVED IN HELL.
ALSO CALLED THE MISSING.
THE ABSENCE.
DISAPPEARED LIKE A PENNY DOWN THE BACK OF THE SOFA.
2006

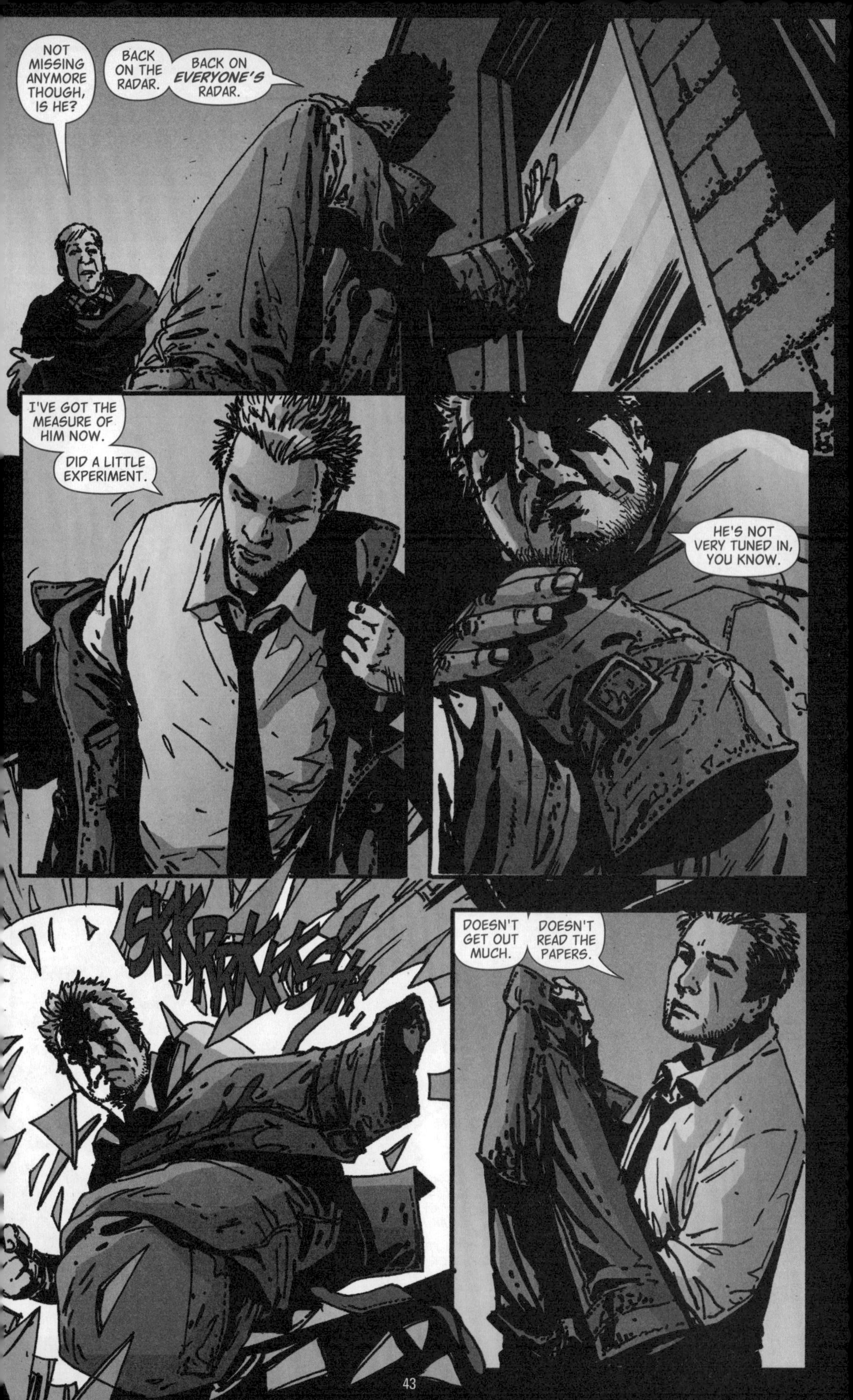
NOT MISSING ANYMORE THOUGH, IS HE?
BACK ON THE RADAR.
BACK ON *EVERYONE'S* RADAR.
I'VE GOT THE MEASURE OF HIM NOW.
DID A LITTLE EXPERIMENT.
HE'S NOT VERY TUNED IN, YOU KNOW.
SKKRKKKSH
DOESN'T GET OUT MUCH.
DOESN'T READ THE PAPERS.

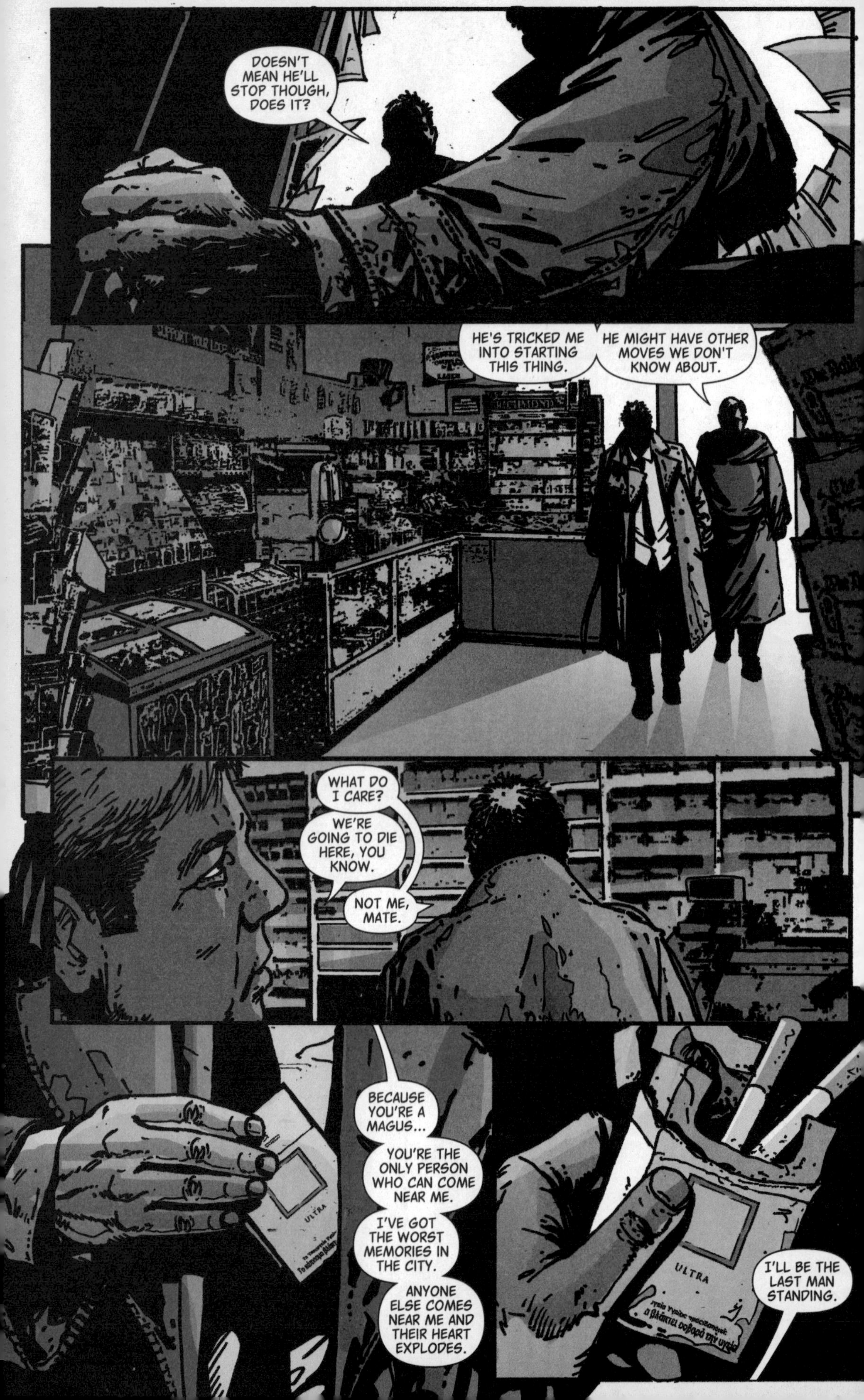
DOESN'T MEAN HE'LL STOP THOUGH, DOES IT?
HE'S TRICKED ME INTO STARTING THIS THING.
HE MIGHT HAVE OTHER MOVES WE DON'T KNOW ABOUT.
WHAT DO I CARE?
WE'RE GOING TO DIE HERE, YOU KNOW.
NOT ME, MATE.
BECAUSE YOU'RE A MAGUS...
YOU'RE THE ONLY PERSON WHO CAN COME NEAR ME.
I'VE GOT THE WORST MEMORIES IN THE CITY.
ANYONE ELSE COMES NEAR ME AND THEIR HEART EXPLODES.
ULTRA
ULTRA
I'LL BE THE LAST MAN STANDING.

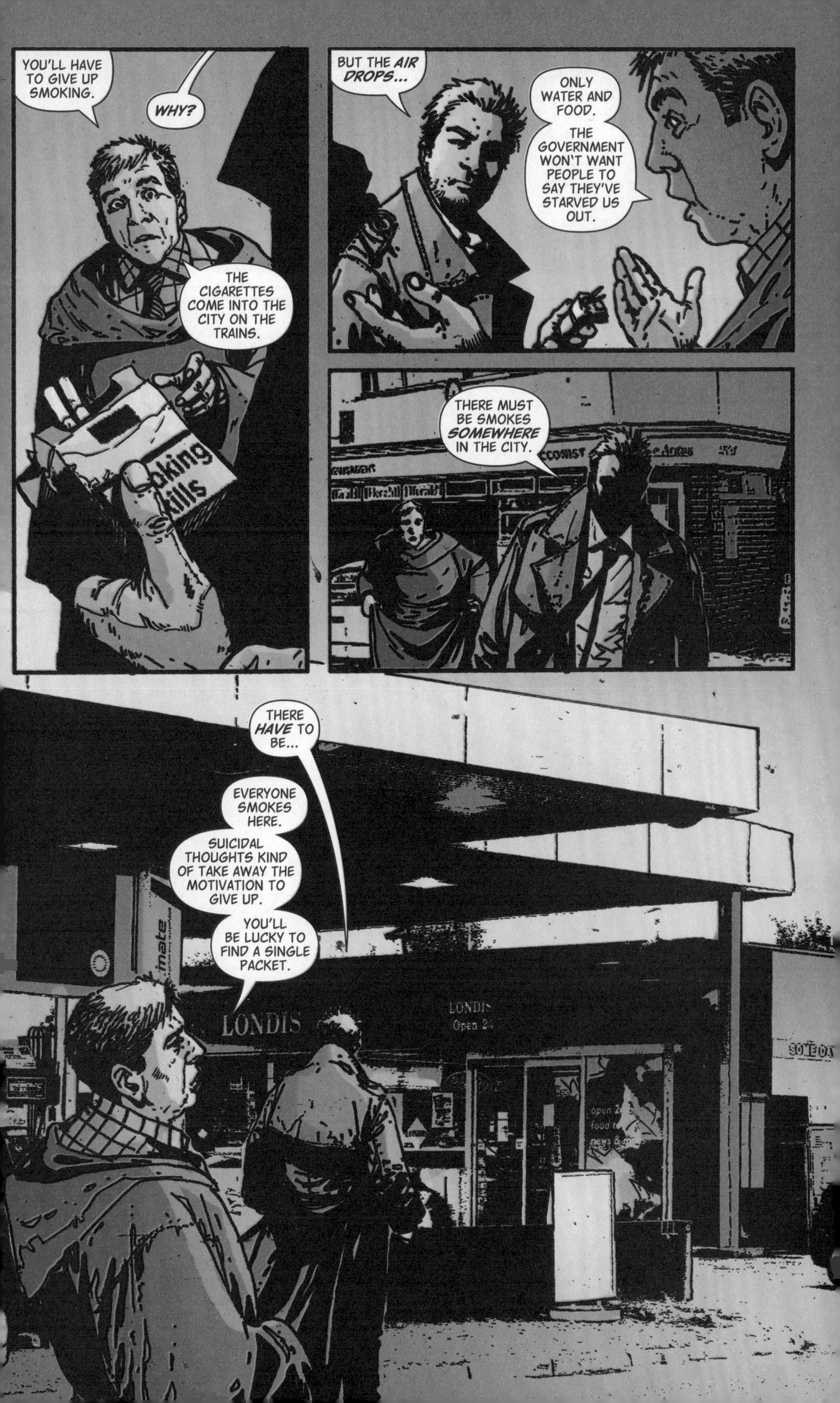
YOU'LL HAVE TO GIVE UP SMOKING.
WHY?
THE CIGARETTES COME INTO THE CITY ON THE TRAINS.
oking kills
BUT THE AIR DROPS...
ONLY WATER AND FOOD.
THE GOVERNMENT WON'T WANT PEOPLE TO SAY THEY'VE STARVED US OUT.
THERE MUST BE SMOKES SOMEWHERE IN THE CITY.
THERE HAVE TO BE...
EVERYONE SMOKES HERE.
SUICIDAL THOUGHTS KIND OF TAKE AWAY THE MOTIVATION TO GIVE UP.
YOU'LL BE LUCKY TO FIND A SINGLE PACKET.
LONDIS
LONDIS
Open 24

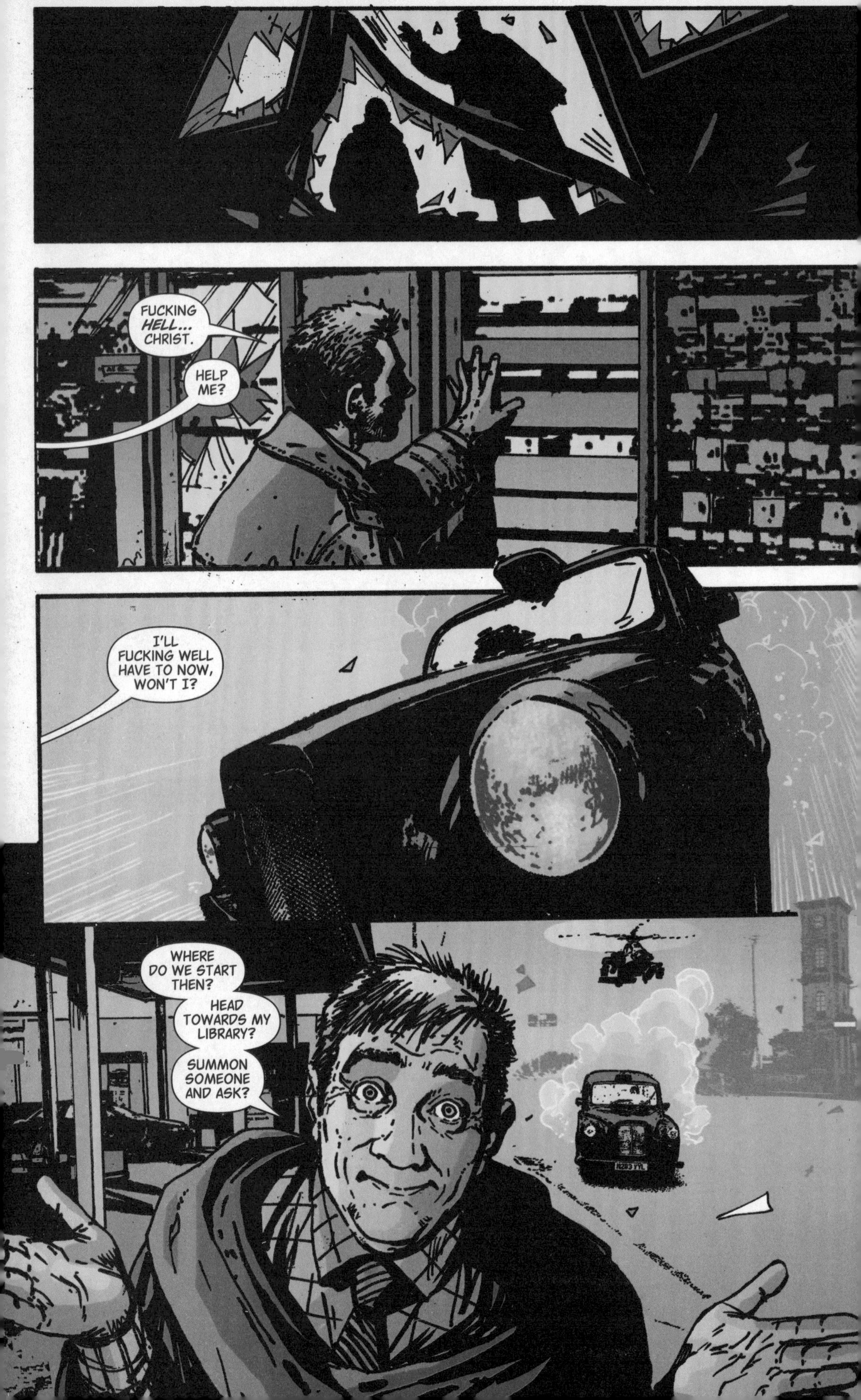
FUCKING *HELL*... CHRIST.
HELP ME?
I'LL FUCKING WELL HAVE TO NOW, WON'T I?
WHERE DO WE START THEN?
HEAD TOWARDS MY LIBRARY?
SUMMON SOMEONE AND ASK?

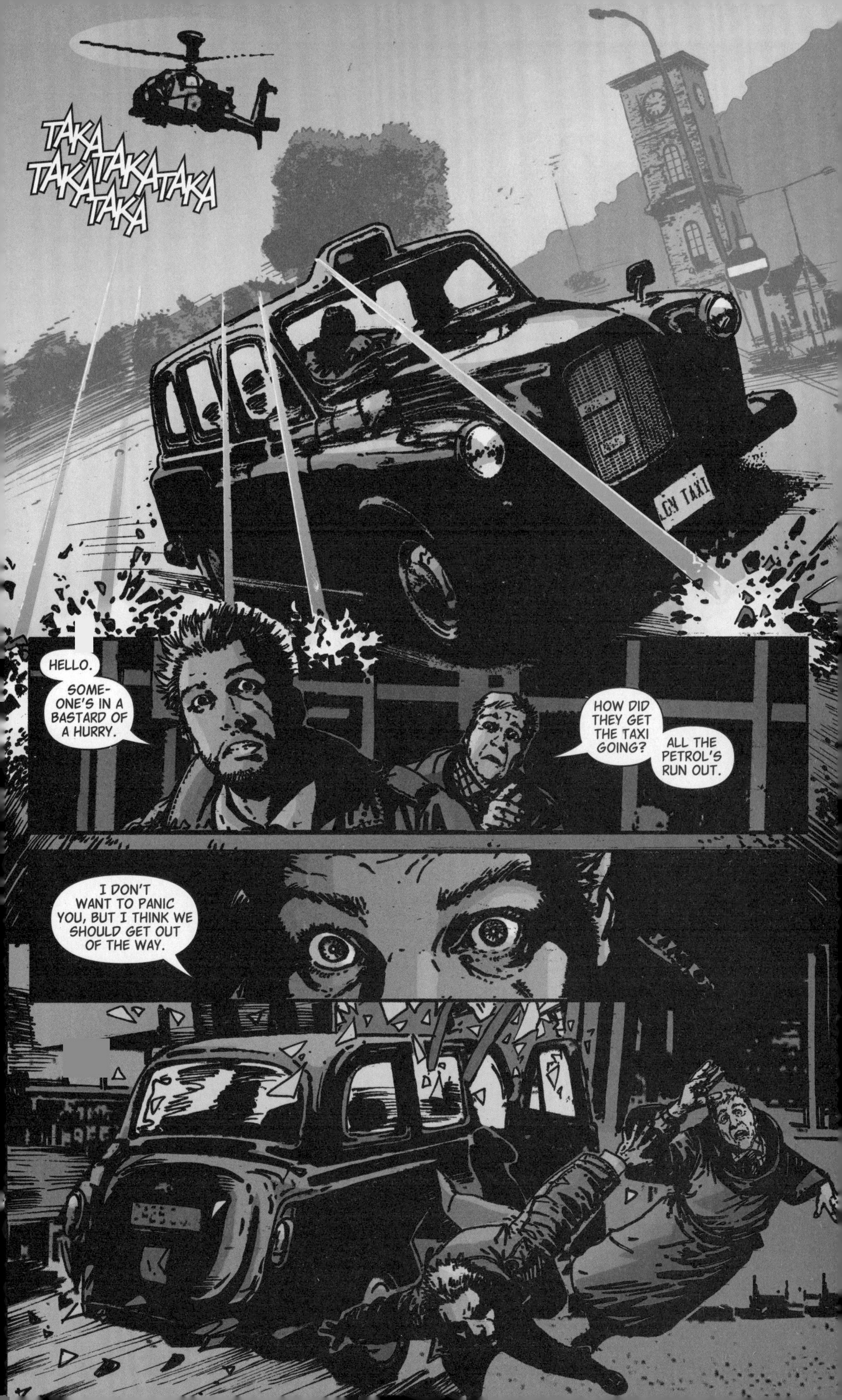
TAKA TAKATAKATAKA TAKA TAKA
LCN TAXI
HELLO.
SOME-ONE'S IN A BASTARD OF A HURRY.
HOW DID THEY GET THE TAXI GOING?
ALL THE PETROL'S RUN OUT.
I DON'T WANT TO PANIC YOU, BUT I THINK WE SHOULD GET OUT OF THE WAY.

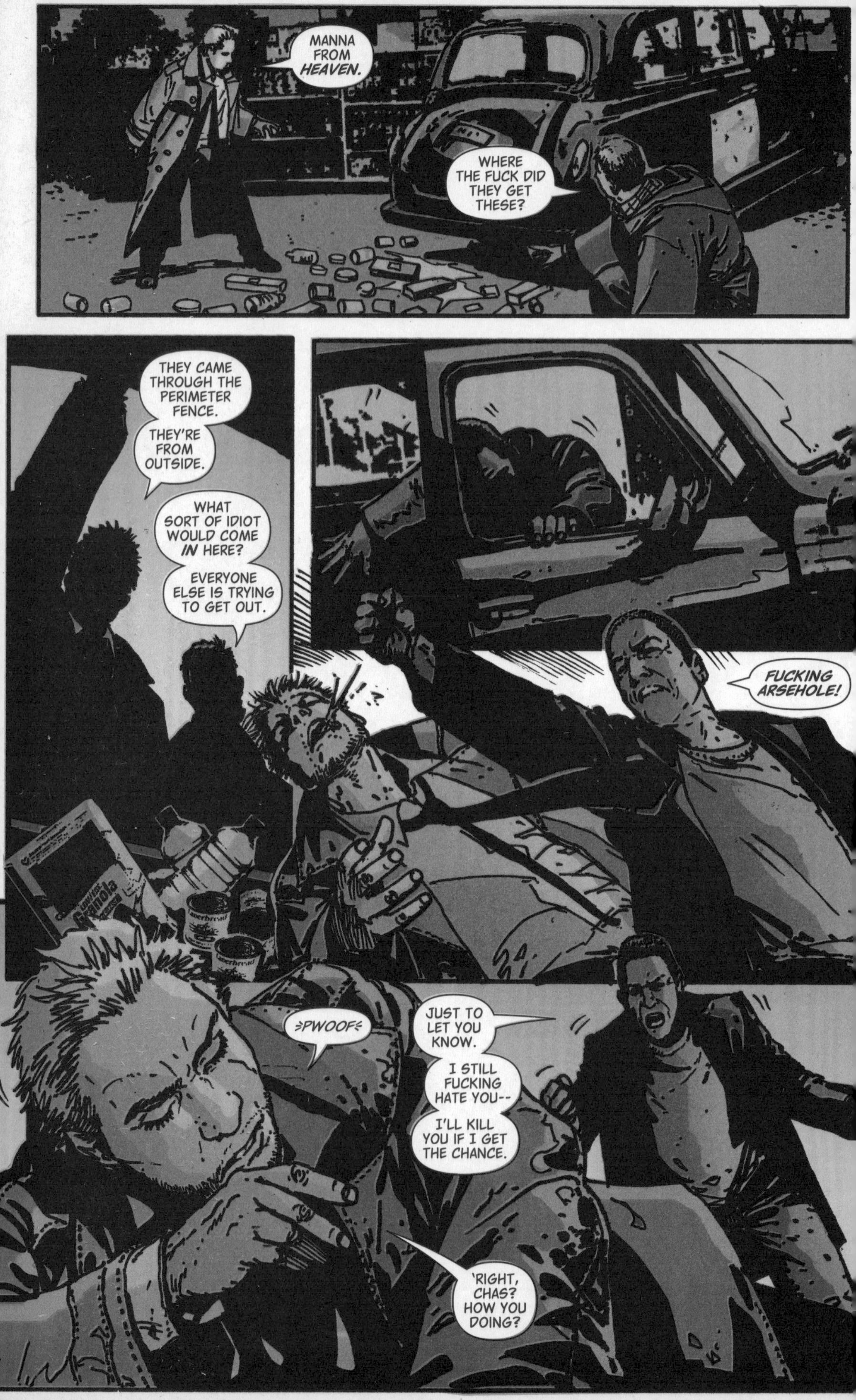
MANNA FROM HEAVEN.
WHERE THE FUCK DID THEY GET THESE?
THEY CAME THROUGH THE PERIMETER FENCE.
THEY'RE FROM OUTSIDE.
WHAT SORT OF IDIOT WOULD COME IN HERE?
EVERYONE ELSE IS TRYING TO GET OUT.
FUCKING ARSEHOLE!
PWOOF
JUST TO LET YOU KNOW.
I STILL FUCKING HATE YOU--
I'LL KILL YOU IF I GET THE CHANCE.
'RIGHT, CHAS? HOW YOU DOING?

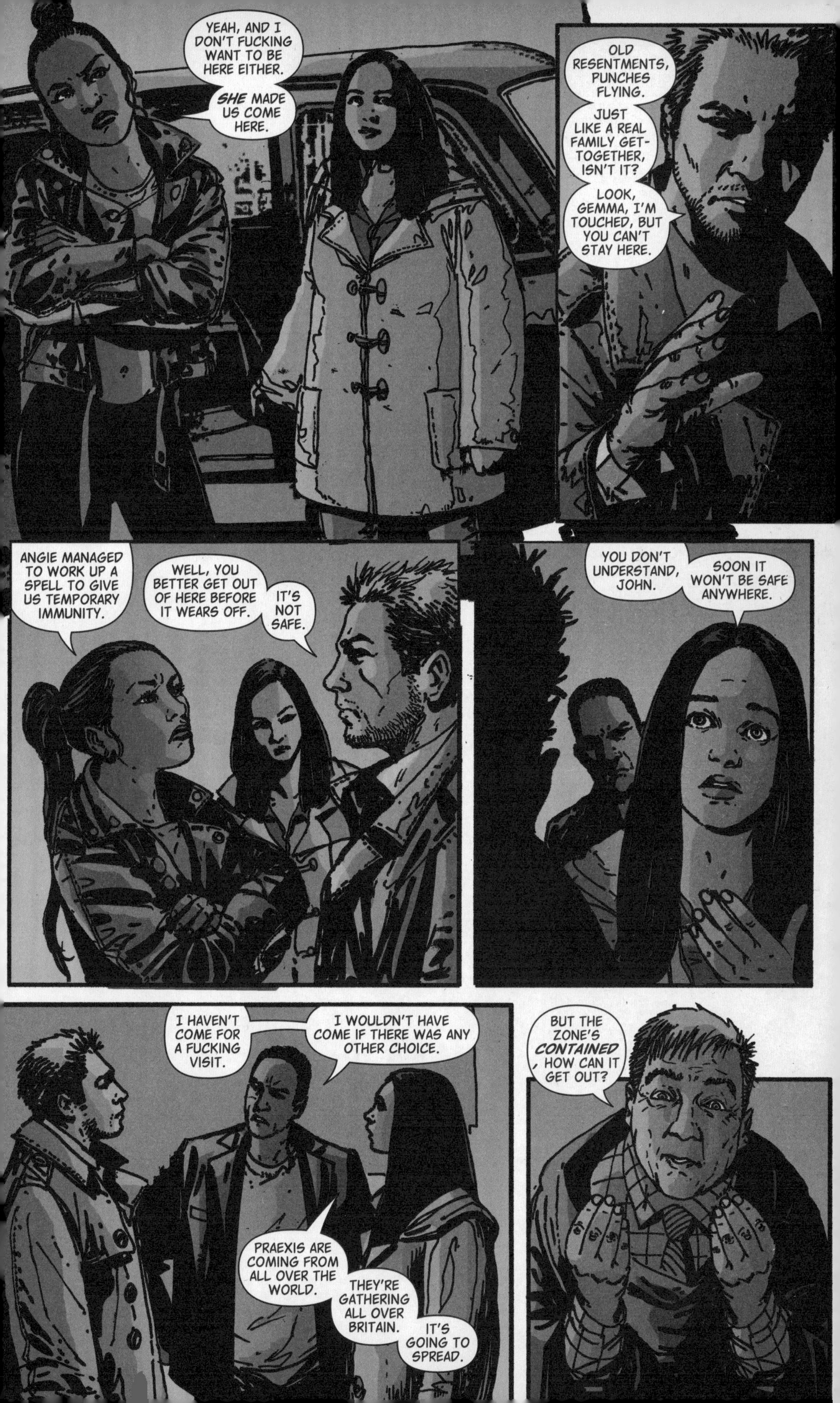
YEAH, AND I DON'T FUCKING WANT TO BE HERE EITHER.
SHE MADE US COME HERE.
OLD RESENTMENTS, PUNCHES FLYING.
JUST LIKE A REAL FAMILY GET-TOGETHER, ISN'T IT?
LOOK, GEMMA, I'M TOUCHED, BUT YOU CAN'T STAY HERE.
ANGIE MANAGED TO WORK UP A SPELL TO GIVE US TEMPORARY IMMUNITY.
WELL, YOU BETTER GET OUT OF HERE BEFORE IT WEARS OFF.
IT'S NOT SAFE.
YOU DON'T UNDERSTAND, JOHN.
SOON IT WON'T BE SAFE ANYWHERE.
I HAVEN'T COME FOR A FUCKING VISIT.
I WOULDN'T HAVE COME IF THERE WAS ANY OTHER CHOICE.
PRAEXIS ARE COMING FROM ALL OVER THE WORLD.
THEY'RE GATHERING ALL OVER BRITAIN.
IT'S GOING TO SPREAD.
BUT THE ZONE'S *CONTAINED*, HOW CAN IT GET OUT?

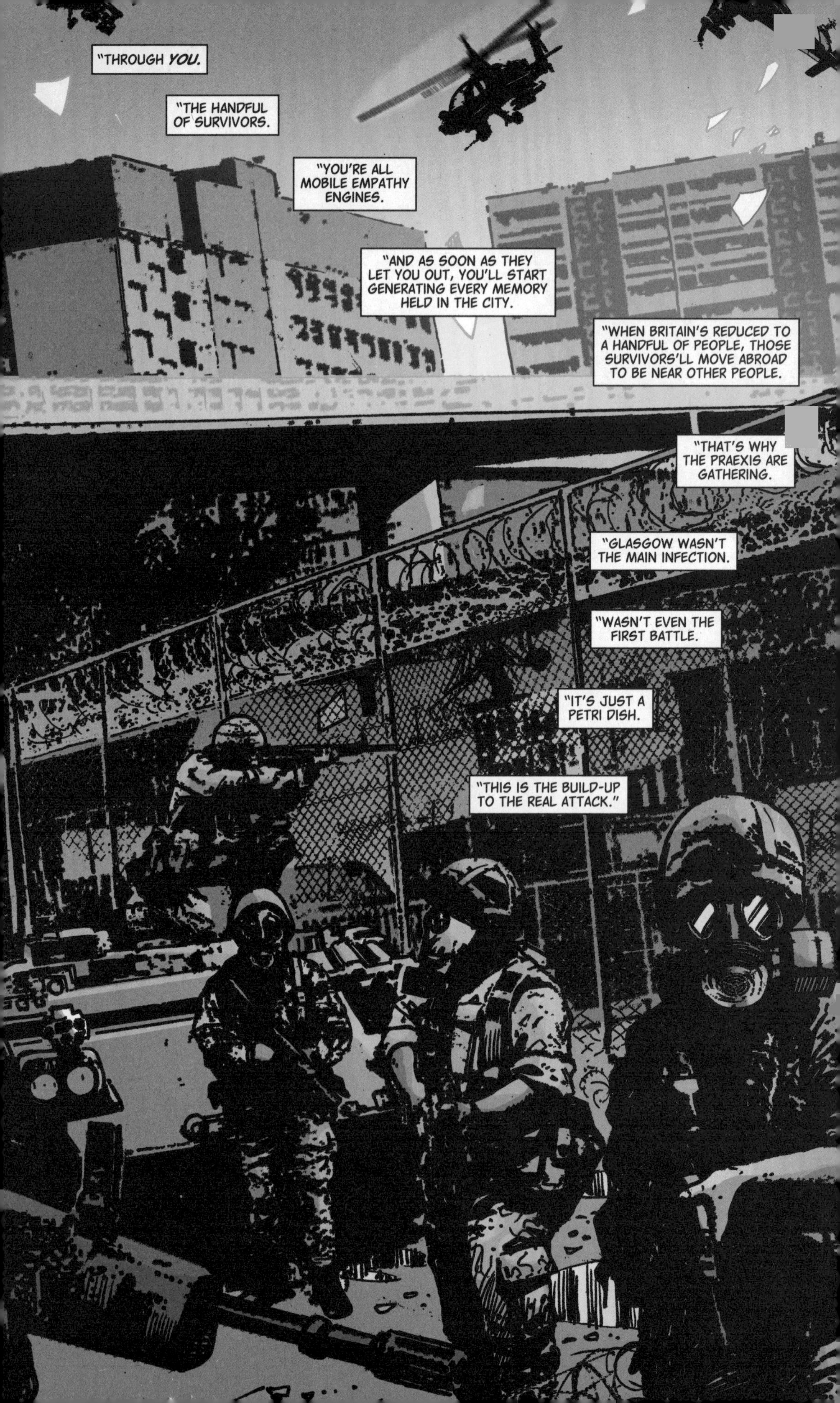
"THROUGH *YOU.*
"THE HANDFUL OF SURVIVORS.
"YOU'RE ALL MOBILE EMPATHY ENGINES.
"AND AS SOON AS THEY LET YOU OUT, YOU'LL START GENERATING EVERY MEMORY HELD IN THE CITY.
"WHEN BRITAIN'S REDUCED TO A HANDFUL OF PEOPLE, THOSE SURVIVORS'LL MOVE ABROAD TO BE NEAR OTHER PEOPLE.
"THAT'S WHY THE PRAEXIS ARE GATHERING.
"GLASGOW WASN'T THE MAIN INFECTION.
"WASN'T EVEN THE FIRST BATTLE.
"IT'S JUST A PETRI DISH.
"THIS IS THE BUILD-UP TO THE REAL ATTACK."

THE RED RIGHT HAND Chapter 2

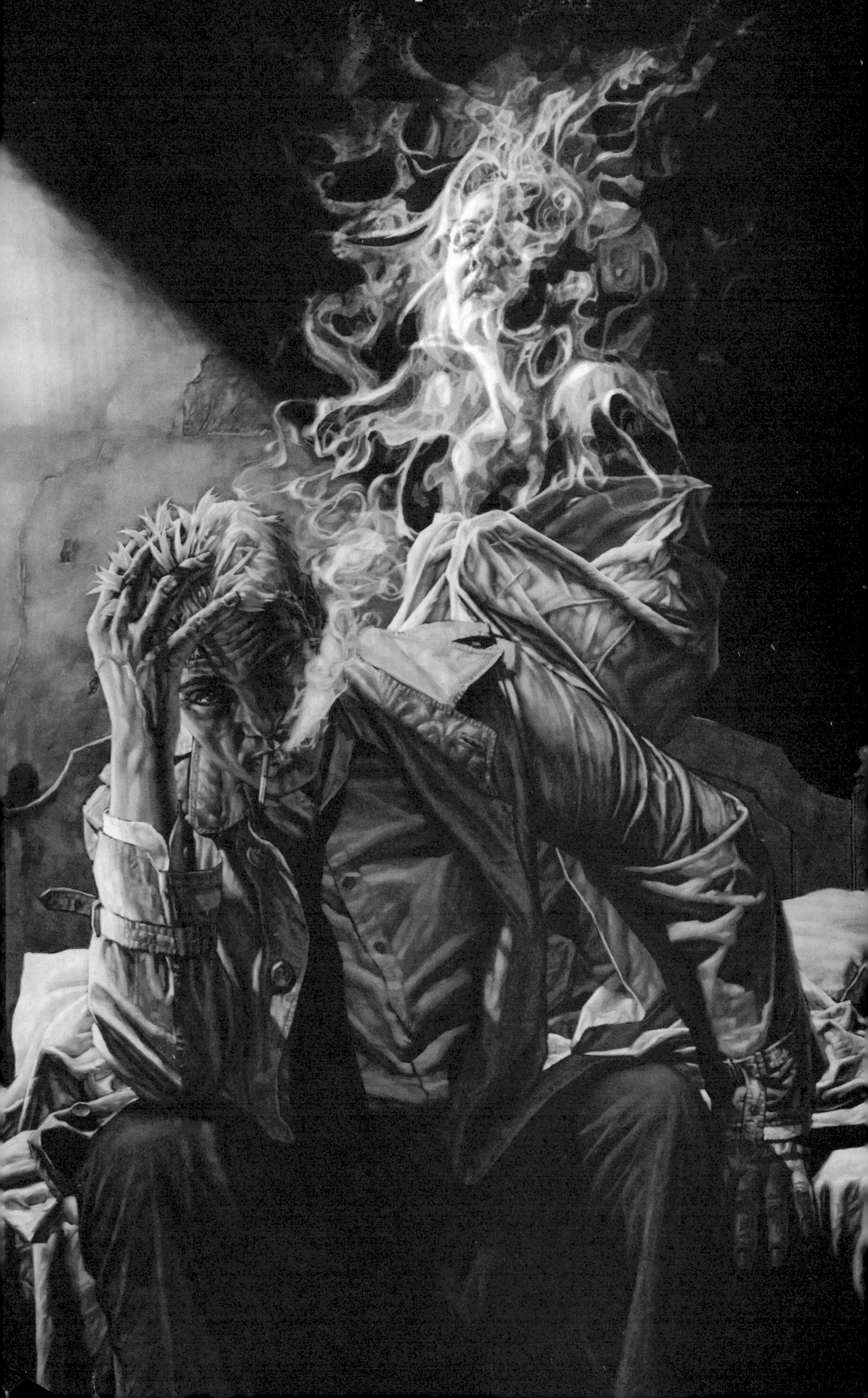

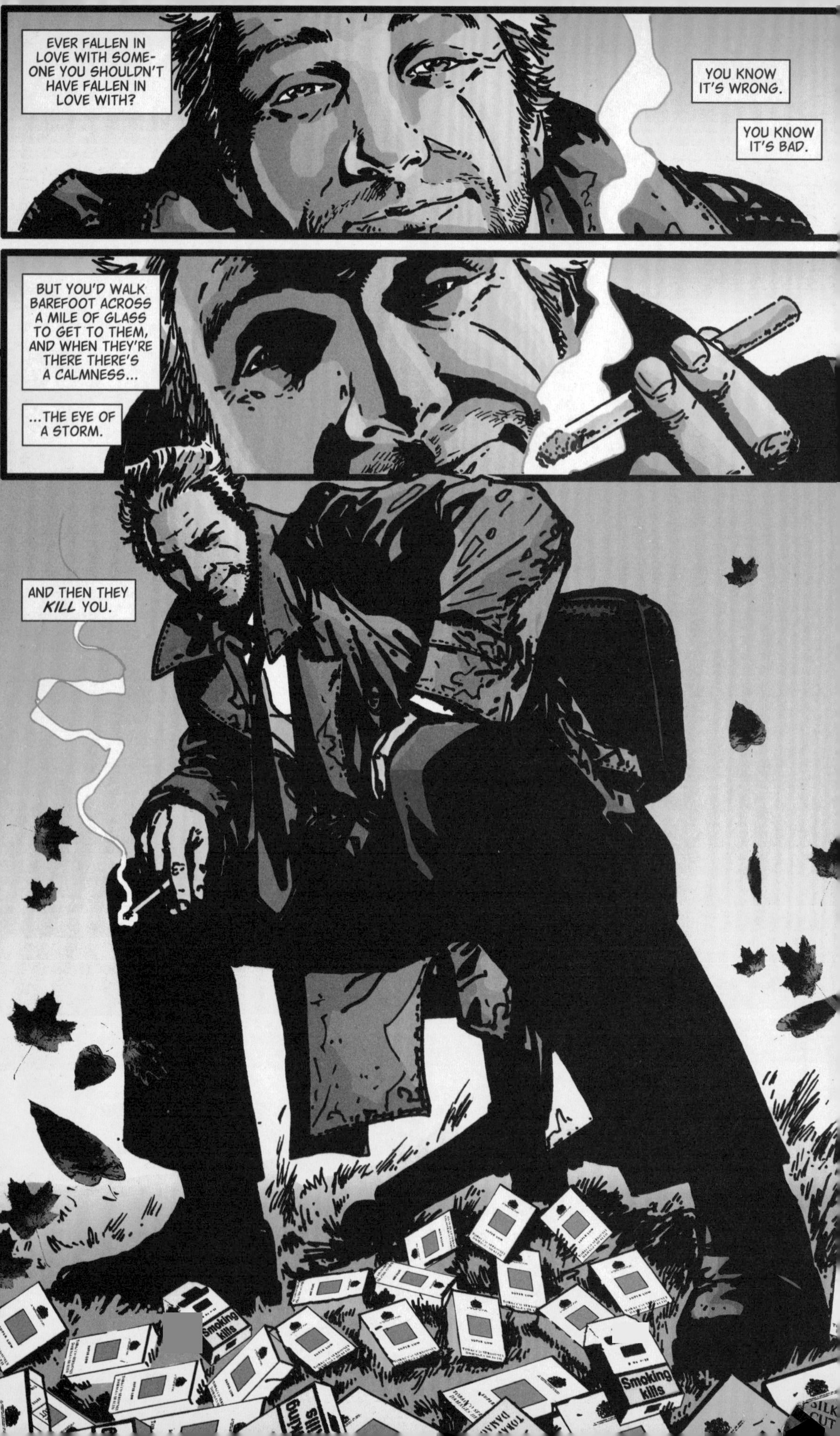
EVER FALLEN IN LOVE WITH SOME-ONE YOU SHOULDN'T HAVE FALLEN IN LOVE WITH?
YOU KNOW IT'S WRONG.
YOU KNOW IT'S BAD.
BUT YOU'D WALK BAREFOOT ACROSS A MILE OF GLASS TO GET TO THEM, AND WHEN THEY'RE THERE THERE'S A CALMNESS...
...THE EYE OF A STORM.
AND THEN THEY *KILL* YOU.
Smoking kills
Smoking kills

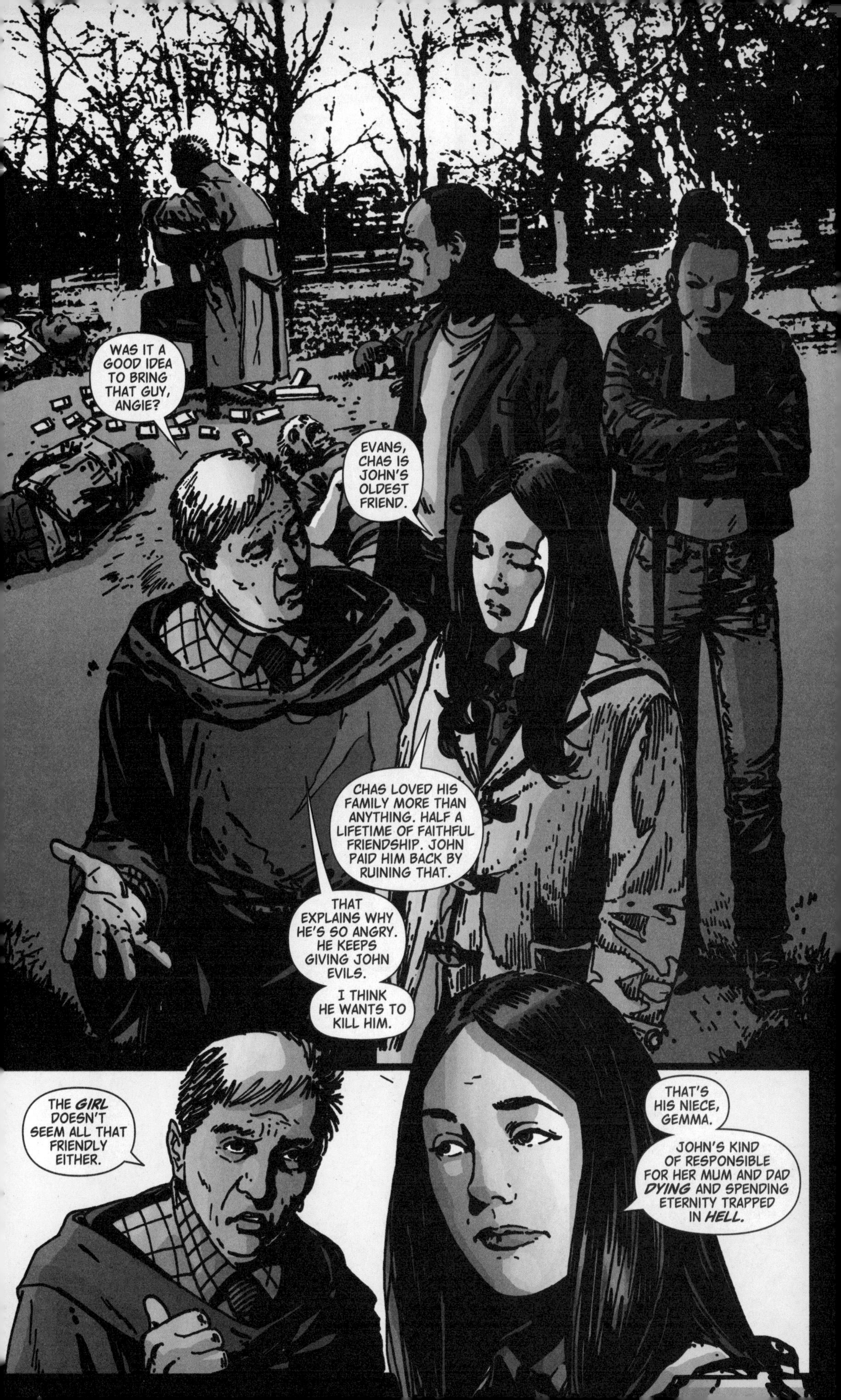
WAS IT A GOOD IDEA TO BRING THAT GUY, ANGIE?
EVANS, CHAS IS JOHN'S OLDEST FRIEND.
CHAS LOVED HIS FAMILY MORE THAN ANYTHING. HALF A LIFETIME OF FAITHFUL FRIENDSHIP. JOHN PAID HIM BACK BY RUINING THAT.
THAT EXPLAINS WHY HE'S SO ANGRY. HE KEEPS GIVING JOHN EVILS.
I THINK HE WANTS TO KILL HIM.
THE GIRL DOESN'T SEEM ALL THAT FRIENDLY EITHER.
THAT'S HIS NIECE, GEMMA.
JOHN'S KIND OF RESPONSIBLE FOR HER MUM AND DAD DYING AND SPENDING ETERNITY TRAPPED IN HELL.

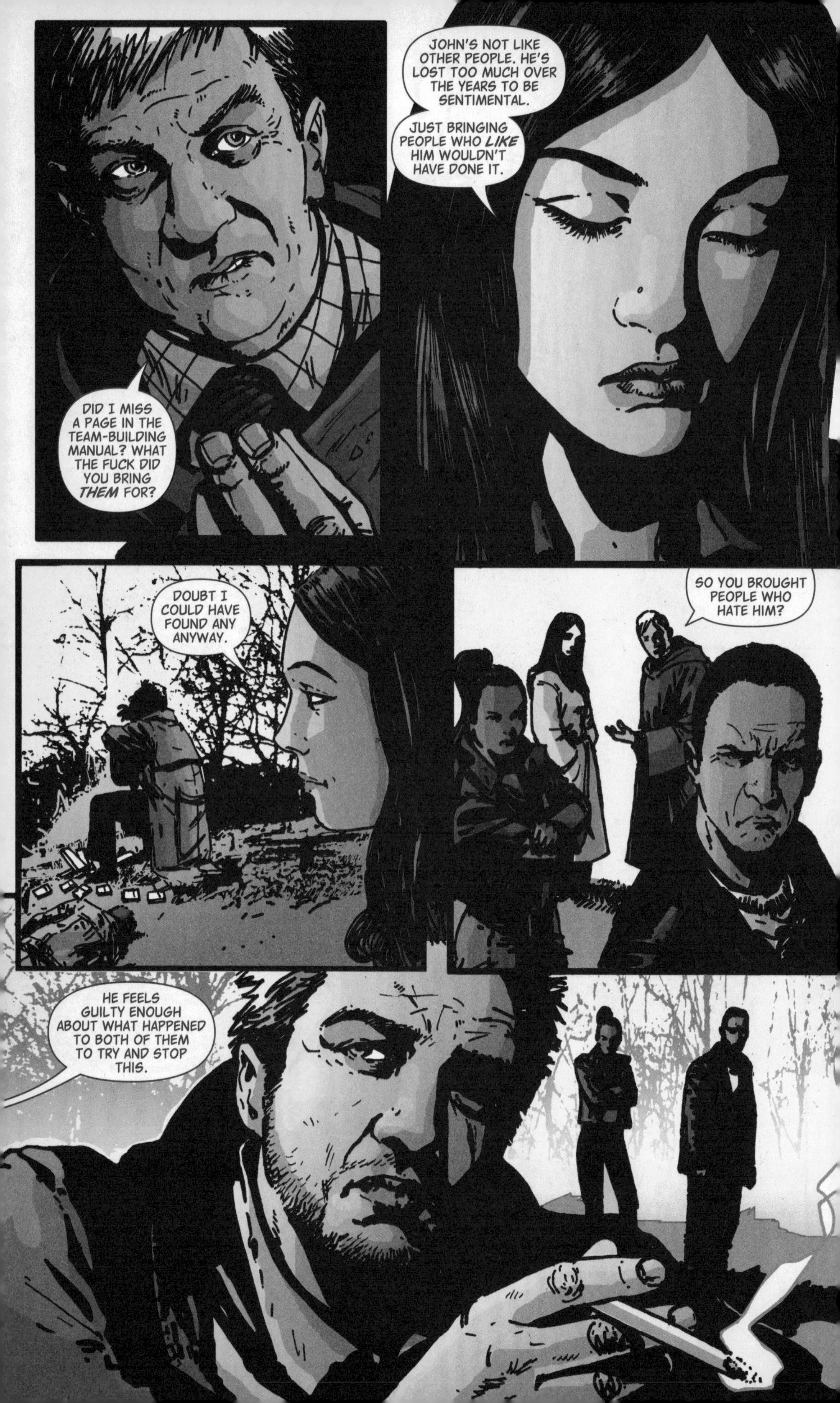
JOHN'S NOT LIKE OTHER PEOPLE. HE'S LOST TOO MUCH OVER THE YEARS TO BE SENTIMENTAL.
JUST BRINGING PEOPLE WHO *LIKE* HIM WOULDN'T HAVE DONE IT.
DID I MISS A PAGE IN THE TEAM-BUILDING MANUAL? WHAT THE FUCK DID YOU BRING *THEM* FOR?
DOUBT I COULD HAVE FOUND ANY ANYWAY.
SO YOU BROUGHT PEOPLE WHO HATE HIM?
HE FEELS GUILTY ENOUGH ABOUT WHAT HAPPENED TO BOTH OF THEM TO TRY AND STOP THIS.

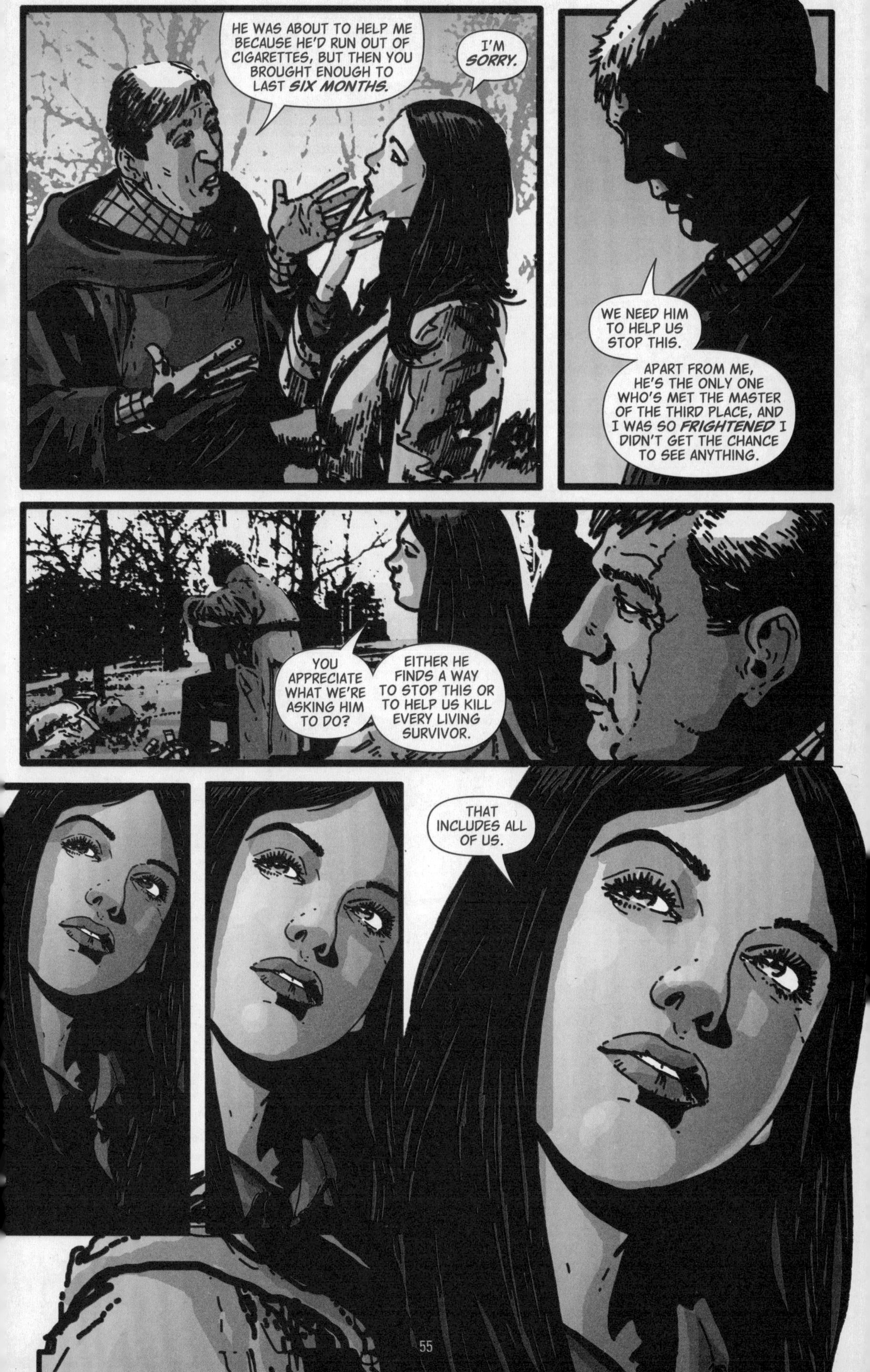
HE WAS ABOUT TO HELP ME BECAUSE HE'D RUN OUT OF CIGARETTES, BUT THEN YOU BROUGHT ENOUGH TO LAST SIX MONTHS.
I'M SORRY.
WE NEED HIM TO HELP US STOP THIS.
APART FROM ME, HE'S THE ONLY ONE WHO'S MET THE MASTER OF THE THIRD PLACE, AND I WAS SO FRIGHTENED I DIDN'T GET THE CHANCE TO SEE ANYTHING.
YOU APPRECIATE WHAT WE'RE ASKING HIM TO DO?
EITHER HE FINDS A WAY TO STOP THIS OR TO HELP US KILL EVERY LIVING SURVIVOR.
THAT INCLUDES ALL OF US.

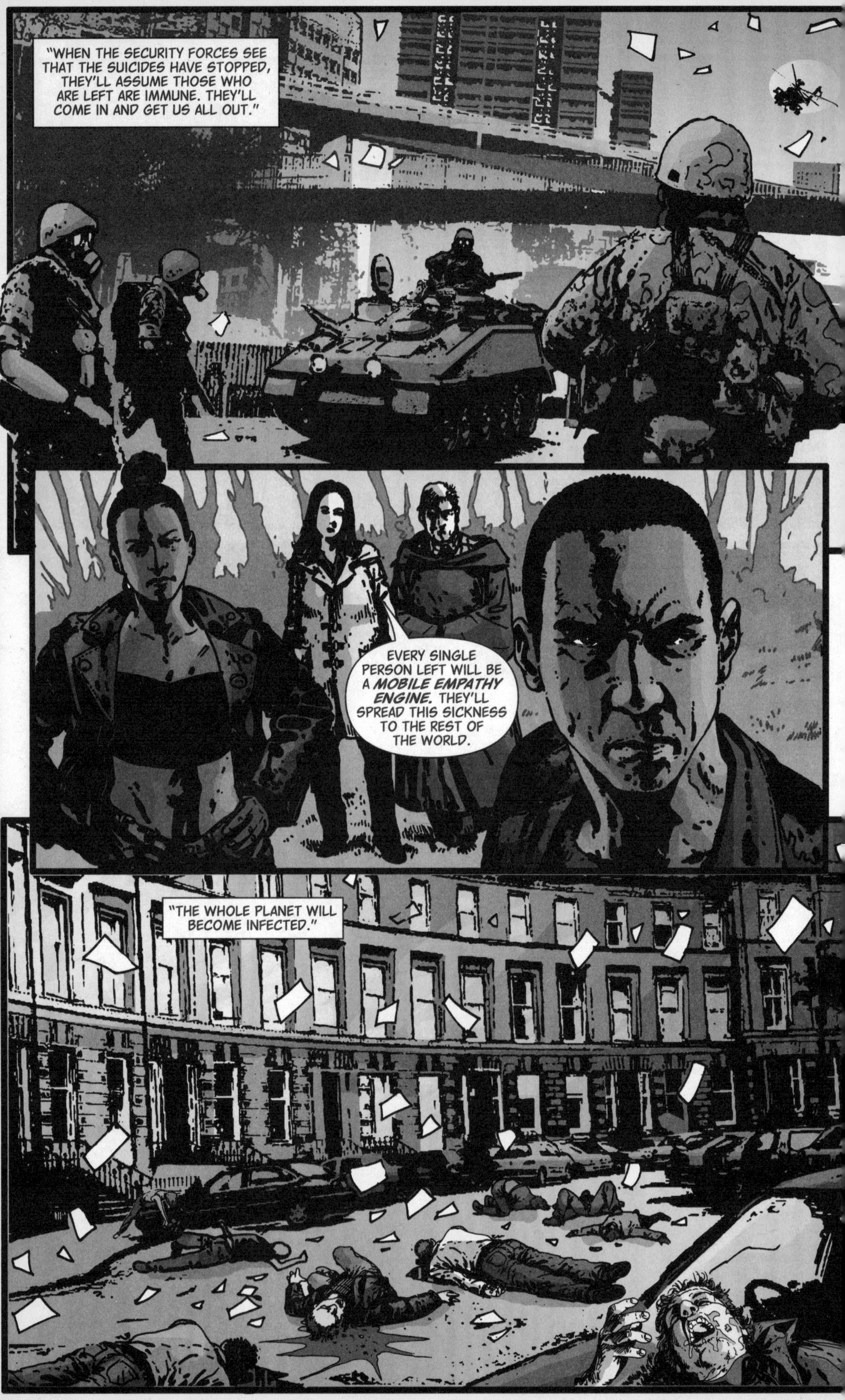
"WHEN THE SECURITY FORCES SEE THAT THE SUICIDES HAVE STOPPED, THEY'LL ASSUME THOSE WHO ARE LEFT ARE IMMUNE. THEY'LL COME IN AND GET US ALL OUT."
EVERY SINGLE PERSON LEFT WILL BE A *MOBILE EMPATHY ENGINE.* THEY'LL SPREAD THIS SICKNESS TO THE REST OF THE WORLD.
"THE WHOLE PLANET WILL BECOME INFECTED."

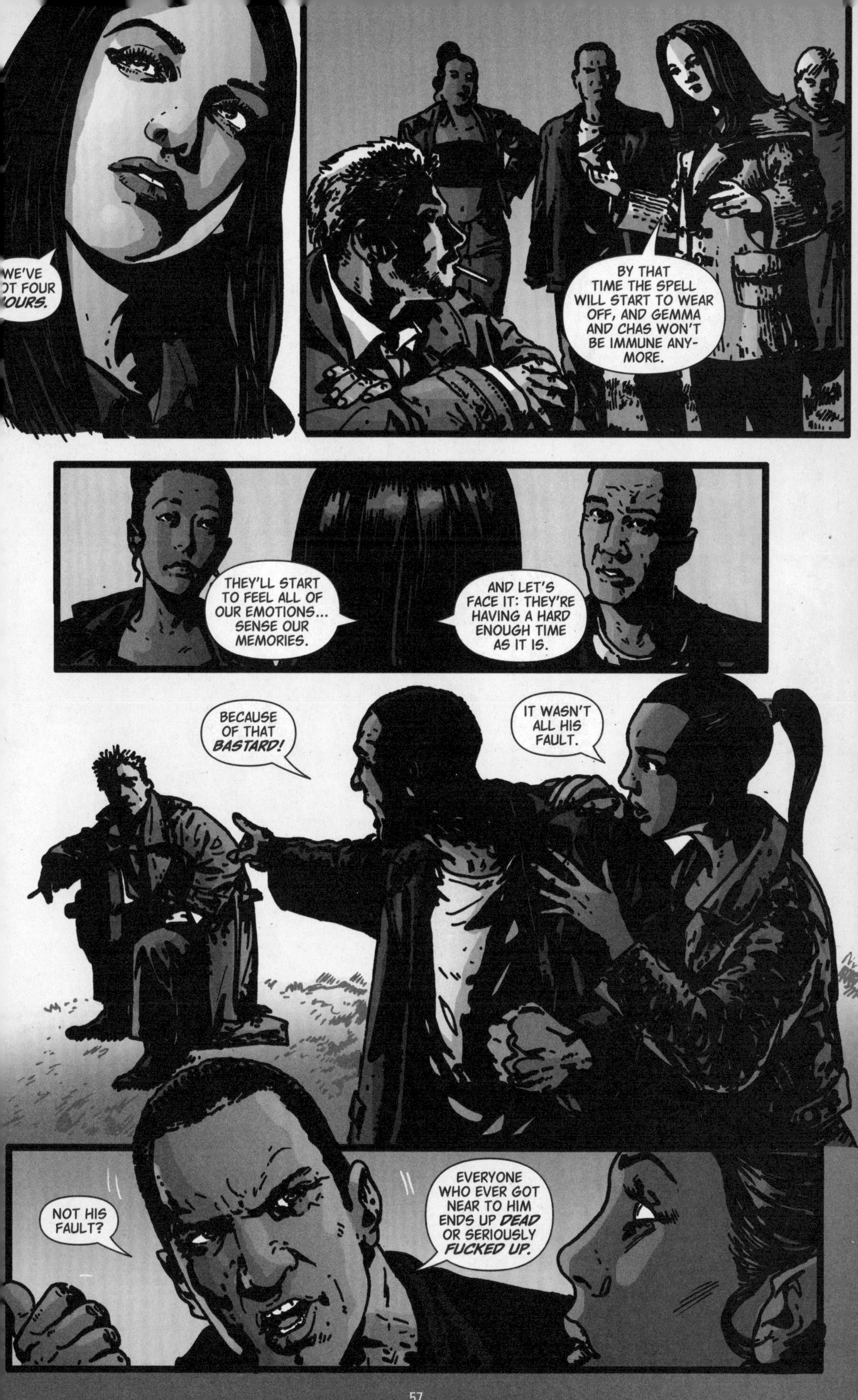
WE'VE
OT FOUR
OURS.
BY THAT TIME THE SPELL WILL START TO WEAR OFF, AND GEMMA AND CHAS WON'T BE IMMUNE ANY-MORE.
THEY'LL START TO FEEL ALL OF OUR EMOTIONS... SENSE OUR MEMORIES.
AND LET'S FACE IT: THEY'RE HAVING A HARD ENOUGH TIME AS IT IS.
BECAUSE OF THAT BASTARD!
IT WASN'T ALL HIS FAULT.
NOT HIS FAULT?
EVERYONE WHO EVER GOT NEAR TO HIM ENDS UP DEAD OR SERIOUSLY FUCKED UP.

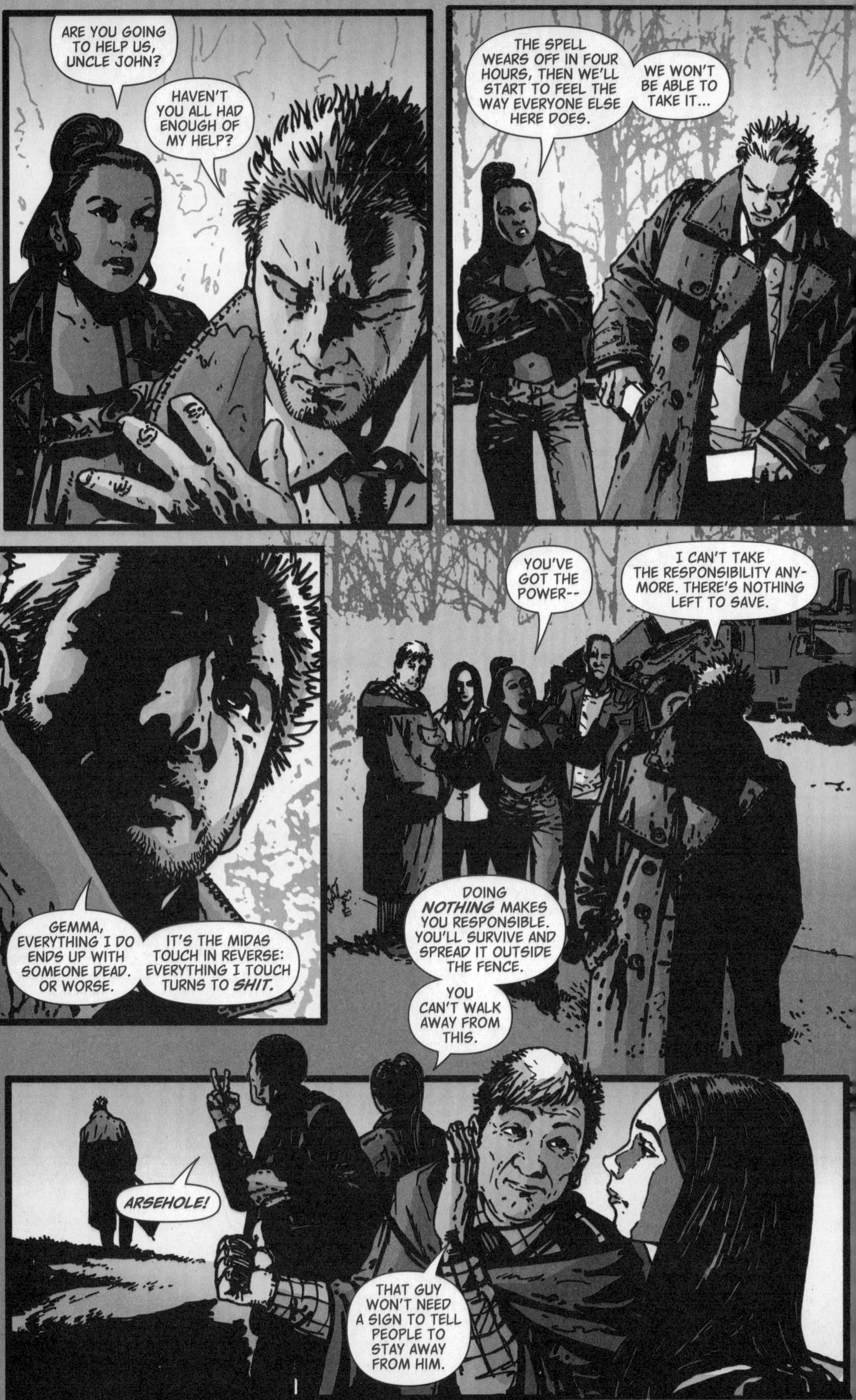

ARE YOU GOING TO HELP US, UNCLE JOHN?
HAVEN'T YOU ALL HAD ENOUGH OF MY HELP?
THE SPELL WEARS OFF IN FOUR HOURS, THEN WE'LL START TO FEEL THE WAY EVERYONE ELSE HERE DOES.
WE WON'T BE ABLE TO TAKE IT...
GEMMA, EVERYTHING I DO ENDS UP WITH SOMEONE DEAD. OR WORSE.
IT'S THE MIDAS TOUCH IN REVERSE: EVERYTHING I TOUCH TURNS TO *SHIT.*
YOU'VE GOT THE POWER--
I CAN'T TAKE THE RESPONSIBILITY ANYMORE. THERE'S NOTHING LEFT TO SAVE.
DOING ***NOTHING*** MAKES YOU RESPONSIBLE. YOU'LL SURVIVE AND SPREAD IT OUTSIDE THE FENCE.
YOU CAN'T WALK AWAY FROM THIS.
ARSEHOLE!
THAT GUY WON'T NEED A SIGN TO TELL PEOPLE TO STAY AWAY FROM HIM.

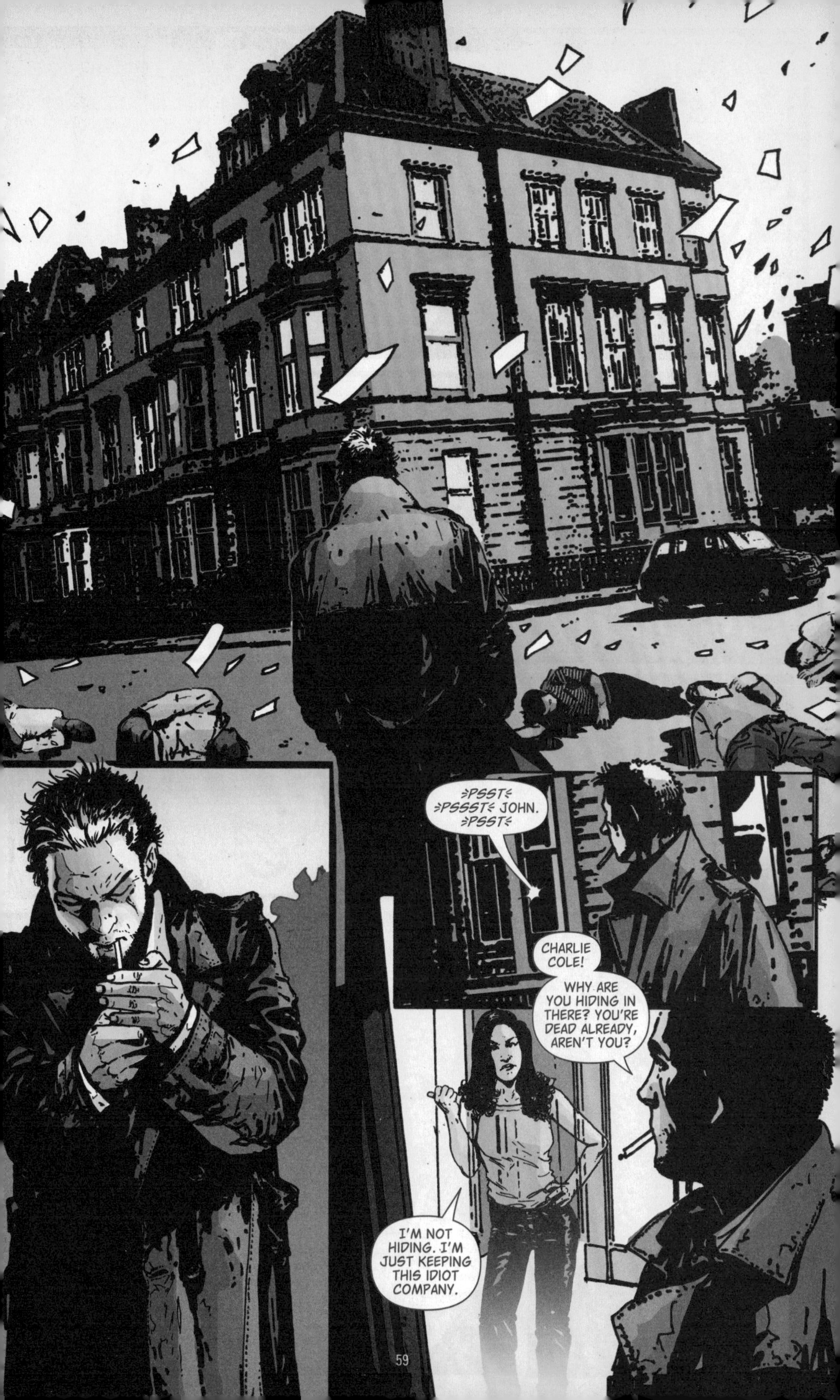

⪢PSST⪡
⪢PSSST⪡ JOHN.
⪢PSST⪡
CHARLIE COLE!
WHY ARE YOU HIDING IN THERE? YOU'RE DEAD ALREADY, AREN'T YOU?
I'M NOT HIDING. I'M JUST KEEPING THIS IDIOT COMPANY.

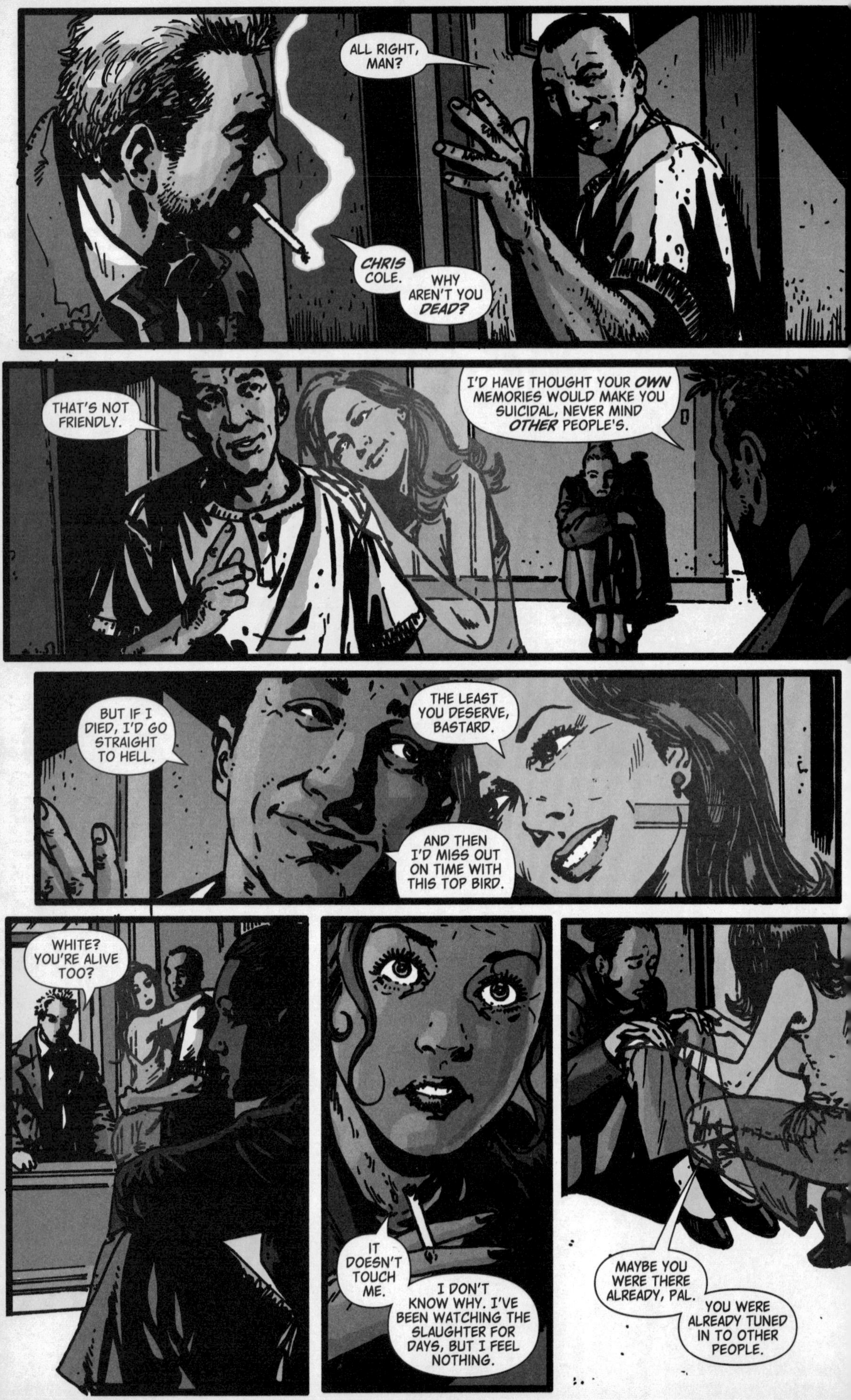

ALL RIGHT, MAN?
CHRIS COLE.
WHY AREN'T YOU DEAD?
THAT'S NOT FRIENDLY.
I'D HAVE THOUGHT YOUR OWN MEMORIES WOULD MAKE YOU SUICIDAL, NEVER MIND OTHER PEOPLE'S.
BUT IF I DIED, I'D GO STRAIGHT TO HELL.
THE LEAST YOU DESERVE, BASTARD.
AND THEN I'D MISS OUT ON TIME WITH THIS TOP BIRD.
WHITE? YOU'RE ALIVE TOO?
IT DOESN'T TOUCH ME.
I DON'T KNOW WHY. I'VE BEEN WATCHING THE SLAUGHTER FOR DAYS, BUT I FEEL NOTHING.
MAYBE YOU WERE THERE ALREADY, PAL.
YOU WERE ALREADY TUNED IN TO OTHER PEOPLE.

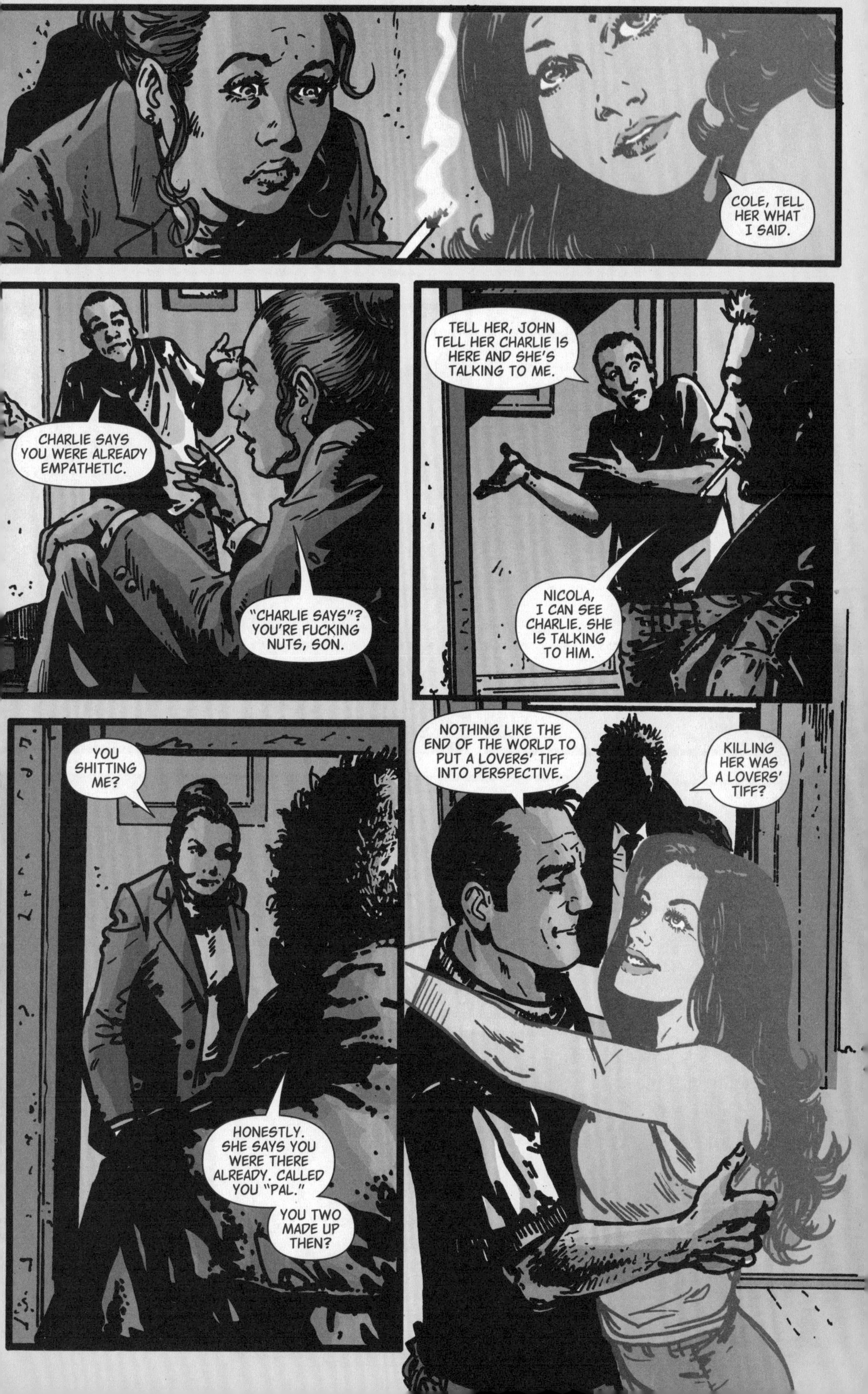
COLE, TELL HER WHAT I SAID.
CHARLIE SAYS YOU WERE ALREADY EMPATHETIC.
"CHARLIE SAYS"? YOU'RE FUCKING NUTS, SON.
TELL HER, JOHN TELL HER CHARLIE IS HERE AND SHE'S TALKING TO ME.
NICOLA, I CAN SEE CHARLIE. SHE IS TALKING TO HIM.
YOU SHITTING ME?
HONESTLY. SHE SAYS YOU WERE THERE ALREADY. CALLED YOU "PAL."
YOU TWO MADE UP THEN?
NOTHING LIKE THE END OF THE WORLD TO PUT A LOVERS' TIFF INTO PERSPECTIVE.
KILLING HER WAS A LOVERS' TIFF?

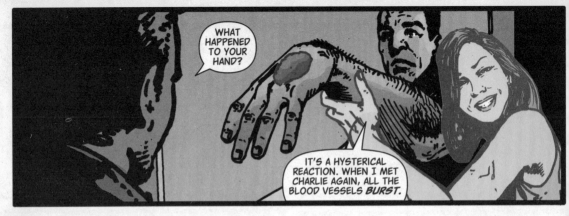

WHAT HAPPENED TO YOUR HAND?

IT'S A HYSTERICAL REACTION. WHEN I MET CHARLIE AGAIN, ALL THE BLOOD VESSELS *BURST*.

A STRAWBERRY BIRTHMARK... STAINING THE SKIN WHERE MY BLOOD RAN DOWN HIS ARM WHEN HE KILLED ME...

ISN'T THAT *SWEET?*

HE COULDN'T GET A TATTOO OF YOUR NAME OR SOMETHING?

THAT WOULD HAVE BEEN NICE TOO.

IS SHE TALKING?

I DIDN'T PLAN IT, IT JUST HAPPENED.

WE'RE GOING TO *DIE* HERE, YOU KNOW.

HARD TO CARE WHEN WE'VE GOT THE AFTERNOON TOGETHER.

CHEERY FUCKER, ISN'T HE?

HEY, JOHN, DO YOU KNOW JOAN EARDLY?

NEVER HEARD OF HER.

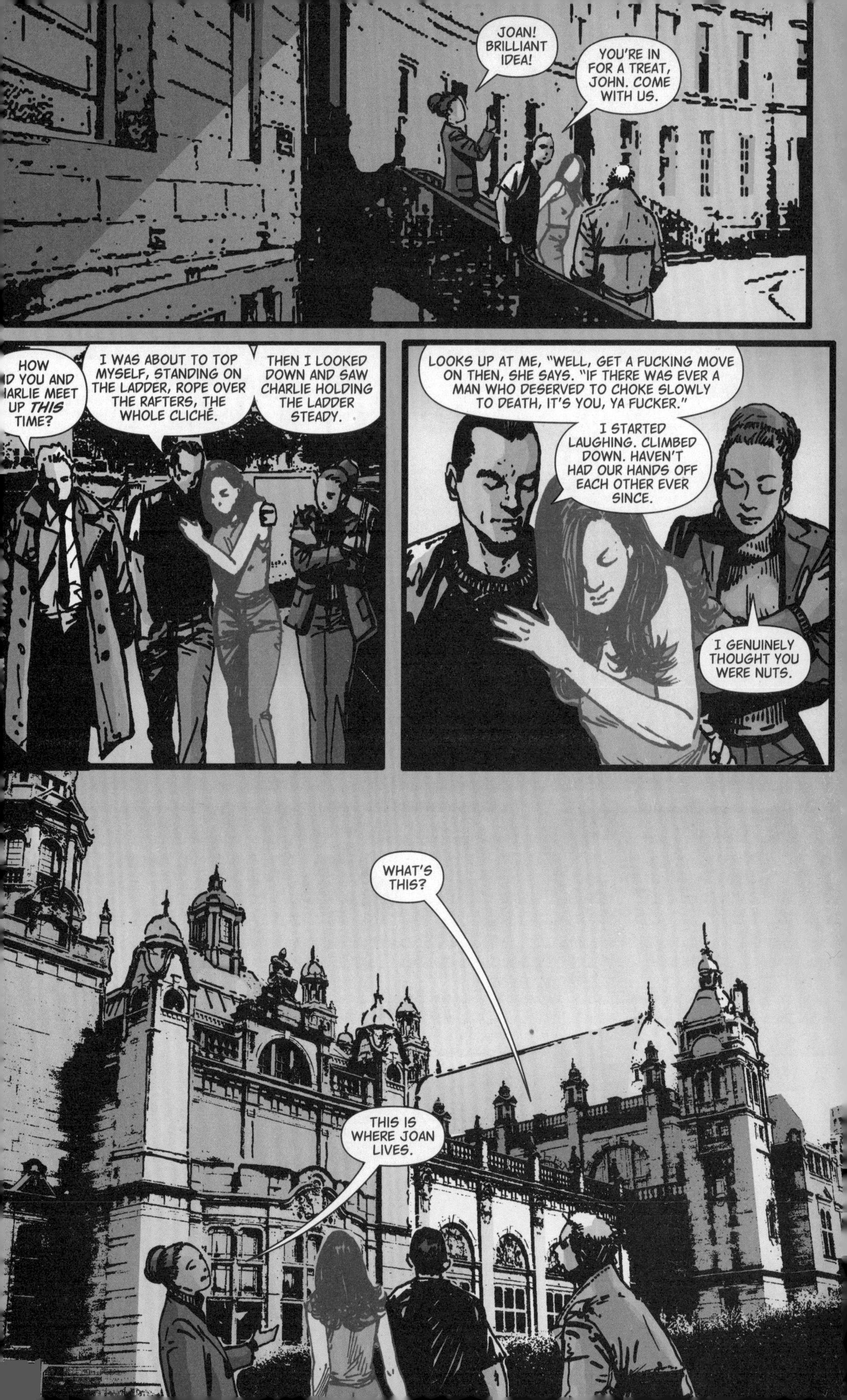
JOAN! BRILLIANT IDEA!
YOU'RE IN FOR A TREAT, JOHN. COME WITH US.
HOW D YOU AND ARLIE MEET UP *THIS* TIME?
I WAS ABOUT TO TOP MYSELF, STANDING ON THE LADDER, ROPE OVER THE RAFTERS, THE WHOLE CLICHÉ.
THEN I LOOKED DOWN AND SAW CHARLIE HOLDING THE LADDER STEADY.
LOOKS UP AT ME, "WELL, GET A FUCKING MOVE ON THEN, SHE SAYS. "IF THERE WAS EVER A MAN WHO DESERVED TO CHOKE SLOWLY TO DEATH, IT'S YOU, YA FUCKER."
I STARTED LAUGHING. CLIMBED DOWN. HAVEN'T HAD OUR HANDS OFF EACH OTHER EVER SINCE.
I GENUINELY THOUGHT YOU WERE NUTS.
WHAT'S THIS?
THIS IS WHERE JOAN LIVES.

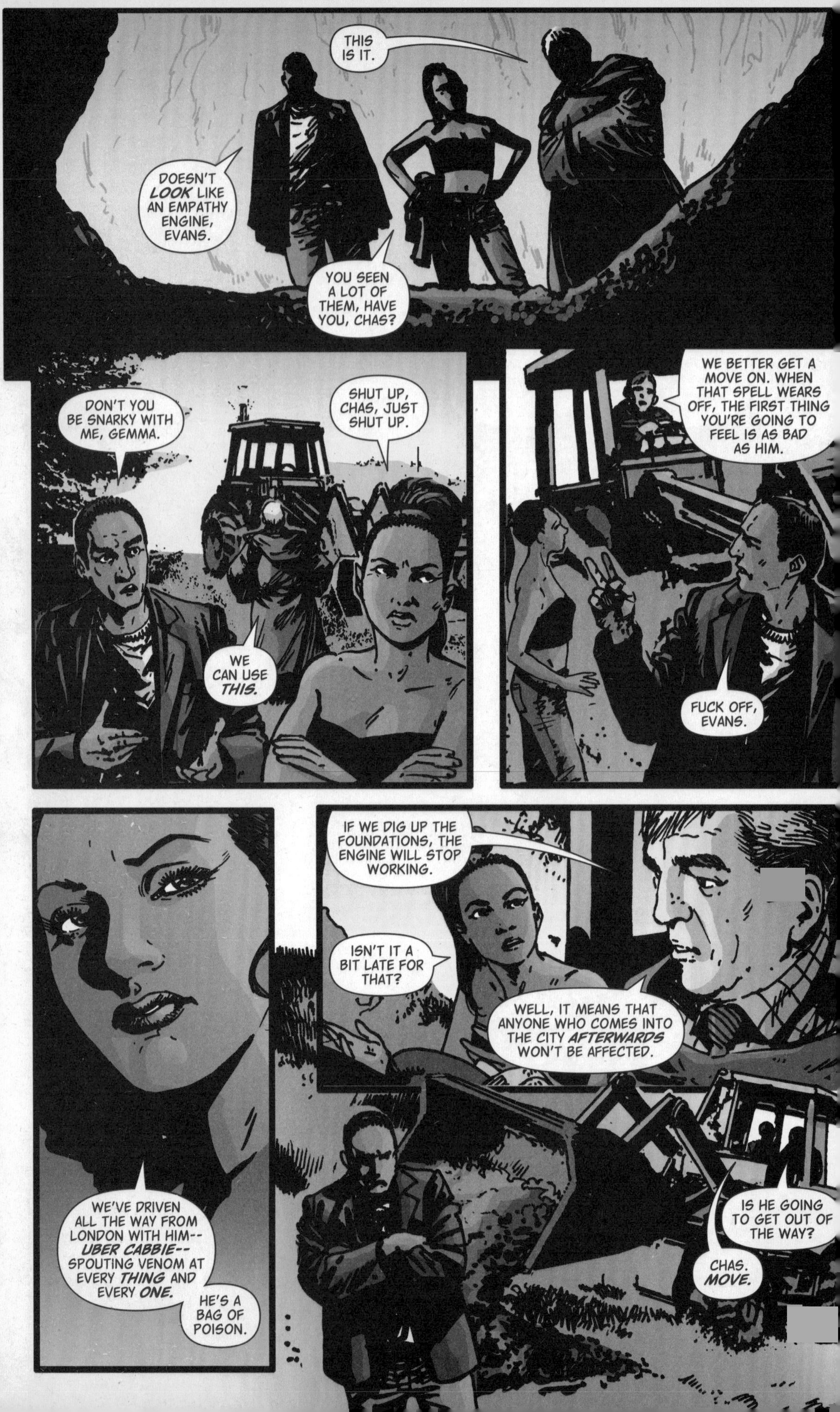
THIS IS IT.
DOESN'T LOOK LIKE AN EMPATHY ENGINE, EVANS.
YOU SEEN A LOT OF THEM, HAVE YOU, CHAS?
DON'T YOU BE SNARKY WITH ME, GEMMA.
SHUT UP, CHAS, JUST SHUT UP.
WE CAN USE THIS.
WE BETTER GET A MOVE ON. WHEN THAT SPELL WEARS OFF, THE FIRST THING YOU'RE GOING TO FEEL IS AS BAD AS HIM.
FUCK OFF, EVANS.
WE'VE DRIVEN ALL THE WAY FROM LONDON WITH HIM-- UBER CABBIE-- SPOUTING VENOM AT EVERY THING AND EVERY ONE.
HE'S A BAG OF POISON.
IF WE DIG UP THE FOUNDATIONS, THE ENGINE WILL STOP WORKING.
ISN'T IT A BIT LATE FOR THAT?
WELL, IT MEANS THAT ANYONE WHO COMES INTO THE CITY AFTERWARDS WON'T BE AFFECTED.
IS HE GOING TO GET OUT OF THE WAY?
CHAS. MOVE.

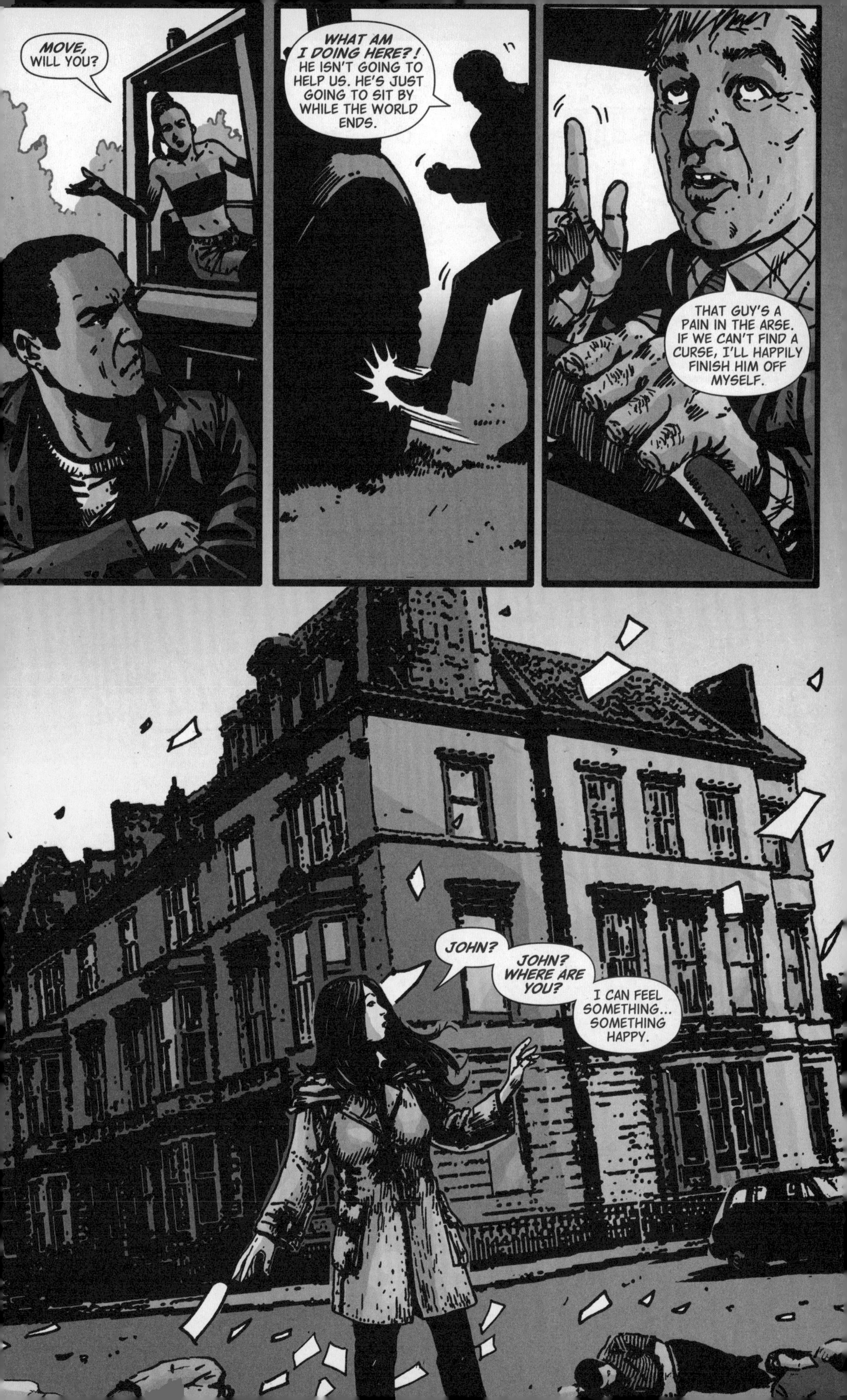

MOVE, WILL YOU?
WHAT AM I DOING HERE?! HE ISN'T GOING TO HELP US. HE'S JUST GOING TO SIT BY WHILE THE WORLD ENDS.
THAT GUY'S A PAIN IN THE ARSE. IF WE CAN'T FIND A CURSE, I'LL HAPPILY FINISH HIM OFF MYSELF.
JOHN?
JOHN? WHERE ARE YOU?
I CAN FEEL SOMETHING... SOMETHING HAPPY.

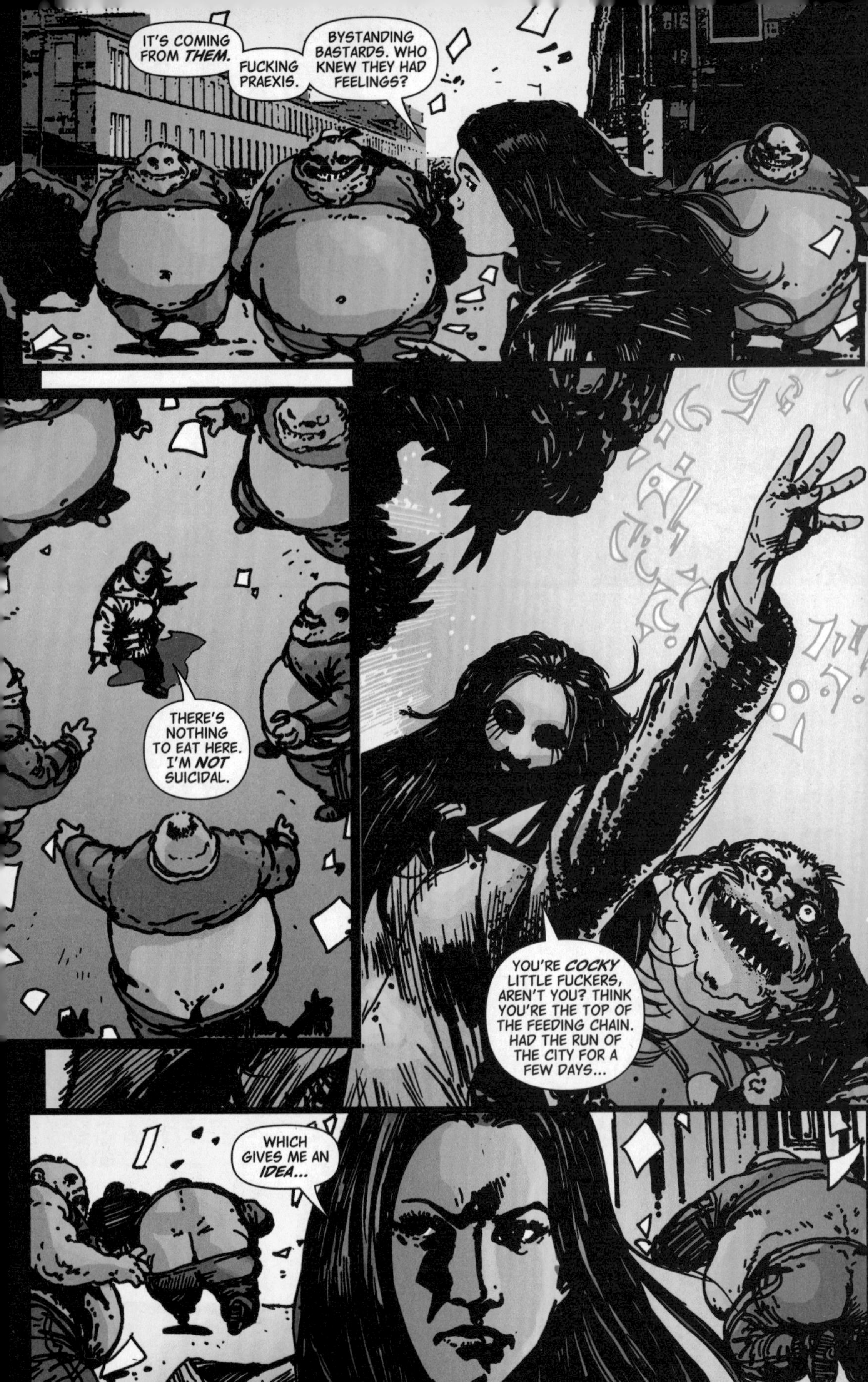
IT'S COMING FROM THEM.
FUCKING PRAEXIS.
BYSTANDING BASTARDS. WHO KNEW THEY HAD FEELINGS?
THERE'S NOTHING TO EAT HERE. I'M NOT SUICIDAL.
YOU'RE COCKY LITTLE FUCKERS, AREN'T YOU? THINK YOU'RE THE TOP OF THE FEEDING CHAIN. HAD THE RUN OF THE CITY FOR A FEW DAYS...
WHICH GIVES ME AN IDEA...

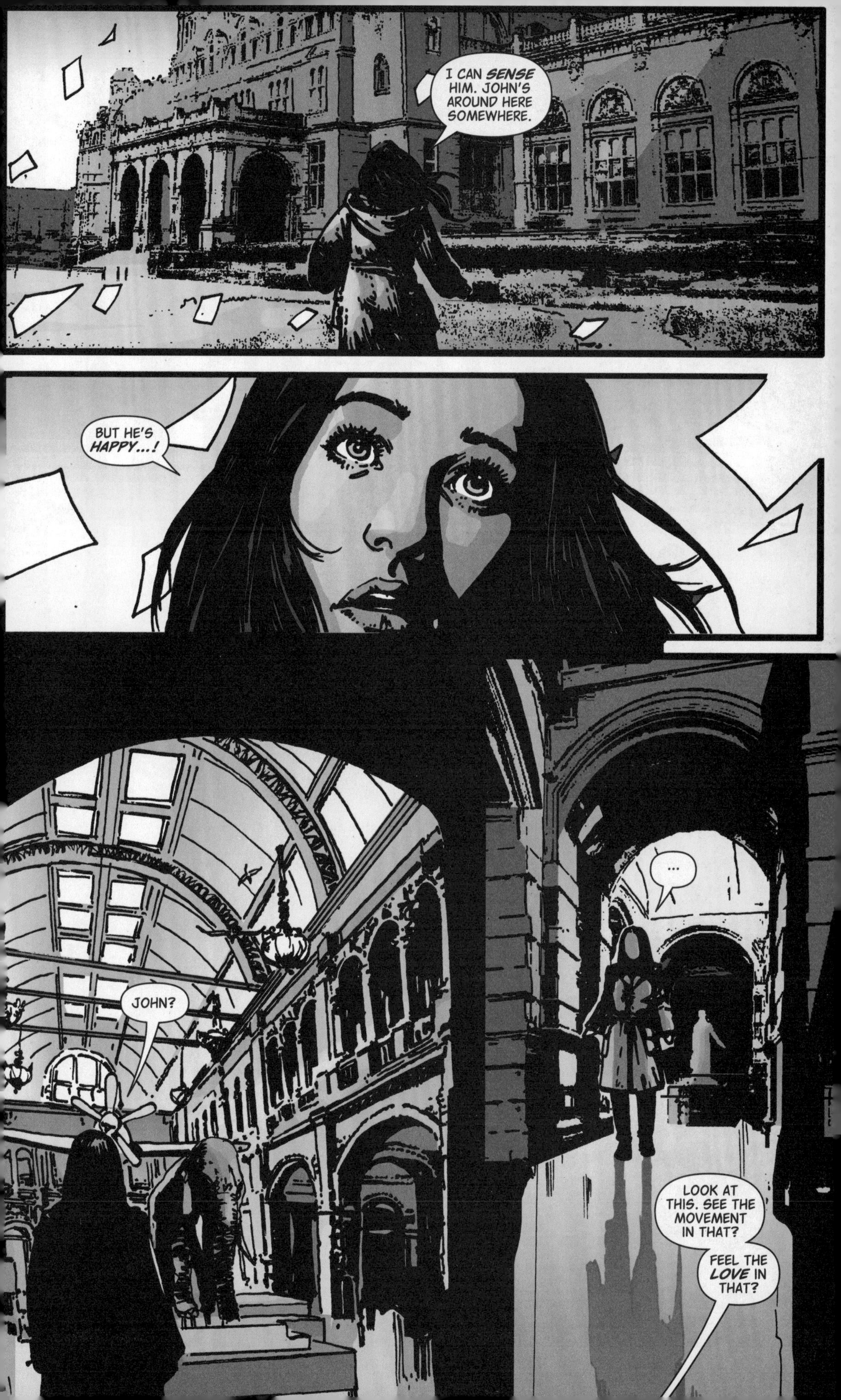
I CAN SENSE HIM. JOHN'S AROUND HERE SOMEWHERE.
BUT HE'S HAPPY...!
JOHN?
...
LOOK AT THIS. SEE THE MOVEMENT IN THAT?
FEEL THE LOVE IN THAT?

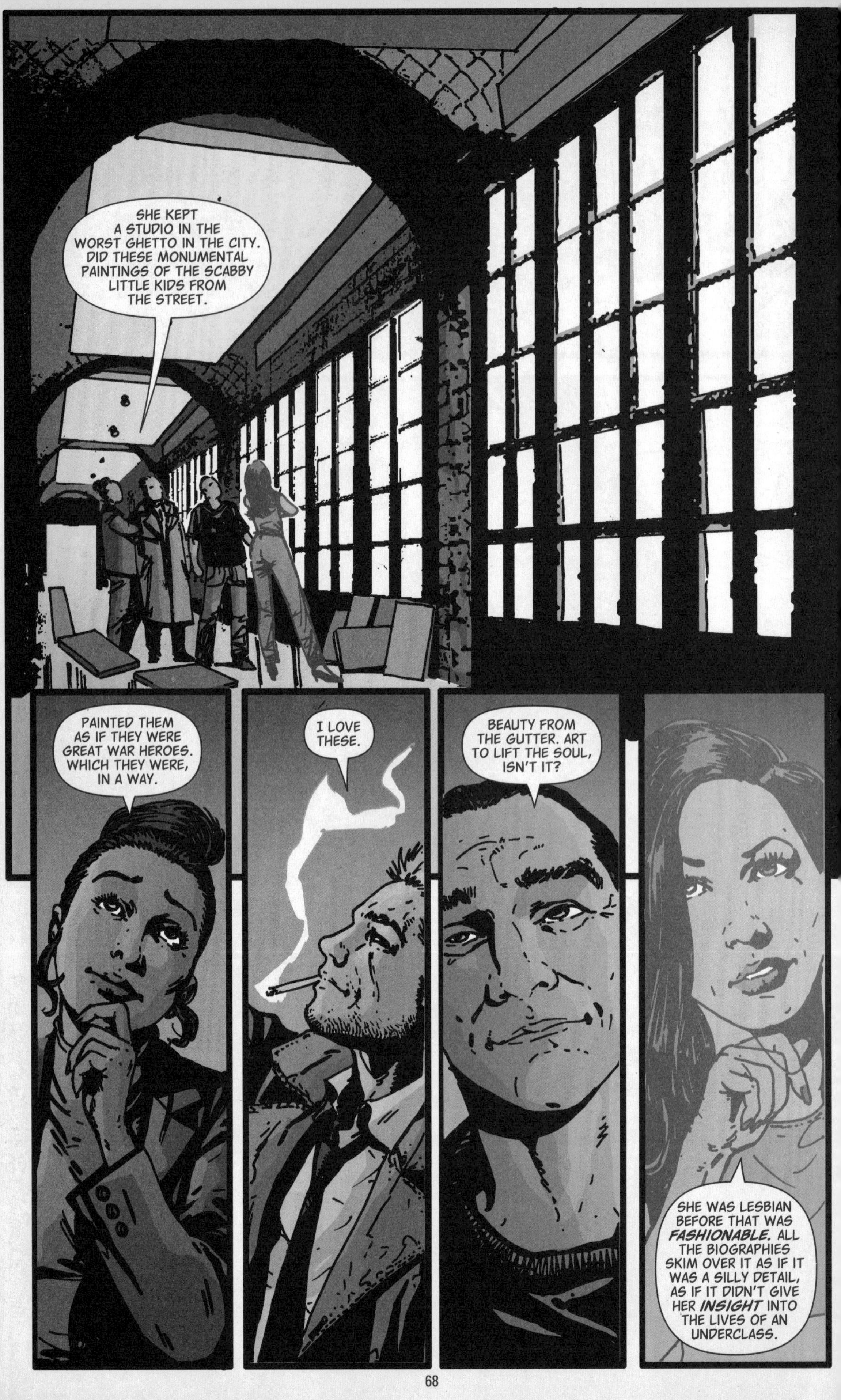
SHE KEPT A STUDIO IN THE WORST GHETTO IN THE CITY. DID THESE MONUMENTAL PAINTINGS OF THE SCABBY LITTLE KIDS FROM THE STREET.
PAINTED THEM AS IF THEY WERE GREAT WAR HEROES. WHICH THEY WERE, IN A WAY.
I LOVE THESE.
BEAUTY FROM THE GUTTER. ART TO LIFT THE SOUL, ISN'T IT?
SHE WAS LESBIAN BEFORE THAT WAS ***FASHIONABLE.*** ALL THE BIOGRAPHIES SKIM OVER IT AS IF IT WAS A SILLY DETAIL, AS IF IT DIDN'T GIVE HER ***INSIGHT*** INTO THE LIVES OF AN UNDERCLASS.

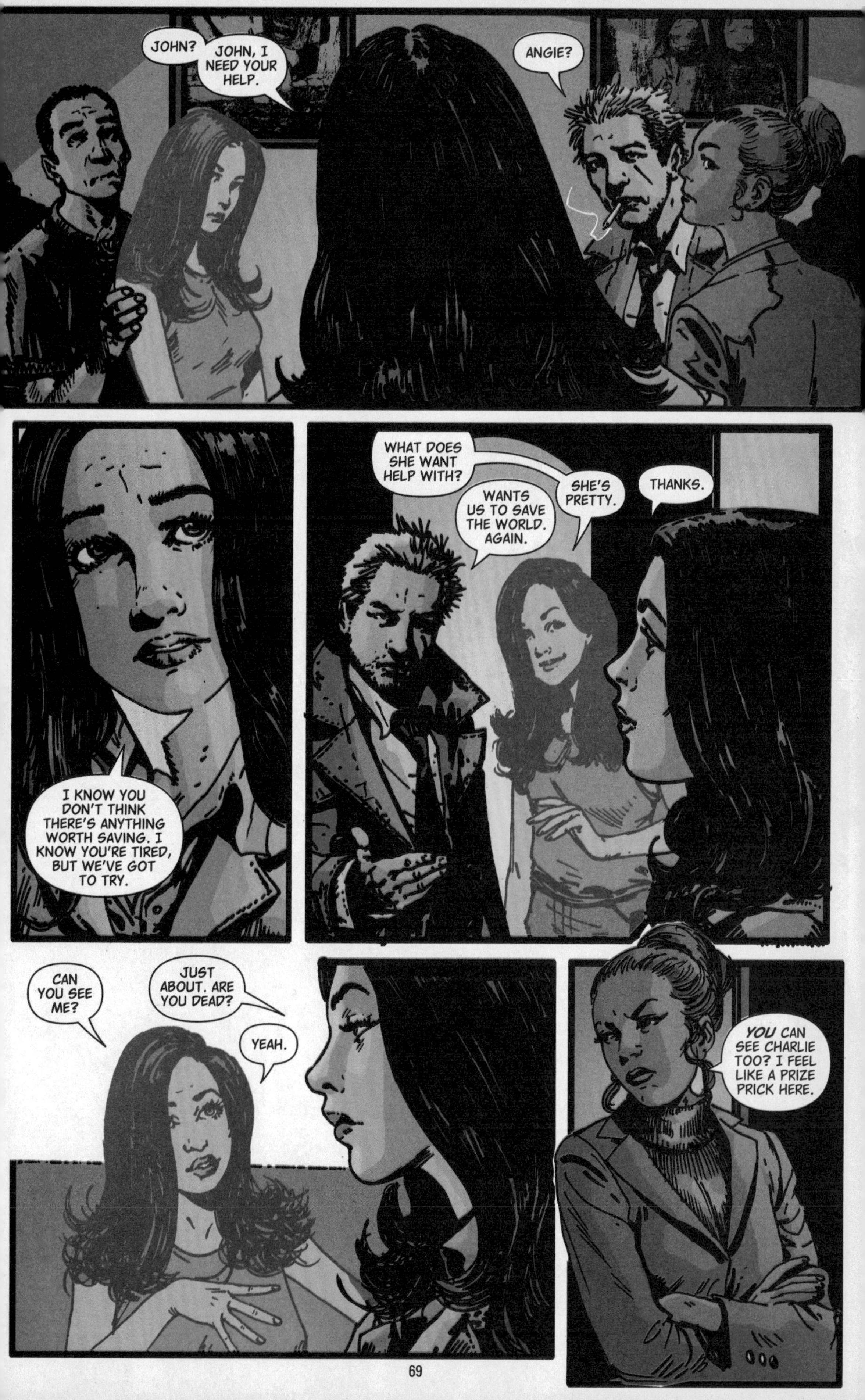
JOHN?
JOHN, I NEED YOUR HELP.
ANGIE?
I KNOW YOU DON'T THINK THERE'S ANYTHING WORTH SAVING. I KNOW YOU'RE TIRED, BUT WE'VE GOT TO TRY.
WHAT DOES SHE WANT HELP WITH?
WANTS US TO SAVE THE WORLD. AGAIN.
SHE'S PRETTY.
THANKS.
CAN YOU SEE ME?
JUST ABOUT. ARE YOU DEAD?
YEAH.
YOU CAN SEE CHARLIE TOO? I FEEL LIKE A PRIZE PRICK HERE.

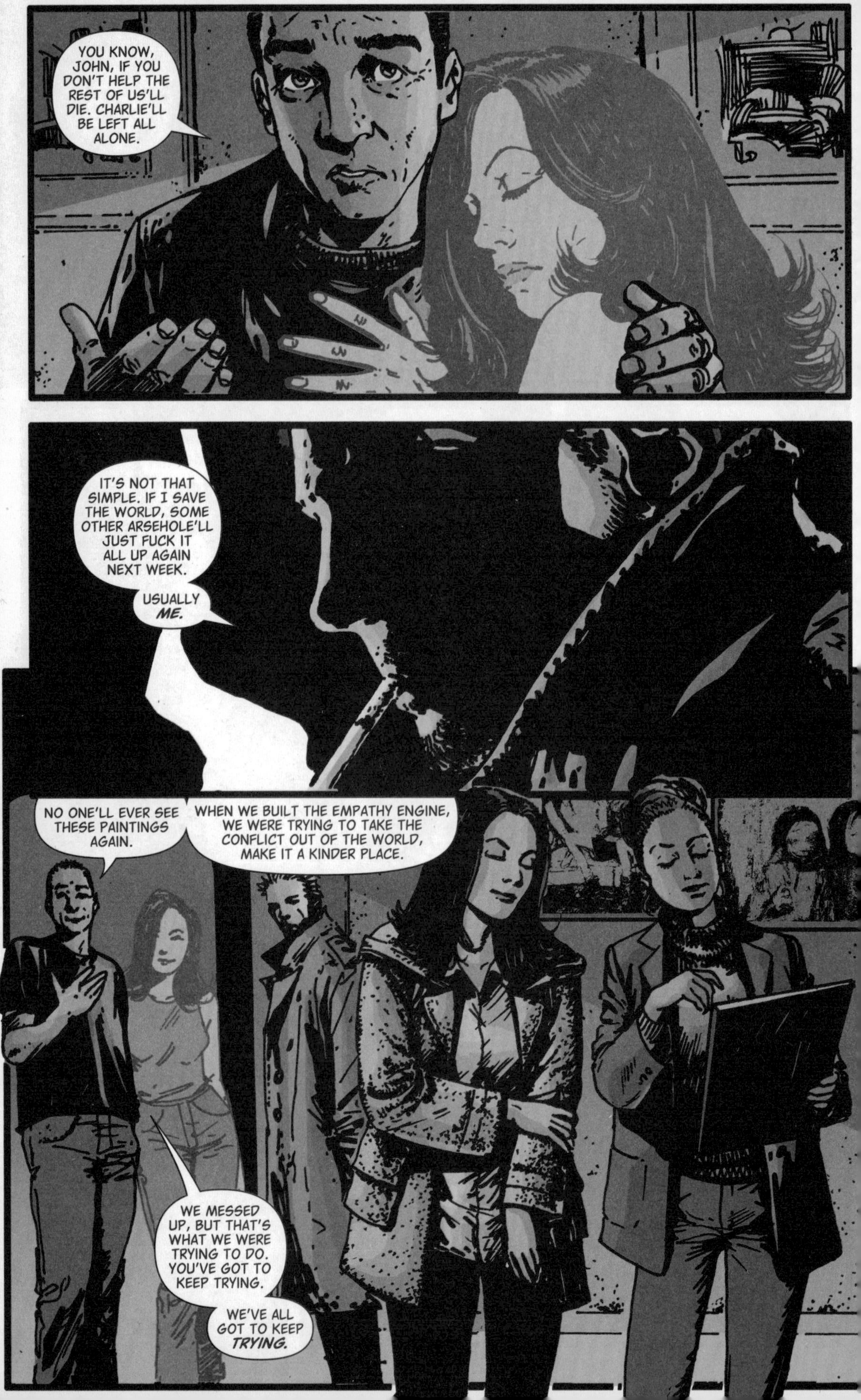
YOU KNOW, JOHN, IF YOU DON'T HELP THE REST OF US'LL DIE. CHARLIE'LL BE LEFT ALL ALONE.
IT'S NOT THAT SIMPLE. IF I SAVE THE WORLD, SOME OTHER ARSEHOLE'LL JUST FUCK IT ALL UP AGAIN NEXT WEEK.
USUALLY *ME.*
NO ONE'LL EVER SEE THESE PAINTINGS AGAIN.
WHEN WE BUILT THE EMPATHY ENGINE, WE WERE TRYING TO TAKE THE CONFLICT OUT OF THE WORLD, MAKE IT A KINDER PLACE.
WE MESSED UP, BUT THAT'S WHAT WE WERE TRYING TO DO. YOU'VE GOT TO KEEP TRYING.
WE'VE ALL GOT TO KEEP *TRYING.*

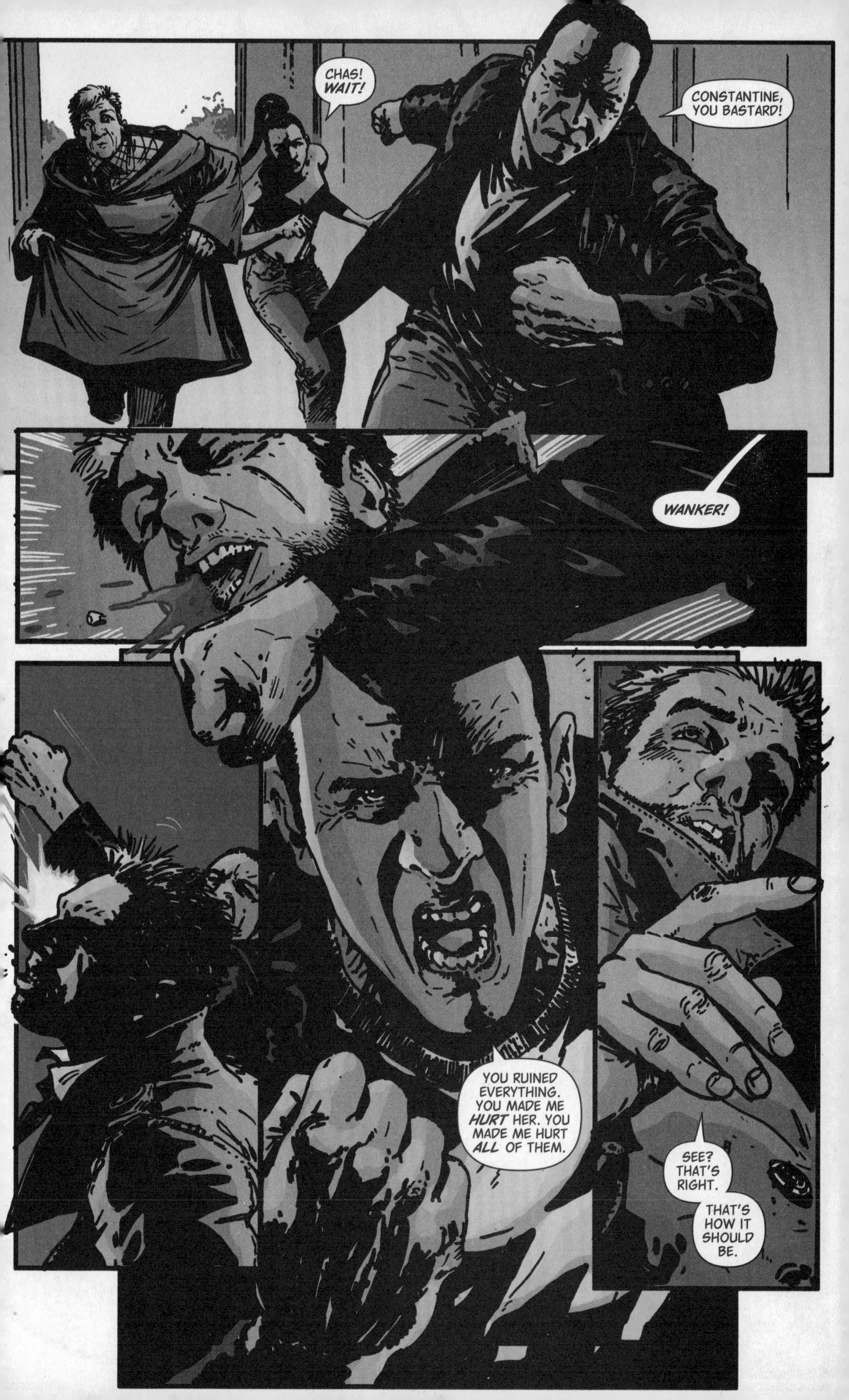
CHAS! WAIT!
CONSTANTINE, YOU BASTARD!
WANKER!
YOU RUINED EVERYTHING. YOU MADE ME HURT HER. YOU MADE ME HURT ALL OF THEM.
SEE? THAT'S RIGHT.
THAT'S HOW IT SHOULD BE.

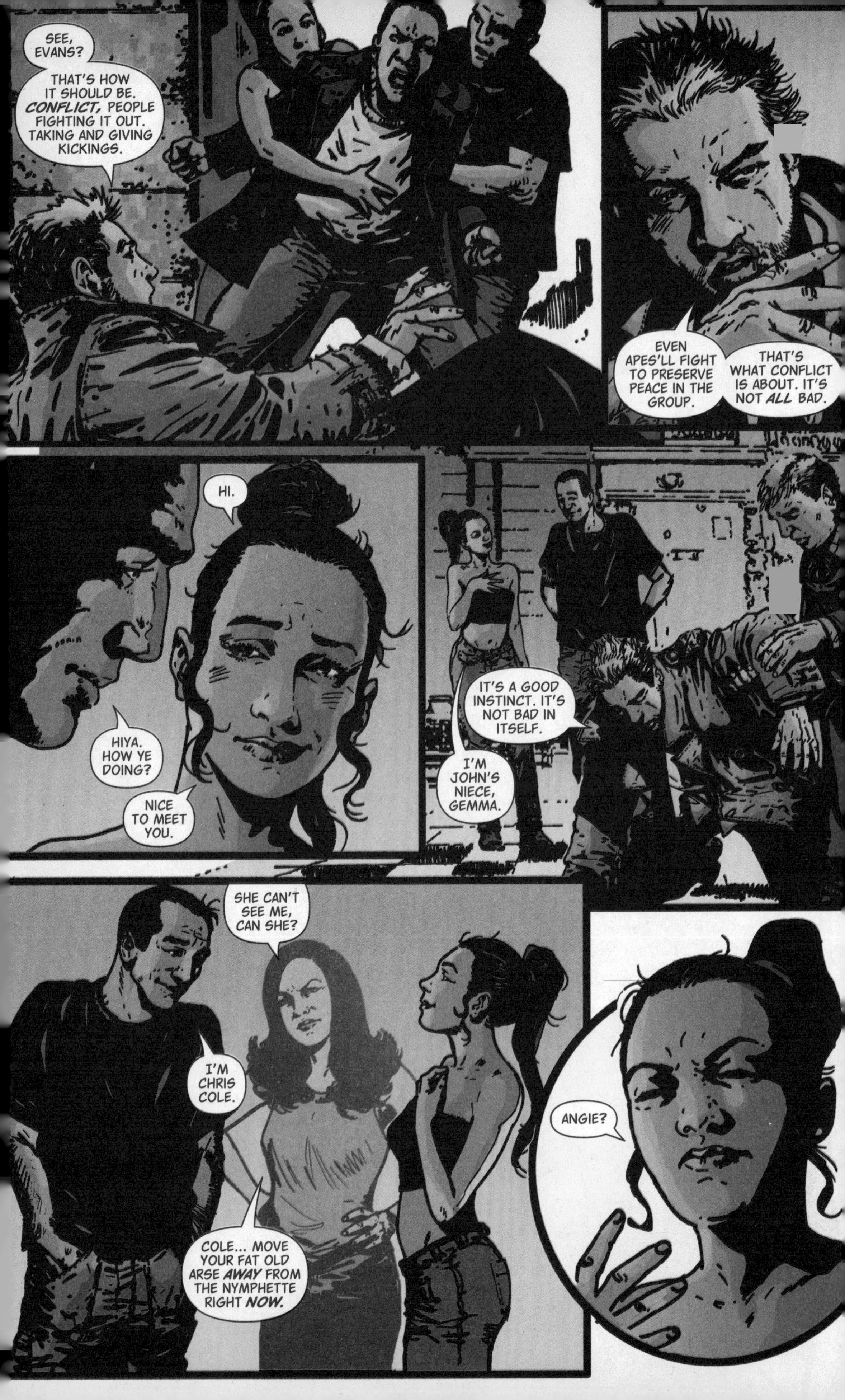
SEE, EVANS?
THAT'S HOW IT SHOULD BE. **CONFLICT,** PEOPLE FIGHTING IT OUT. TAKING AND GIVING KICKINGS.
EVEN APES'LL FIGHT TO PRESERVE PEACE IN THE GROUP.
THAT'S WHAT CONFLICT IS ABOUT. IT'S NOT ***ALL*** BAD.
HI.
HIYA. HOW YE DOING?
NICE TO MEET YOU.
IT'S A GOOD INSTINCT. IT'S NOT BAD IN ITSELF.
I'M JOHN'S NIECE, GEMMA.
SHE CAN'T SEE ME, CAN SHE?
I'M CHRIS COLE.
COLE... MOVE YOUR FAT OLD ARSE ***AWAY*** FROM THE NYMPHETTE RIGHT ***NOW.***
ANGIE?

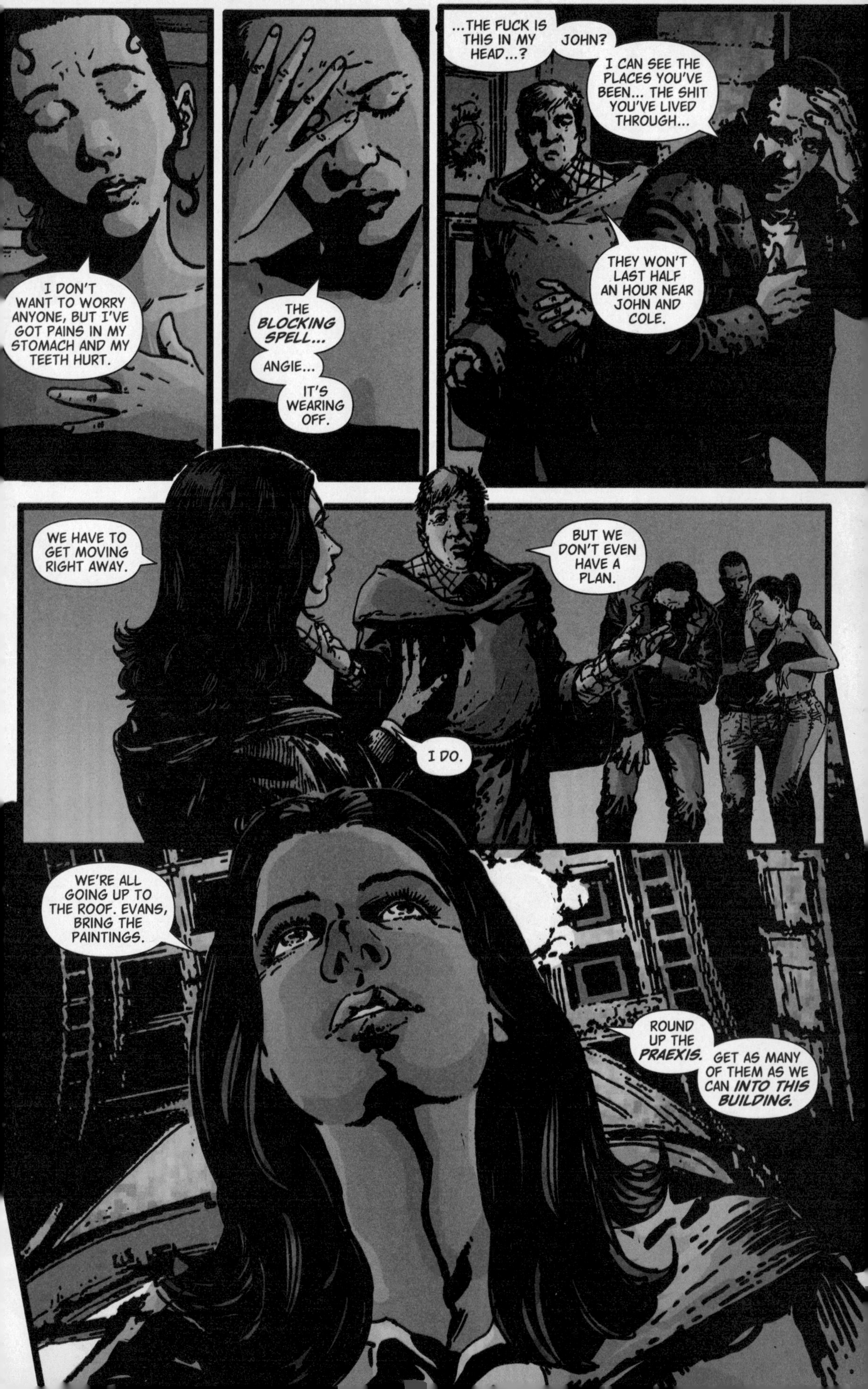
I DON'T WANT TO WORRY ANYONE, BUT I'VE GOT PAINS IN MY STOMACH AND MY TEETH HURT.
THE BLOCKING SPELL...
ANGIE...
IT'S WEARING OFF.
...THE FUCK IS THIS IN MY HEAD...?
JOHN?
I CAN SEE THE PLACES YOU'VE BEEN... THE SHIT YOU'VE LIVED THROUGH...
THEY WON'T LAST HALF AN HOUR NEAR JOHN AND COLE.
WE HAVE TO GET MOVING RIGHT AWAY.
BUT WE DON'T EVEN HAVE A PLAN.
I DO.
WE'RE ALL GOING UP TO THE ROOF. EVANS, BRING THE PAINTINGS.
ROUND UP THE PRAEXIS.
GET AS MANY OF THEM AS WE CAN INTO THIS BUILDING.

THE RED RIGHT HAND Chapter 3

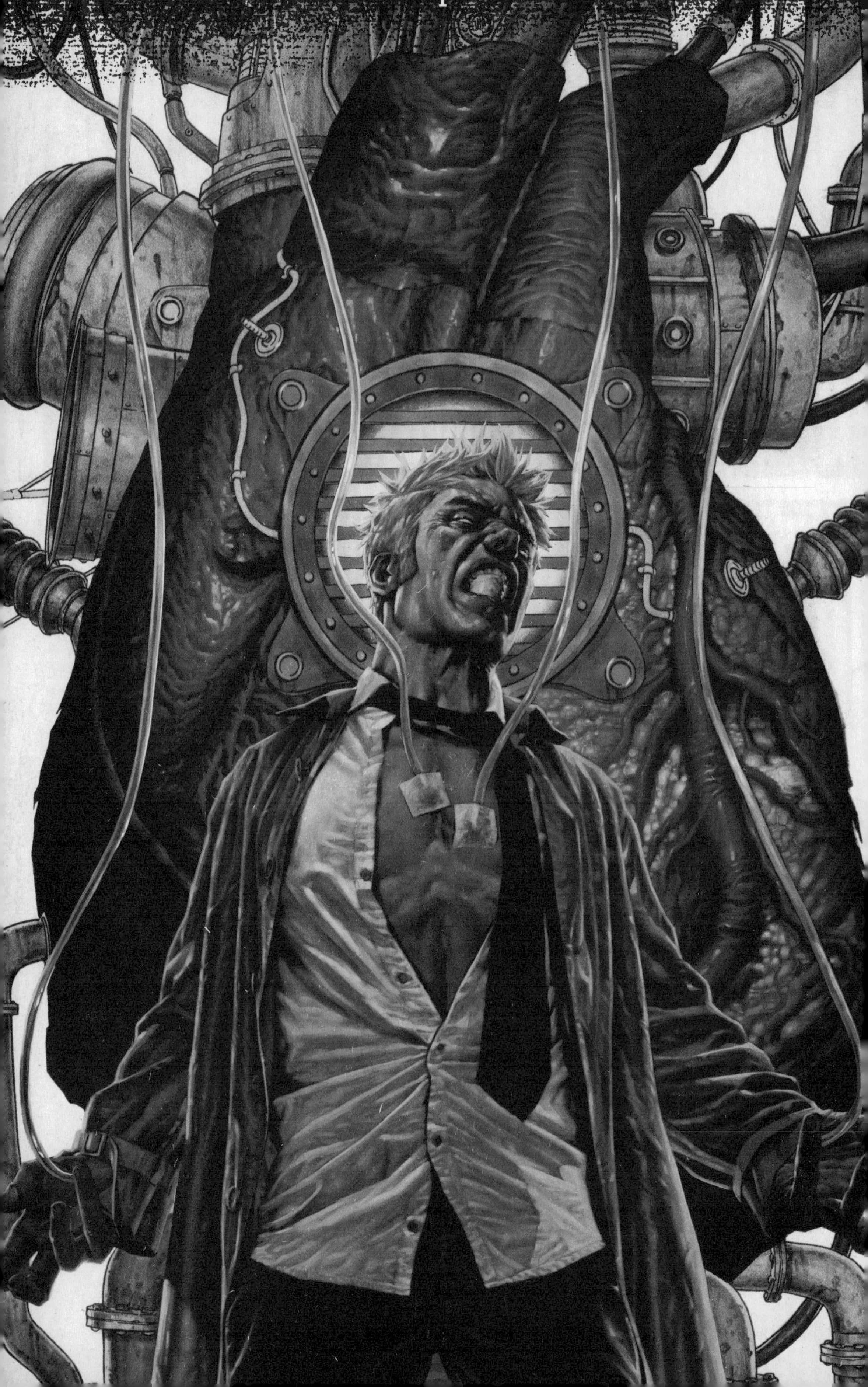

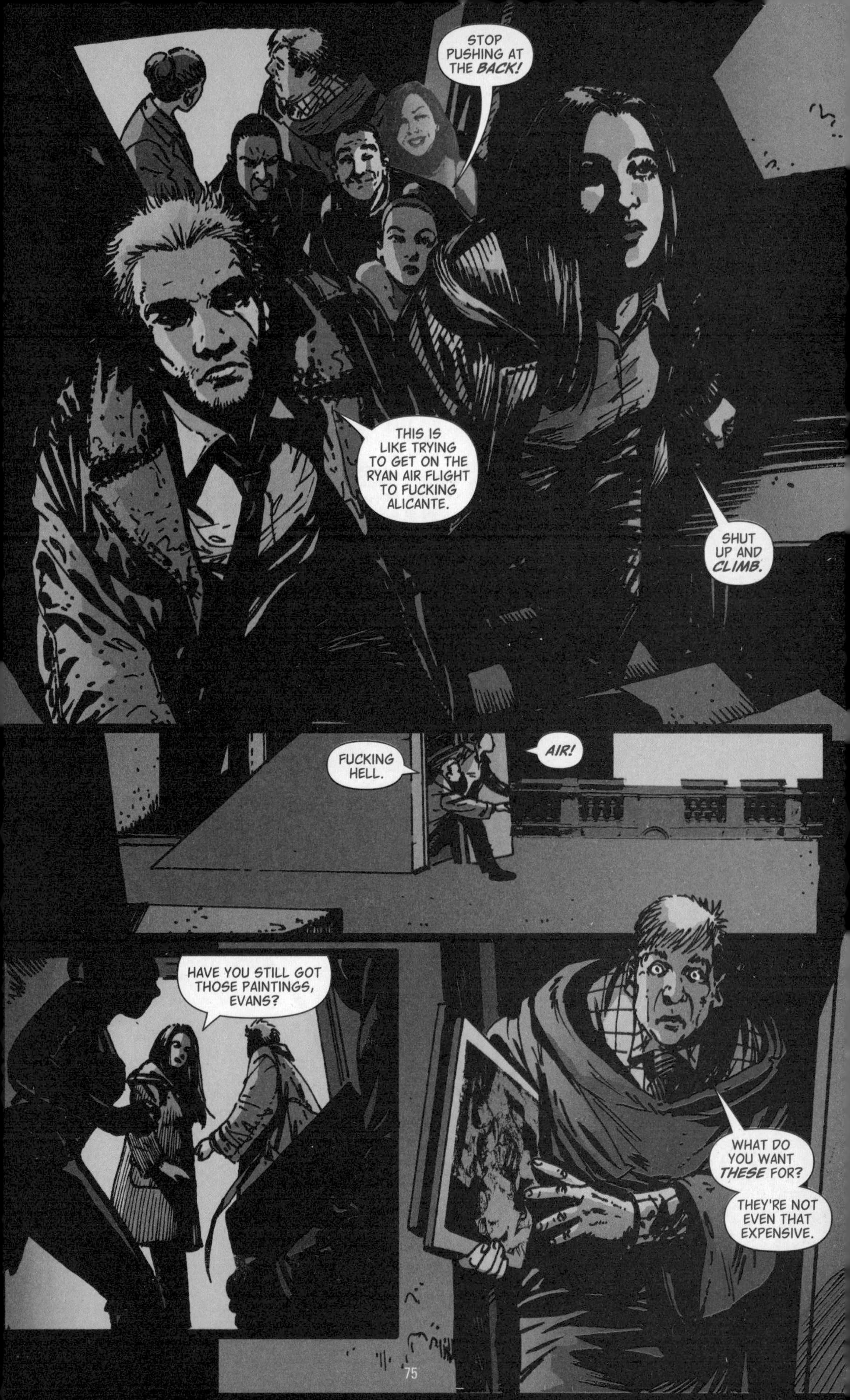
STOP PUSHING AT THE BACK!
THIS IS LIKE TRYING TO GET ON THE RYAN AIR FLIGHT TO FUCKING ALICANTE.
SHUT UP AND CLIMB.
FUCKING HELL.
AIR!
HAVE YOU STILL GOT THOSE PAINTINGS, EVANS?
WHAT DO YOU WANT THESE FOR?
THEY'RE NOT EVEN THAT EXPENSIVE.

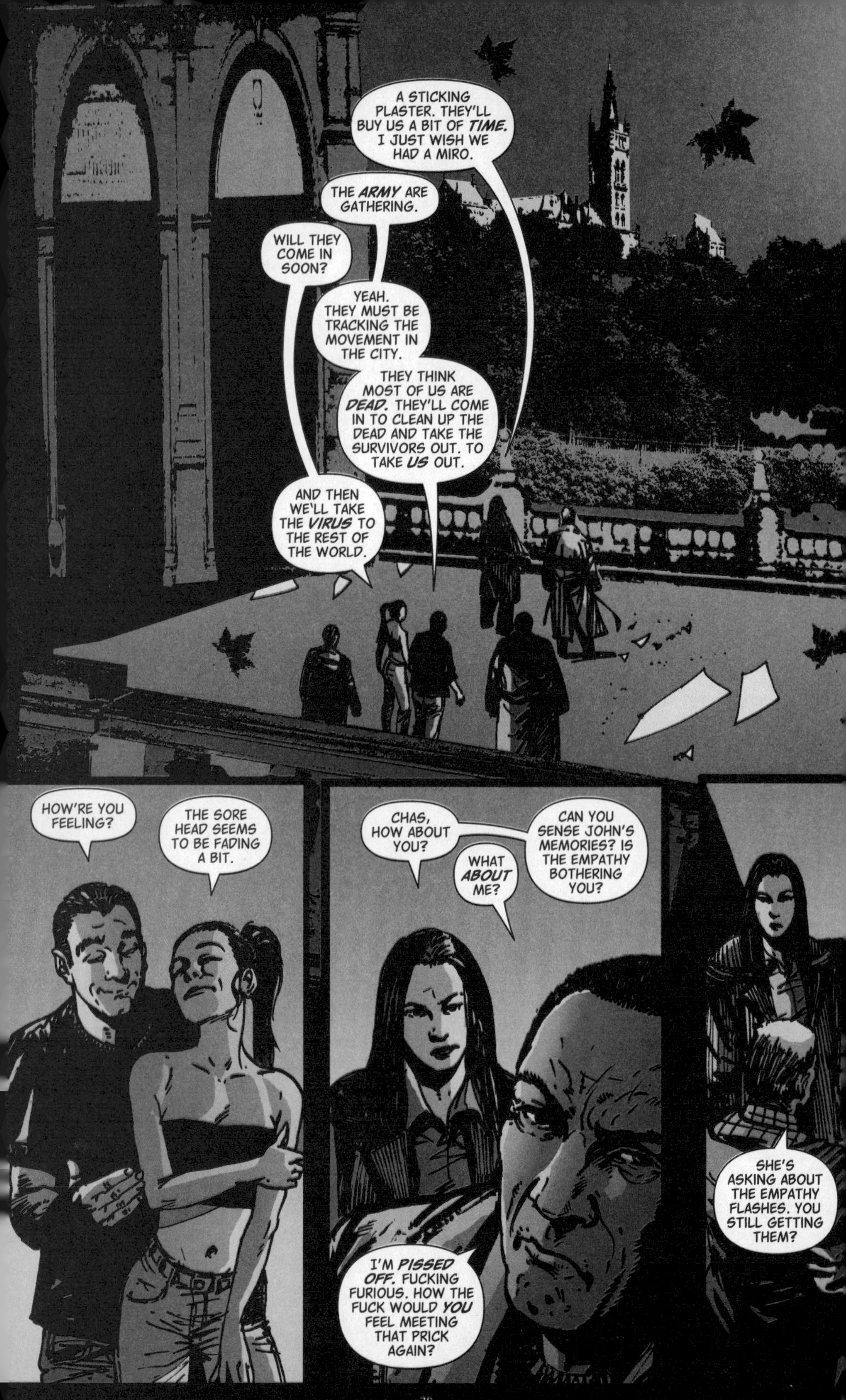
A STICKING PLASTER. THEY'LL BUY US A BIT OF TIME. I JUST WISH WE HAD A MIRO.
THE ARMY ARE GATHERING.
WILL THEY COME IN SOON?
YEAH. THEY MUST BE TRACKING THE MOVEMENT IN THE CITY.
THEY THINK MOST OF US ARE DEAD. THEY'LL COME IN TO CLEAN UP THE DEAD AND TAKE THE SURVIVORS OUT. TO TAKE US OUT.
AND THEN WE'LL TAKE THE VIRUS TO THE REST OF THE WORLD.
HOW'RE YOU FEELING?
THE SORE HEAD SEEMS TO BE FADING A BIT.
CHAS, HOW ABOUT YOU?
WHAT ABOUT ME?
CAN YOU SENSE JOHN'S MEMORIES? IS THE EMPATHY BOTHERING YOU?
I'M PISSED OFF. FUCKING FURIOUS. HOW THE FUCK WOULD YOU FEEL MEETING THAT PRICK AGAIN?
SHE'S ASKING ABOUT THE EMPATHY FLASHES. YOU STILL GETTING THEM?

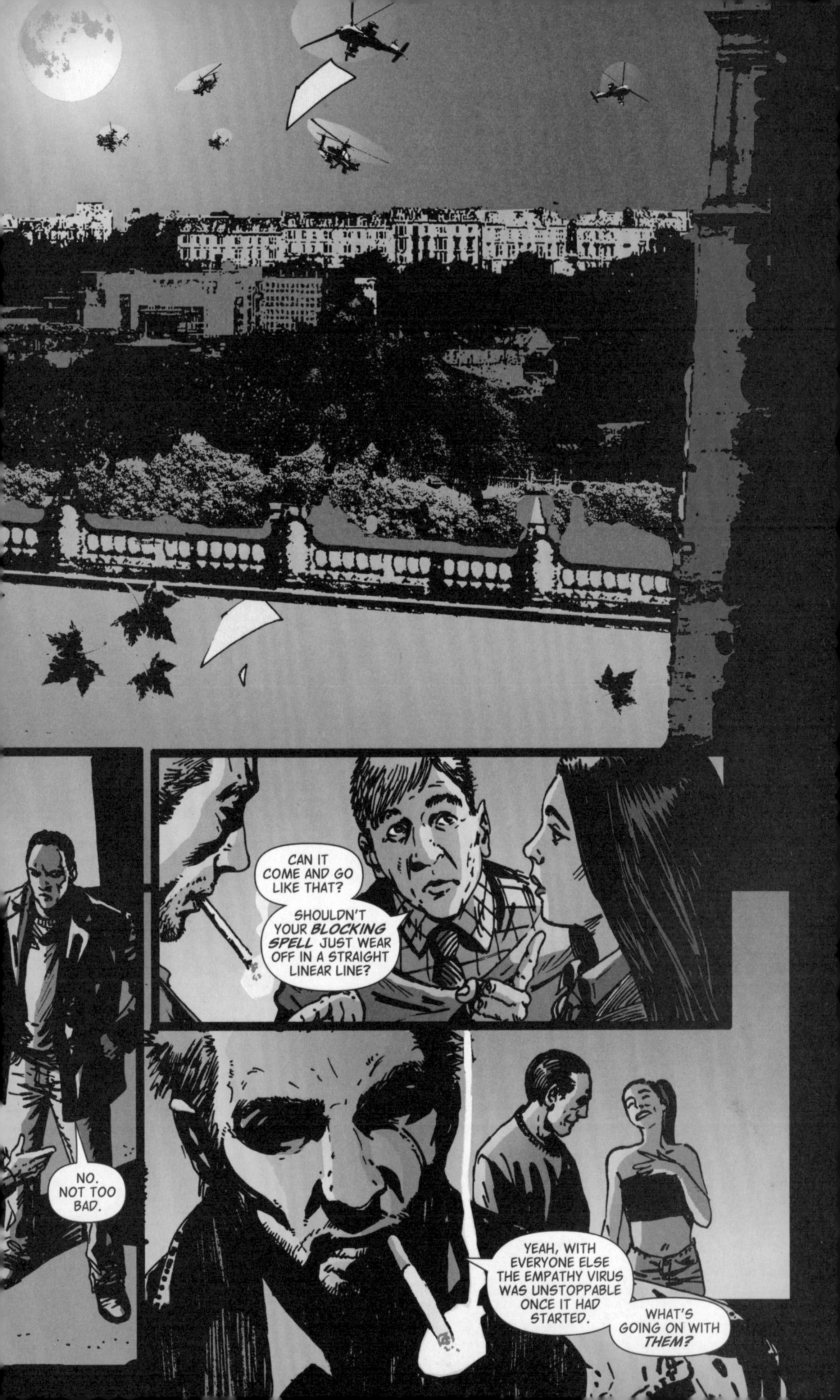

CAN IT COME AND GO LIKE THAT?
SHOULDN'T YOUR BLOCKING SPELL JUST WEAR OFF IN A STRAIGHT LINEAR LINE?
NO. NOT TOO BAD.
YEAH, WITH EVERYONE ELSE THE EMPATHY VIRUS WAS UNSTOPPABLE ONCE IT HAD STARTED.
WHAT'S GOING ON WITH THEM?

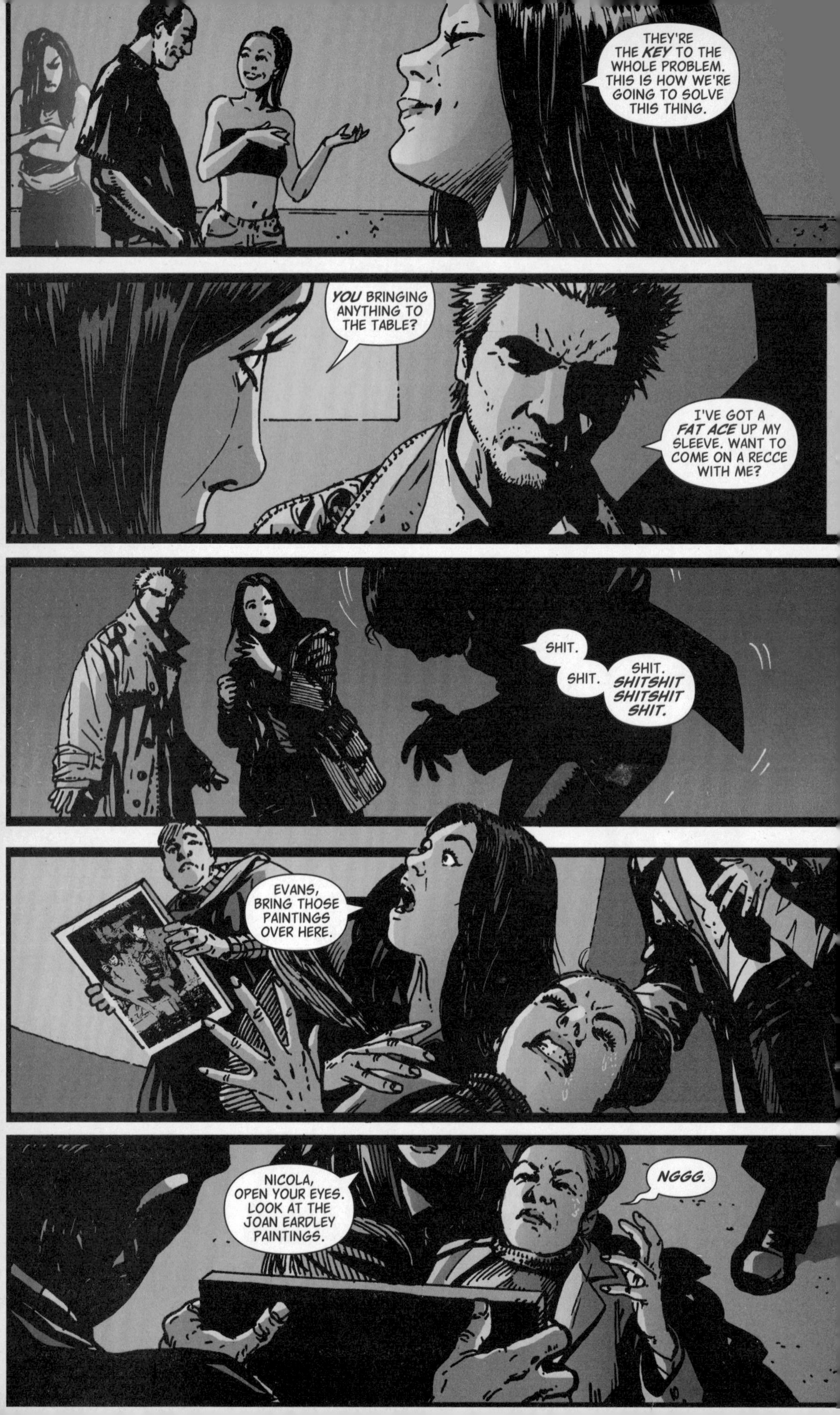

THEY'RE THE KEY TO THE WHOLE PROBLEM. THIS IS HOW WE'RE GOING TO SOLVE THIS THING.
YOU BRINGING ANYTHING TO THE TABLE?
I'VE GOT A FAT ACE UP MY SLEEVE. WANT TO COME ON A RECCE WITH ME?
SHIT.
SHIT.
SHIT. SHITSHIT SHITSHIT SHIT.
EVANS, BRING THOSE PAINTINGS OVER HERE.
NICOLA, OPEN YOUR EYES. LOOK AT THE JOAN EARDLEY PAINTINGS.
NGGG.

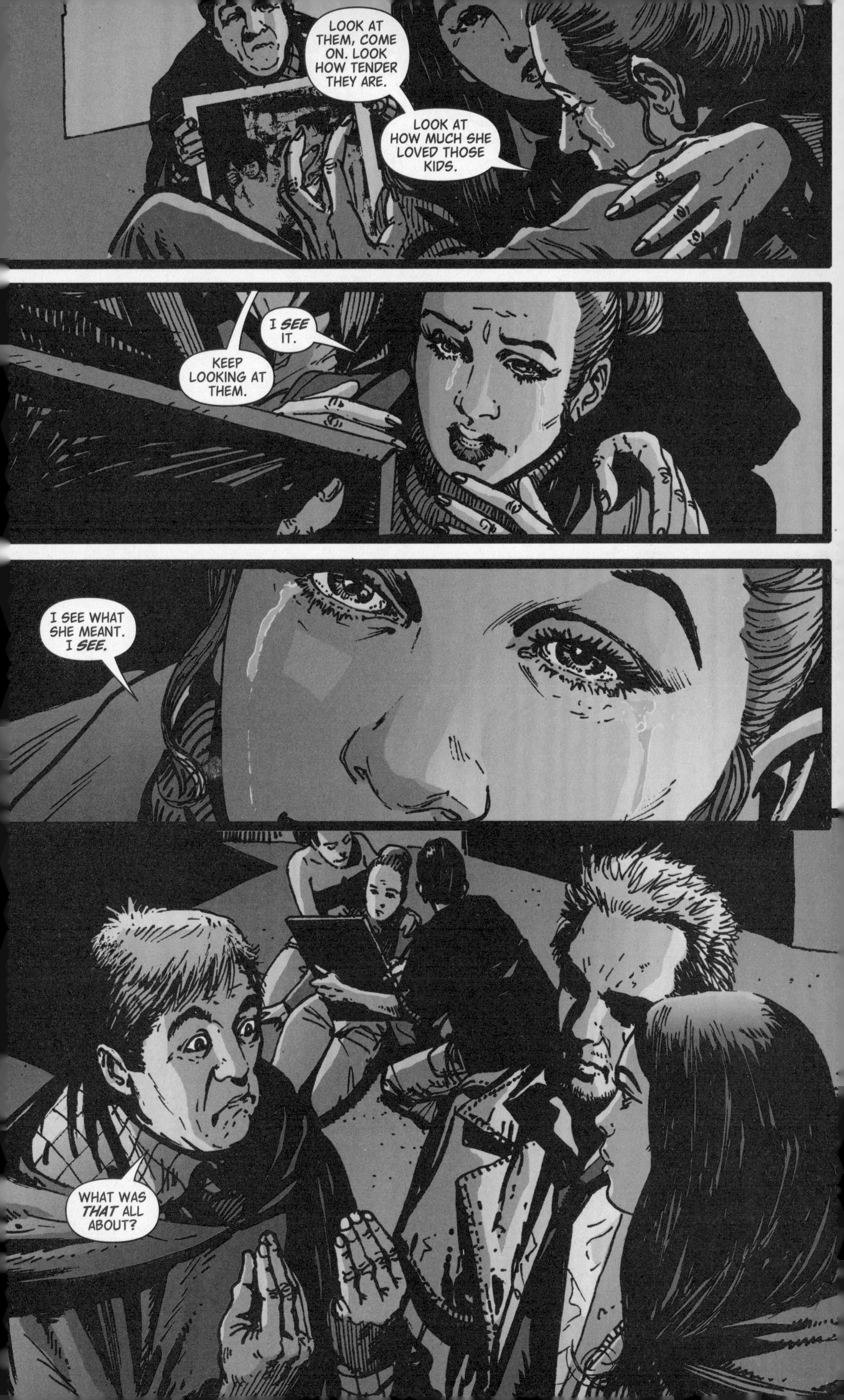
LOOK AT THEM, COME ON. LOOK HOW TENDER THEY ARE.
LOOK AT HOW MUCH SHE LOVED THOSE KIDS.
KEEP LOOKING AT THEM.
I *SEE* IT.
I SEE WHAT SHE MEANT. I *SEE.*
WHAT WAS *THAT* ALL ABOUT?

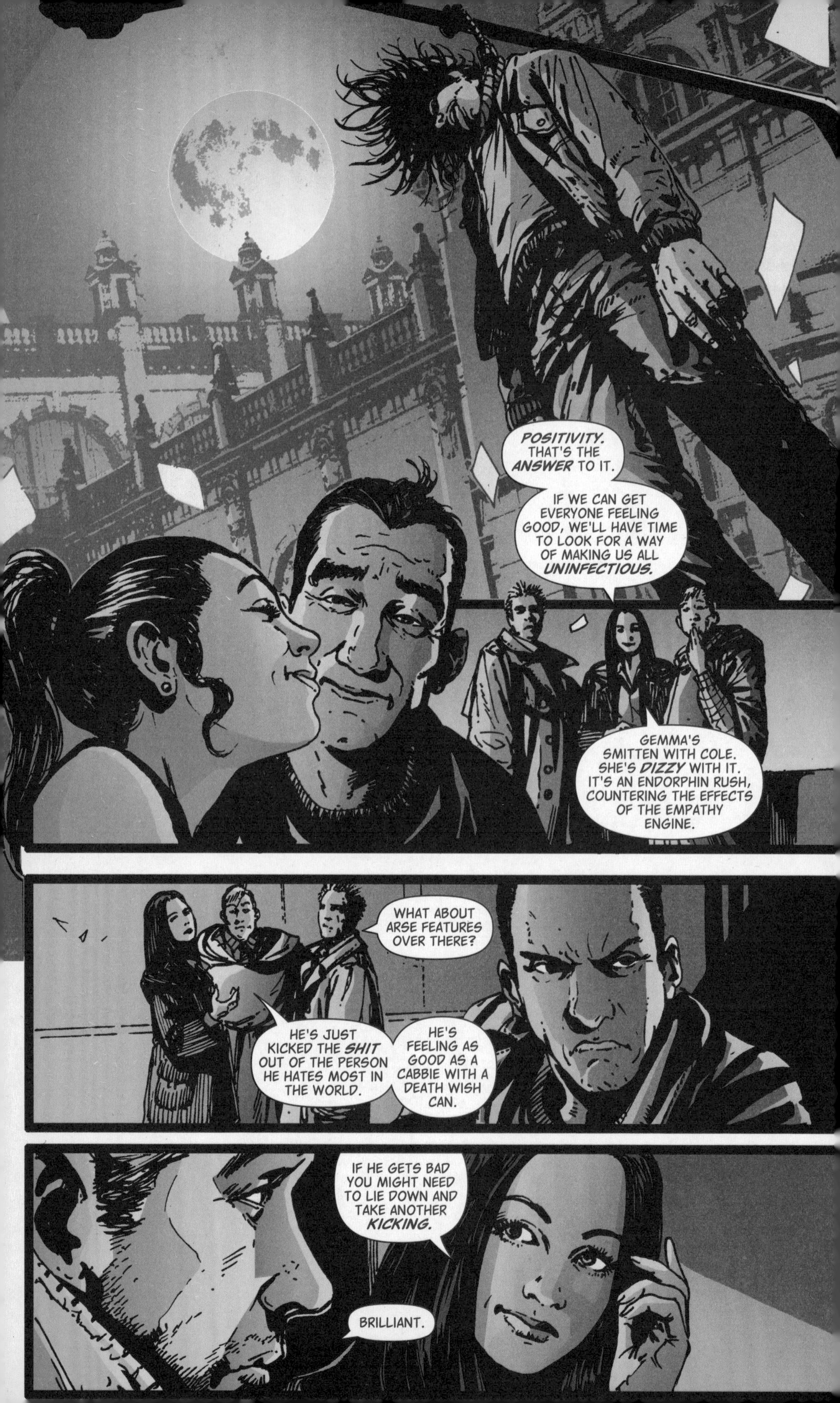
POSITIVITY. THAT'S THE ANSWER TO IT.
IF WE CAN GET EVERYONE FEELING GOOD, WE'LL HAVE TIME TO LOOK FOR A WAY OF MAKING US ALL UNINFECTIOUS.
GEMMA'S SMITTEN WITH COLE. SHE'S DIZZY WITH IT. IT'S AN ENDORPHIN RUSH, COUNTERING THE EFFECTS OF THE EMPATHY ENGINE.
WHAT ABOUT ARSE FEATURES OVER THERE?
HE'S JUST KICKED THE SHIT OUT OF THE PERSON HE HATES MOST IN THE WORLD.
HE'S FEELING AS GOOD AS A CABBIE WITH A DEATH WISH CAN.
IF HE GETS BAD YOU MIGHT NEED TO LIE DOWN AND TAKE ANOTHER KICKING.
BRILLIANT.

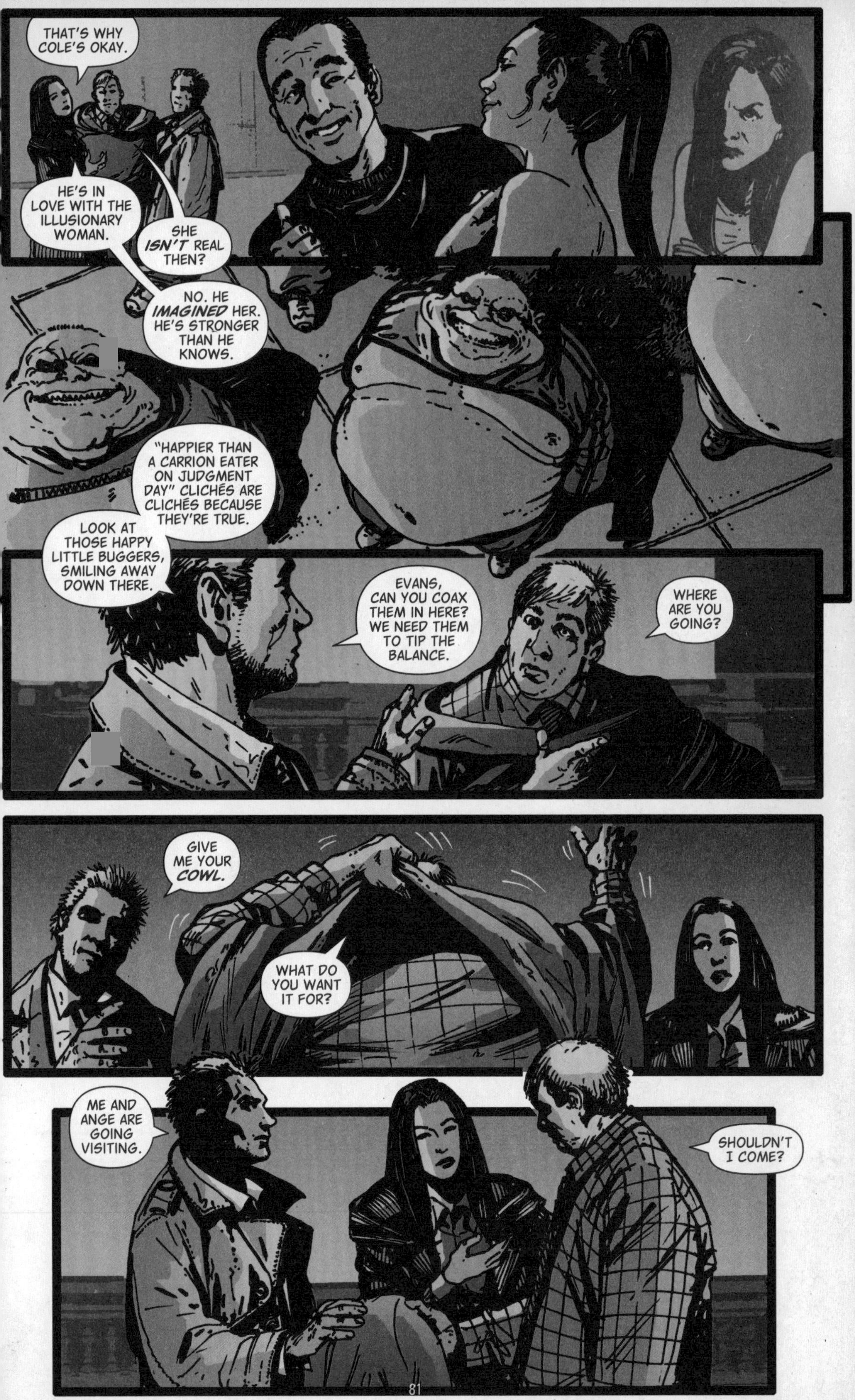
THAT'S WHY COLE'S OKAY.
HE'S IN LOVE WITH THE ILLUSIONARY WOMAN.
SHE ISN'T REAL THEN?
NO. HE IMAGINED HER. HE'S STRONGER THAN HE KNOWS.
"HAPPIER THAN A CARRION EATER ON JUDGMENT DAY" CLICHÉS ARE CLICHÉS BECAUSE THEY'RE TRUE.
LOOK AT THOSE HAPPY LITTLE BUGGERS, SMILING AWAY DOWN THERE.
EVANS, CAN YOU COAX THEM IN HERE? WE NEED THEM TO TIP THE BALANCE.
WHERE ARE YOU GOING?
GIVE ME YOUR COWL.
WHAT DO YOU WANT IT FOR?
ME AND ANGE ARE GOING VISITING.
SHOULDN'T I COME?

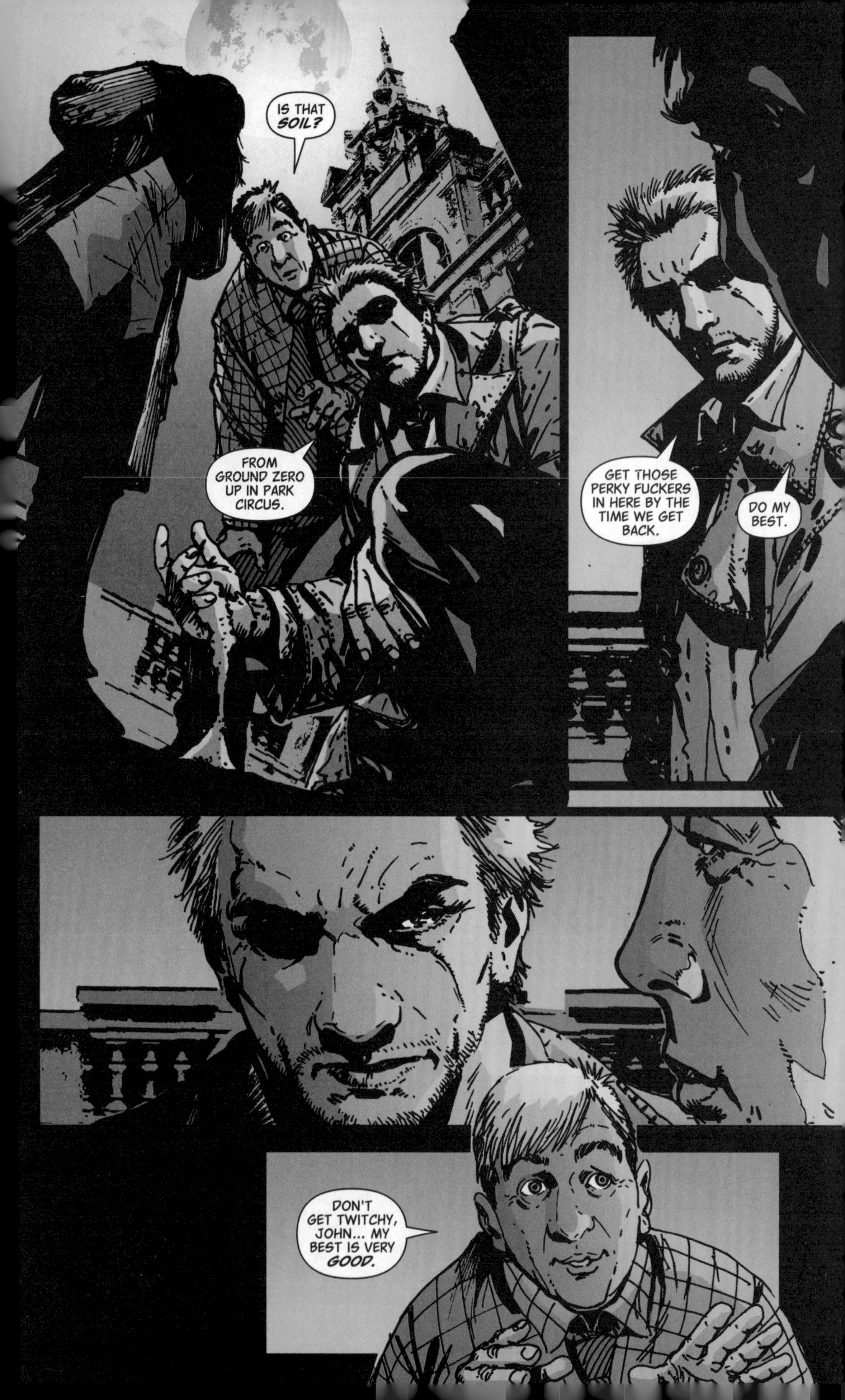
IS THAT SOIL?
FROM GROUND ZERO UP IN PARK CIRCUS.
GET THOSE PERKY FUCKERS IN HERE BY THE TIME WE GET BACK.
DO MY BEST.
DON'T GET TWITCHY, JOHN... MY BEST IS VERY GOOD.

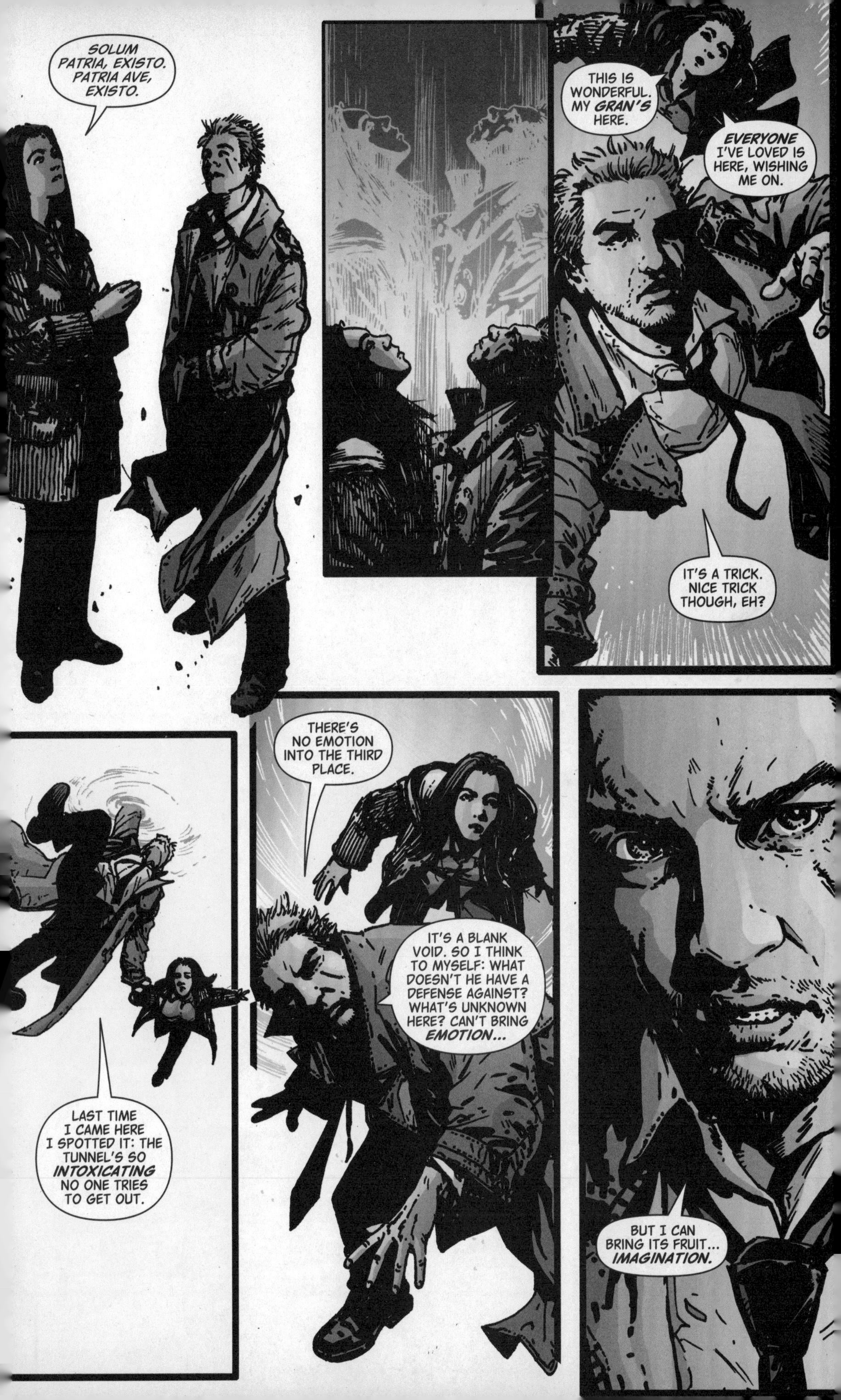
SOLUM PATRIA, EXISTO. PATRIA AVE, EXISTO.
THIS IS WONDERFUL. MY GRAN'S HERE.
EVERYONE I'VE LOVED IS HERE, WISHING ME ON.
IT'S A TRICK. NICE TRICK THOUGH, EH?
LAST TIME I CAME HERE I SPOTTED IT: THE TUNNEL'S SO INTOXICATING NO ONE TRIES TO GET OUT.
THERE'S NO EMOTION INTO THE THIRD PLACE.
IT'S A BLANK VOID. SO I THINK TO MYSELF: WHAT DOESN'T HE HAVE A DEFENSE AGAINST? WHAT'S UNKNOWN HERE? CAN'T BRING EMOTION...
BUT I CAN BRING ITS FRUIT... IMAGINATION.

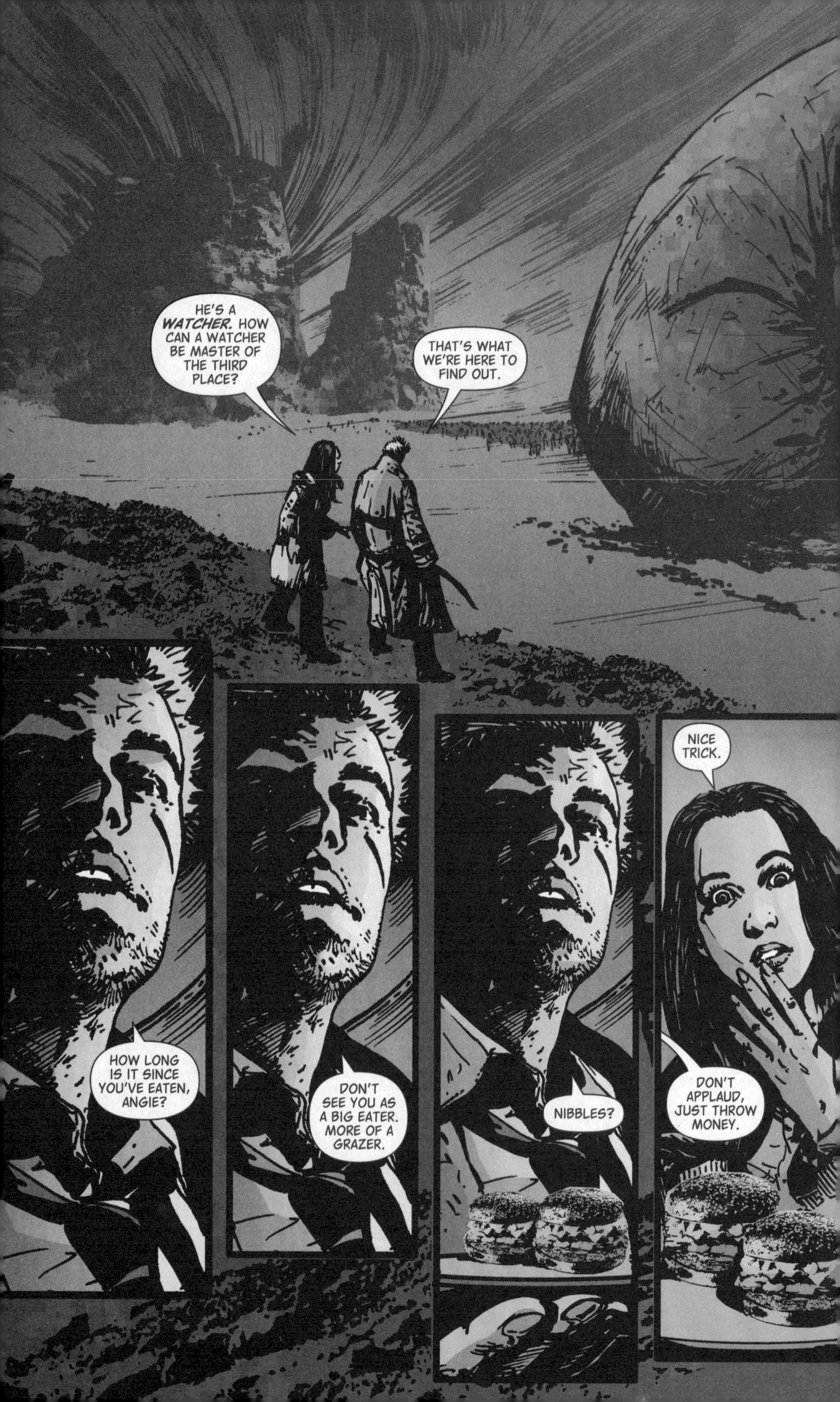
HE'S A WATCHER. HOW CAN A WATCHER BE MASTER OF THE THIRD PLACE?
THAT'S WHAT WE'RE HERE TO FIND OUT.
HOW LONG IS IT SINCE YOU'VE EATEN, ANGIE?
DON'T SEE YOU AS A BIG EATER. MORE OF A GRAZER.
NIBBLES?
NICE TRICK.
DON'T APPLAUD, JUST THROW MONEY.

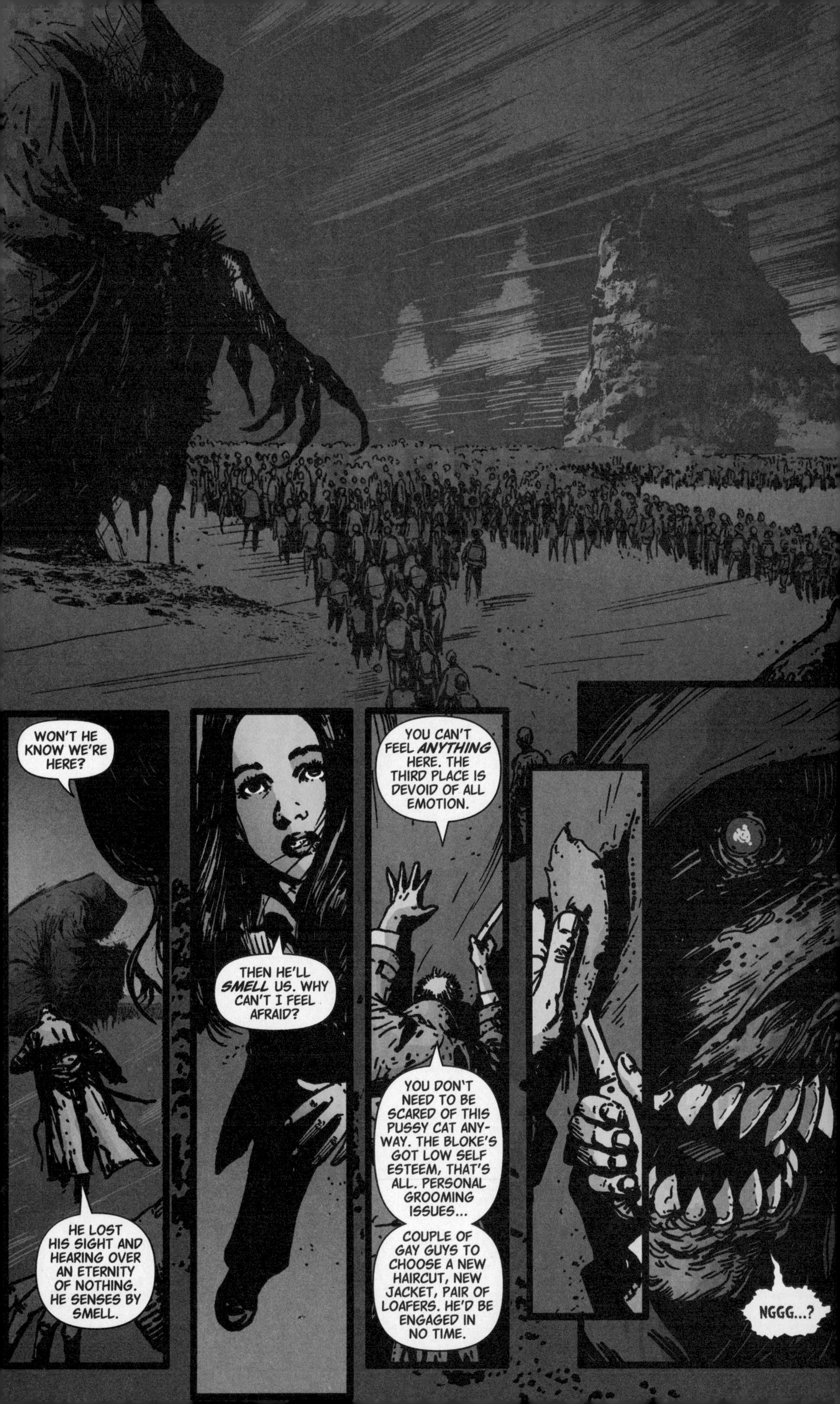
WON'T HE KNOW WE'RE HERE?
HE LOST HIS SIGHT AND HEARING OVER AN ETERNITY OF NOTHING. HE SENSES BY SMELL.
THEN HE'LL SMELL US. WHY CAN'T I FEEL AFRAID?
YOU CAN'T FEEL ANYTHING HERE. THE THIRD PLACE IS DEVOID OF ALL EMOTION.
YOU DON'T NEED TO BE SCARED OF THIS PUSSY CAT ANY-WAY. THE BLOKE'S GOT LOW SELF ESTEEM, THAT'S ALL. PERSONAL GROOMING ISSUES...
COUPLE OF GAY GUYS TO CHOOSE A NEW HAIRCUT, NEW JACKET, PAIR OF LOAFERS. HE'D BE ENGAGED IN NO TIME.
NGGG...?

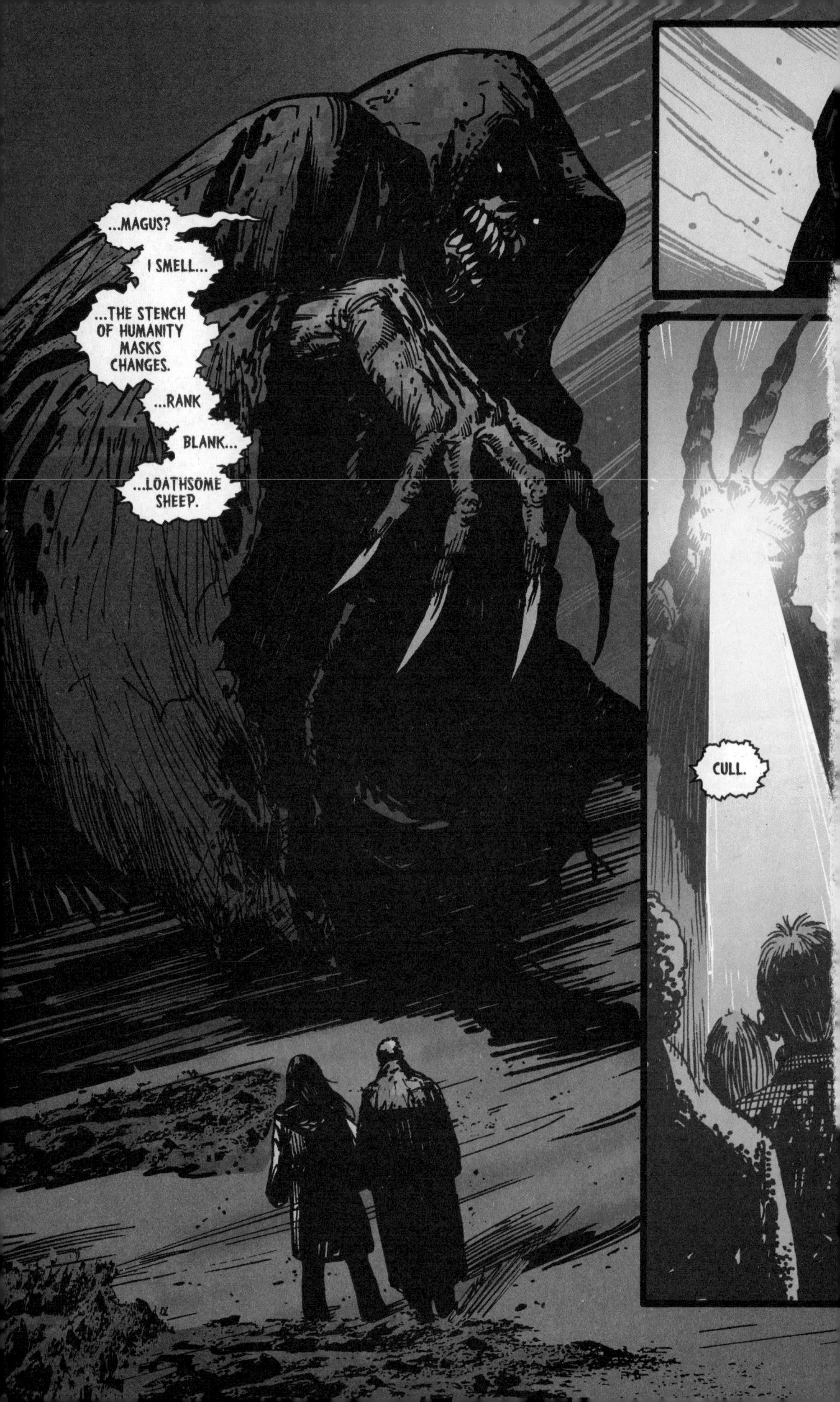
...MAGUS?
I SMELL...
...THE STENCH OF HUMANITY MASKS CHANGES.
...RANK
BLANK...
...LOATHSOME SHEEP.
CULL.

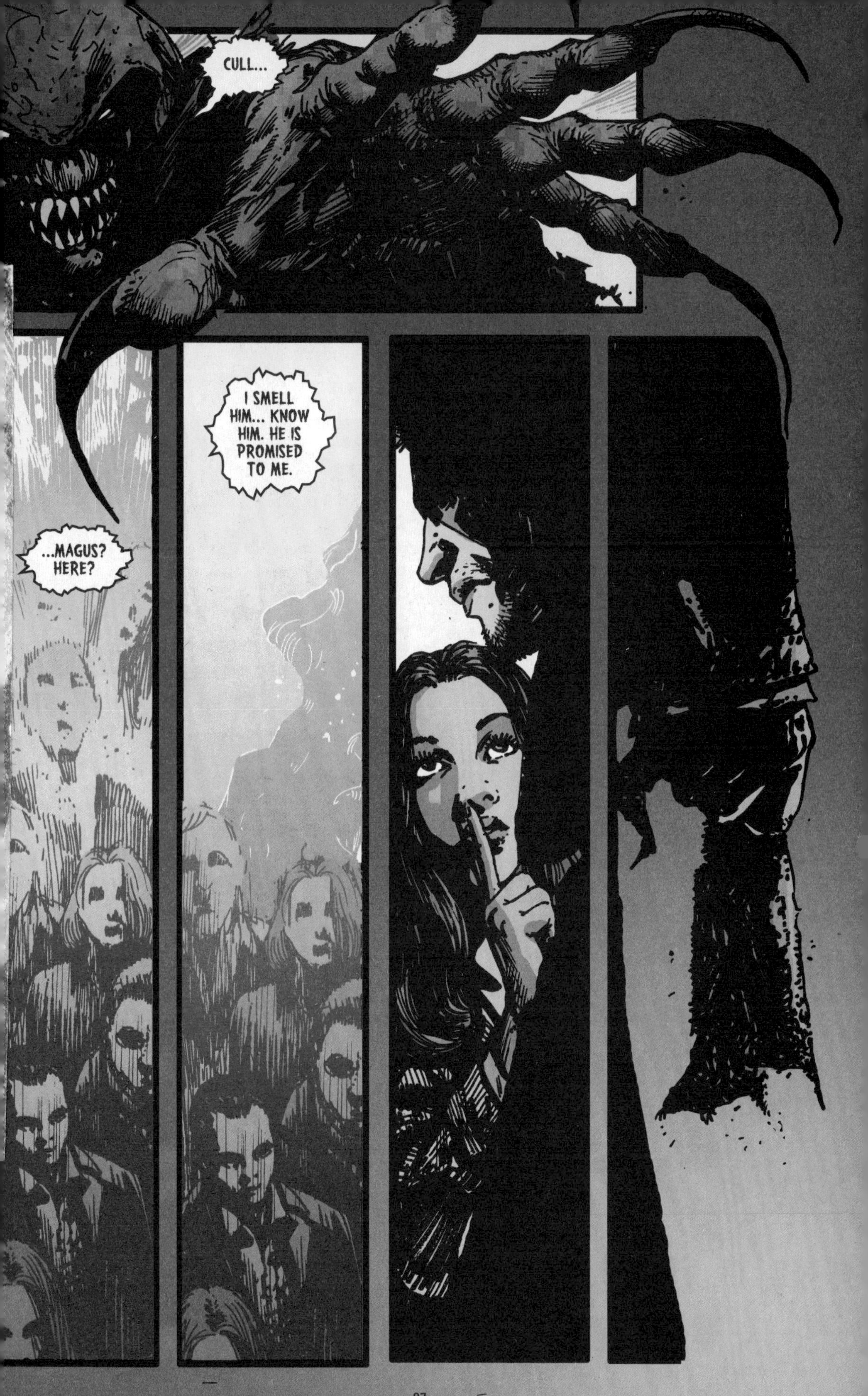
CULL...
...MAGUS? HERE?
I SMELL HIM... KNOW HIM. HE IS PROMISED TO ME.

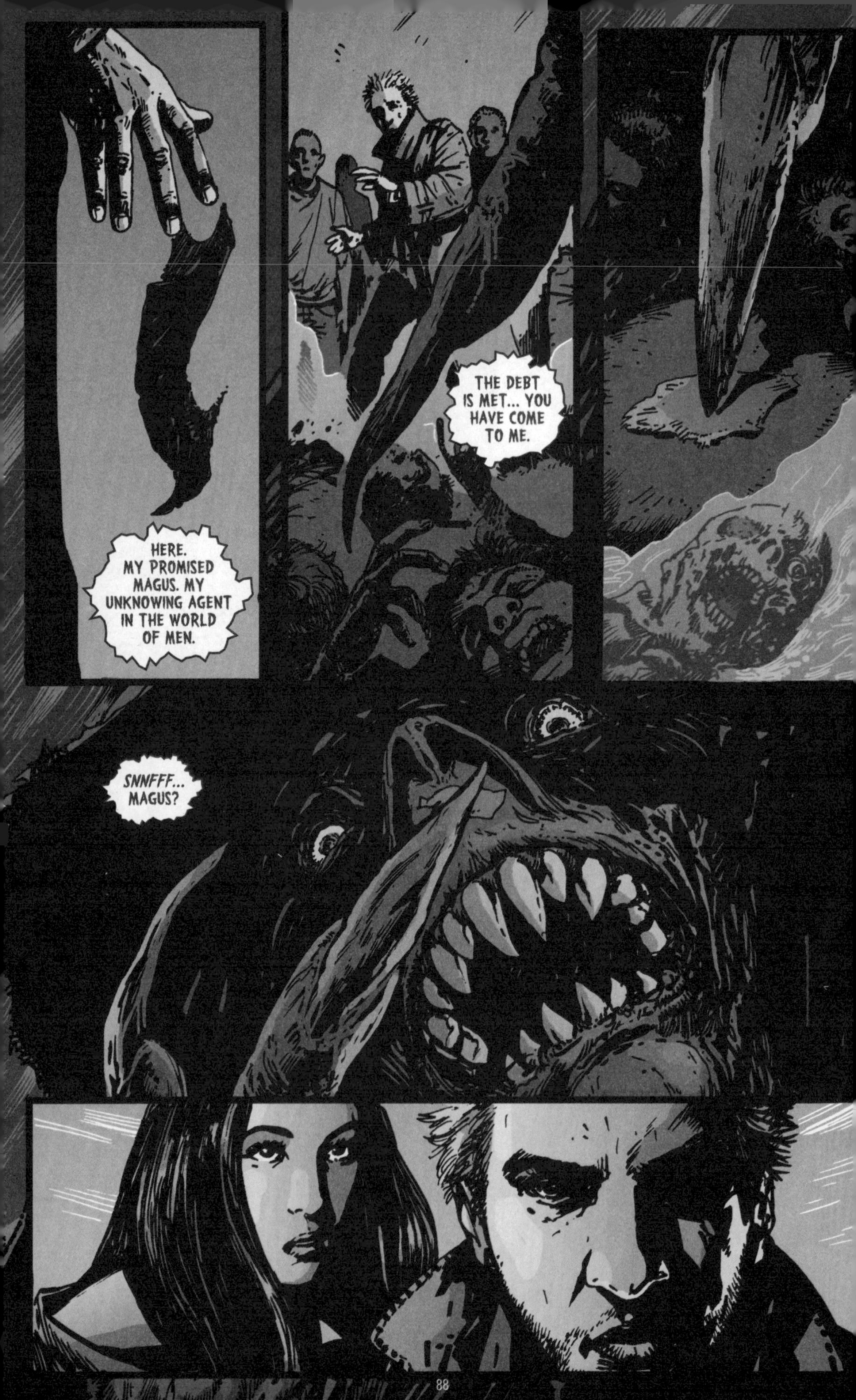
HERE. MY PROMISED MAGUS. MY UNKNOWING AGENT IN THE WORLD OF MEN.
THE DEBT IS MET... YOU HAVE COME TO ME.
SNNFFF... MAGUS?

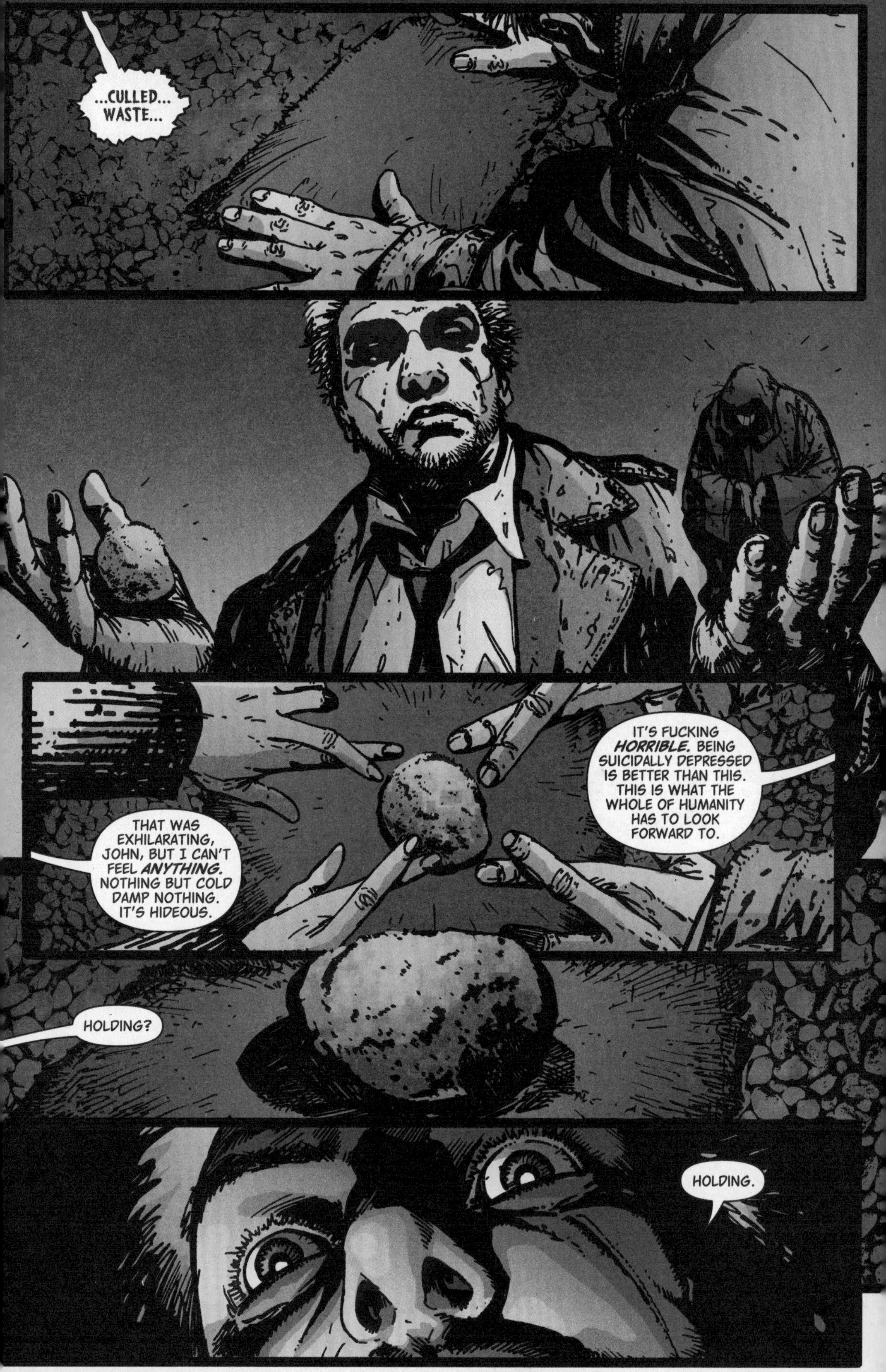
...CULLED... WASTE...
THAT WAS EXHILARATING, JOHN, BUT I CAN'T FEEL *ANYTHING.* NOTHING BUT COLD DAMP NOTHING. IT'S HIDEOUS.
IT'S FUCKING **HORRIBLE.** BEING SUICIDALLY DEPRESSED IS BETTER THAN THIS. THIS IS WHAT THE WHOLE OF HUMANITY HAS TO LOOK FORWARD TO.
HOLDING?
HOLDING.

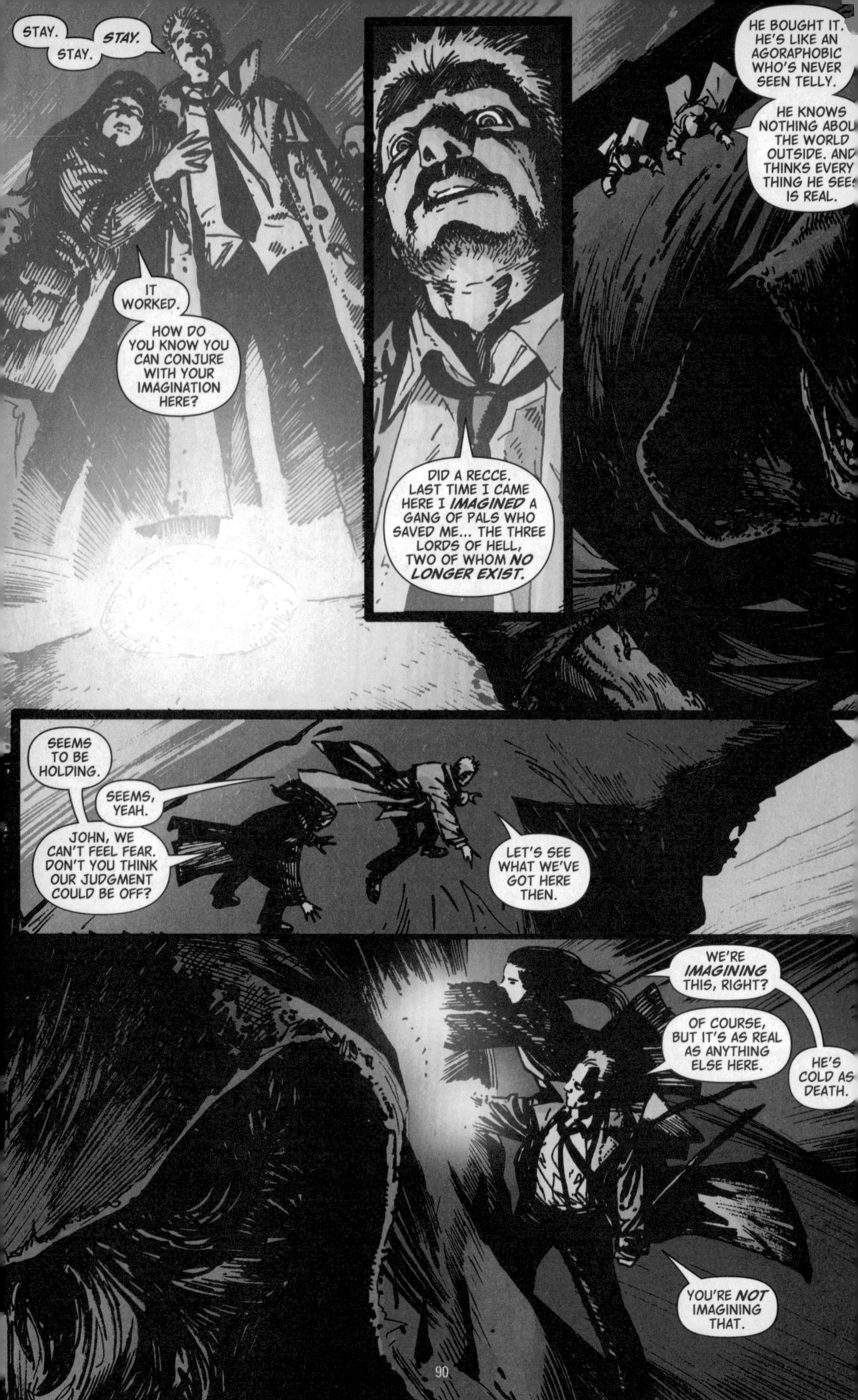
STAY. STAY. STAY.
IT WORKED.
HOW DO YOU KNOW YOU CAN CONJURE WITH YOUR IMAGINATION HERE?
DID A RECCE. LAST TIME I CAME HERE I IMAGINED A GANG OF PALS WHO SAVED ME... THE THREE LORDS OF HELL, TWO OF WHOM NO LONGER EXIST.
HE BOUGHT IT. HE'S LIKE AN AGORAPHOBIC WHO'S NEVER SEEN TELLY.
HE KNOWS NOTHING ABOU THE WORLD OUTSIDE. AND THINKS EVERY THING HE SEE IS REAL.
SEEMS TO BE HOLDING.
SEEMS, YEAH.
JOHN, WE CAN'T FEEL FEAR. DON'T YOU THINK OUR JUDGMENT COULD BE OFF?
LET'S SEE WHAT WE'VE GOT HERE THEN.
WE'RE IMAGINING THIS, RIGHT?
OF COURSE, BUT IT'S AS REAL AS ANYTHING ELSE HERE.
HE'S COLD AS DEATH.
YOU'RE NOT IMAGINING THAT.

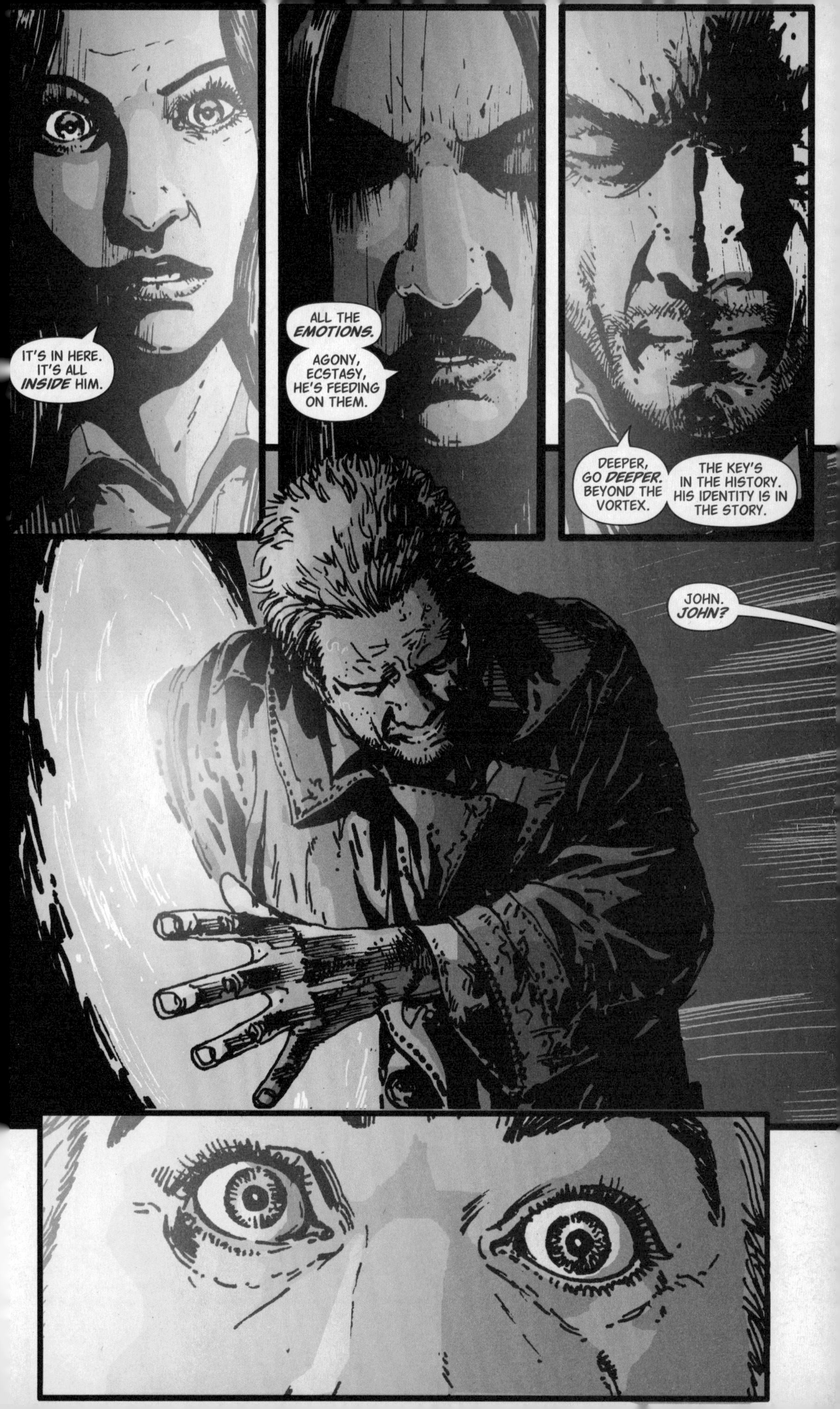
IT'S IN HERE. IT'S ALL INSIDE HIM.
ALL THE EMOTIONS.
AGONY, ECSTASY, HE'S FEEDING ON THEM.
DEEPER, GO DEEPER. BEYOND THE VORTEX.
THE KEY'S IN THE HISTORY. HIS IDENTITY IS IN THE STORY.
JOHN. JOHN?

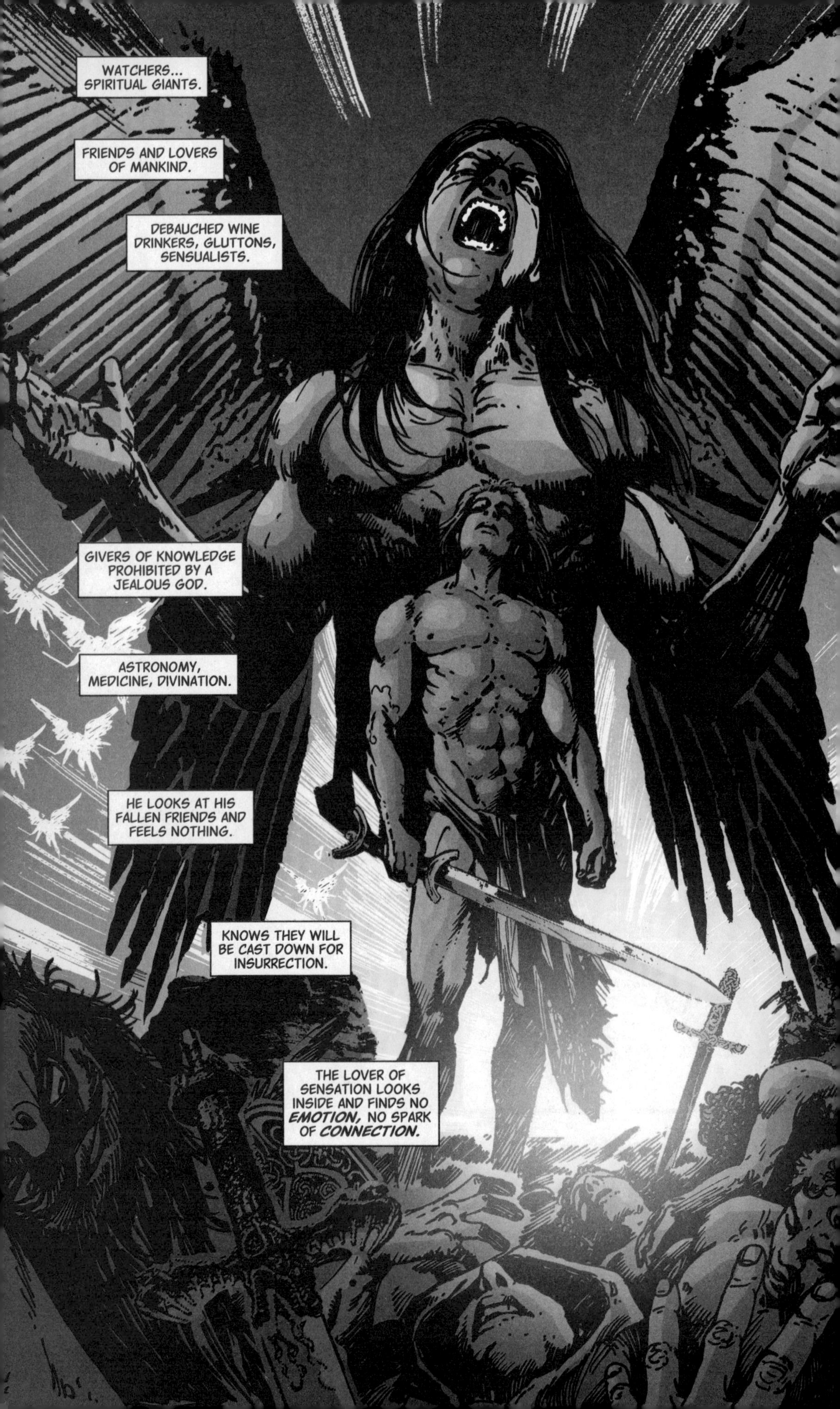
WATCHERS...
SPIRITUAL GIANTS.
FRIENDS AND LOVERS OF MANKIND.
DEBAUCHED WINE DRINKERS, GLUTTONS, SENSUALISTS.
GIVERS OF KNOWLEDGE PROHIBITED BY A JEALOUS GOD.
ASTRONOMY, MEDICINE, DIVINATION.
HE LOOKS AT HIS FALLEN FRIENDS AND FEELS NOTHING.
KNOWS THEY WILL BE CAST DOWN FOR INSURRECTION.
THE LOVER OF SENSATION LOOKS INSIDE AND FINDS NO *EMOTION,* NO SPARK OF *CONNECTION.*

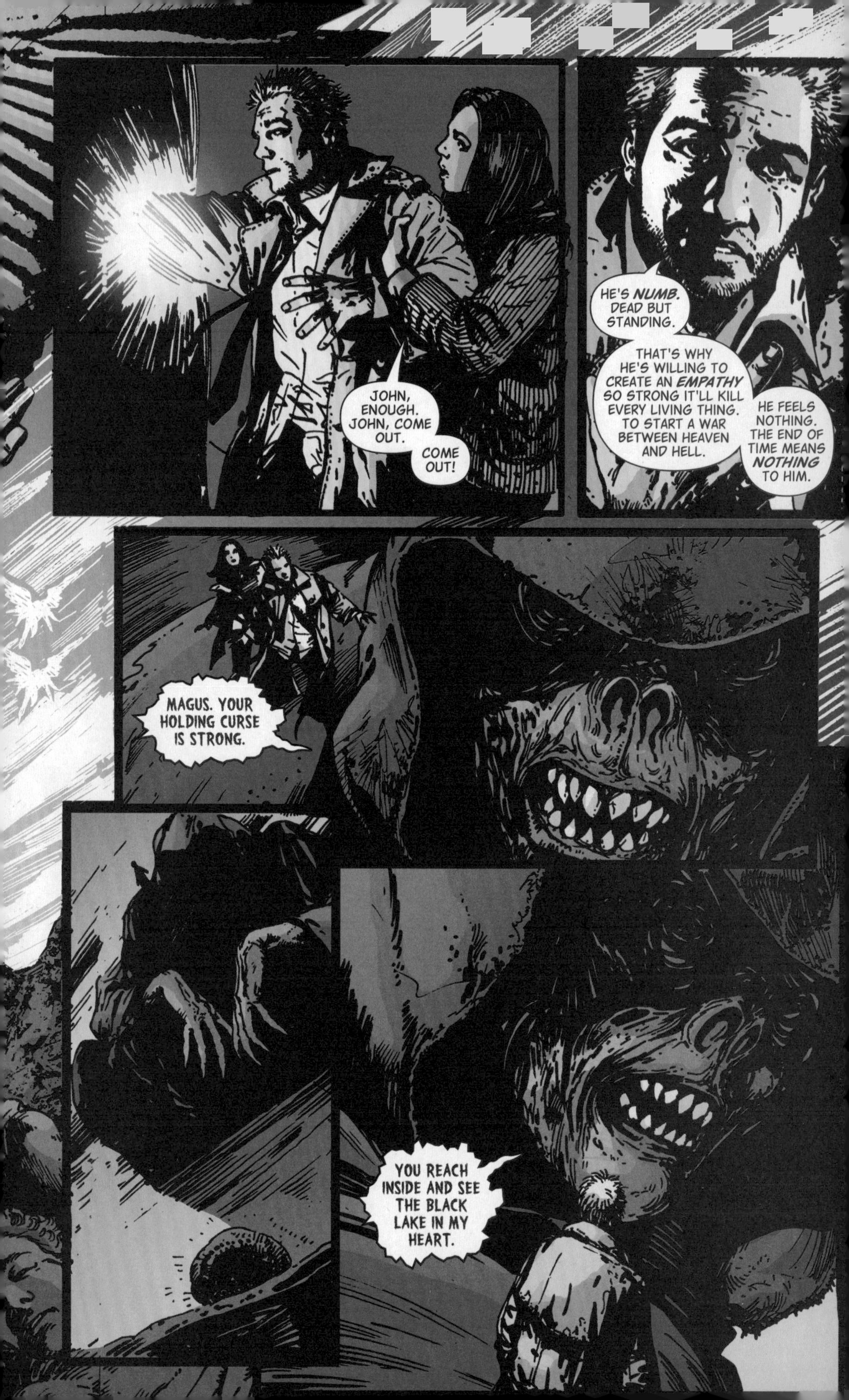
JOHN, ENOUGH. JOHN, COME OUT.
COME OUT!
HE'S NUMB. DEAD BUT STANDING.
THAT'S WHY HE'S WILLING TO CREATE AN EMPATHY SO STRONG IT'LL KILL EVERY LIVING THING. TO START A WAR BETWEEN HEAVEN AND HELL.
HE FEELS NOTHING. THE END OF TIME MEANS NOTHING TO HIM.
MAGUS. YOUR HOLDING CURSE IS STRONG.
YOU REACH INSIDE AND SEE THE BLACK LAKE IN MY HEART.

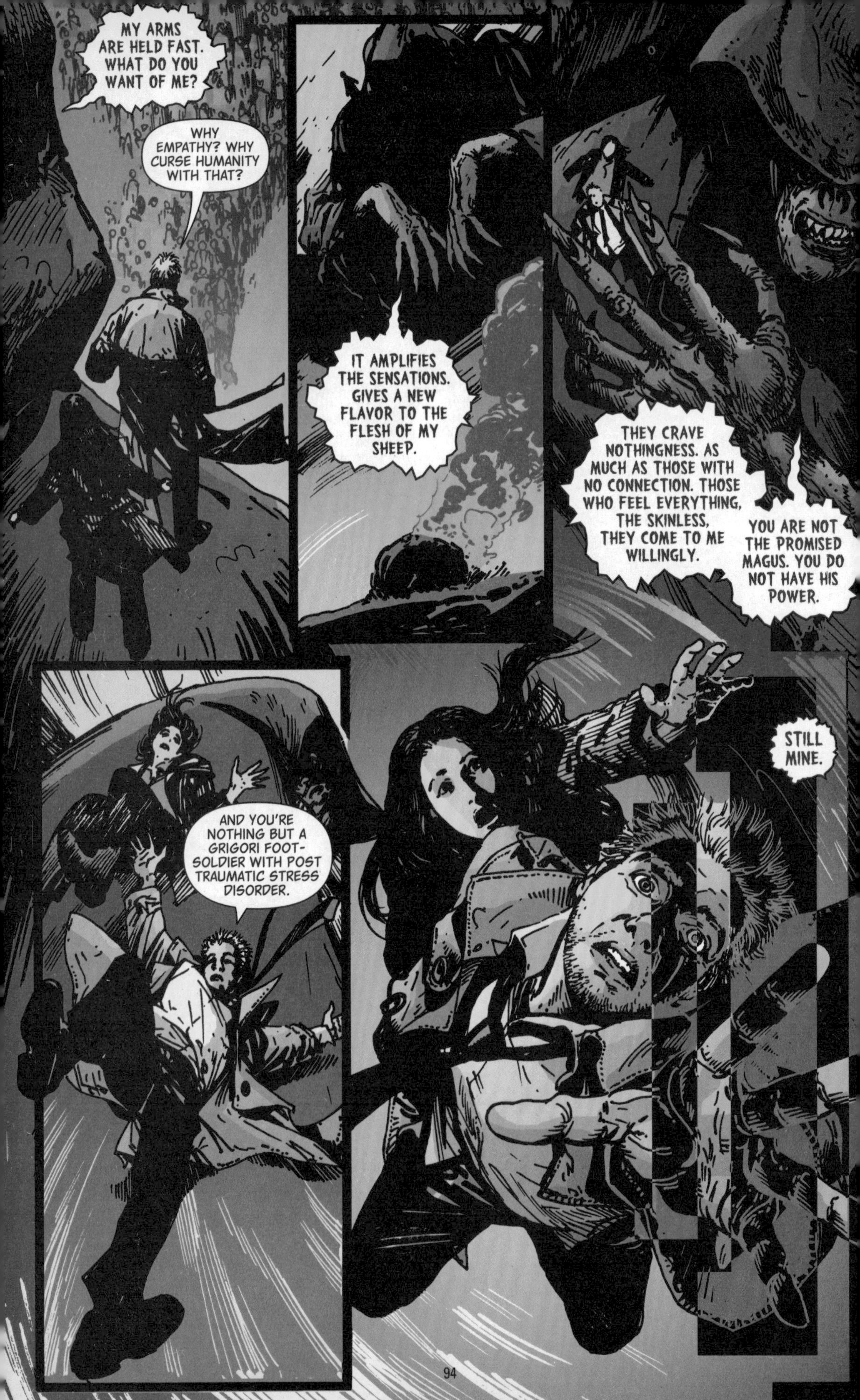

MY ARMS ARE HELD FAST. WHAT DO YOU WANT OF ME?
WHY EMPATHY? WHY CURSE HUMANITY WITH THAT?
IT AMPLIFIES THE SENSATIONS. GIVES A NEW FLAVOR TO THE FLESH OF MY SHEEP.
THEY CRAVE NOTHINGNESS. AS MUCH AS THOSE WITH NO CONNECTION. THOSE WHO FEEL EVERYTHING, THE SKINLESS, THEY COME TO ME WILLINGLY.
YOU ARE NOT THE PROMISED MAGUS. YOU DO NOT HAVE HIS POWER.
AND YOU'RE NOTHING BUT A GRIGORI FOOT-SOLDIER WITH POST TRAUMATIC STRESS DISORDER.
STILL MINE.

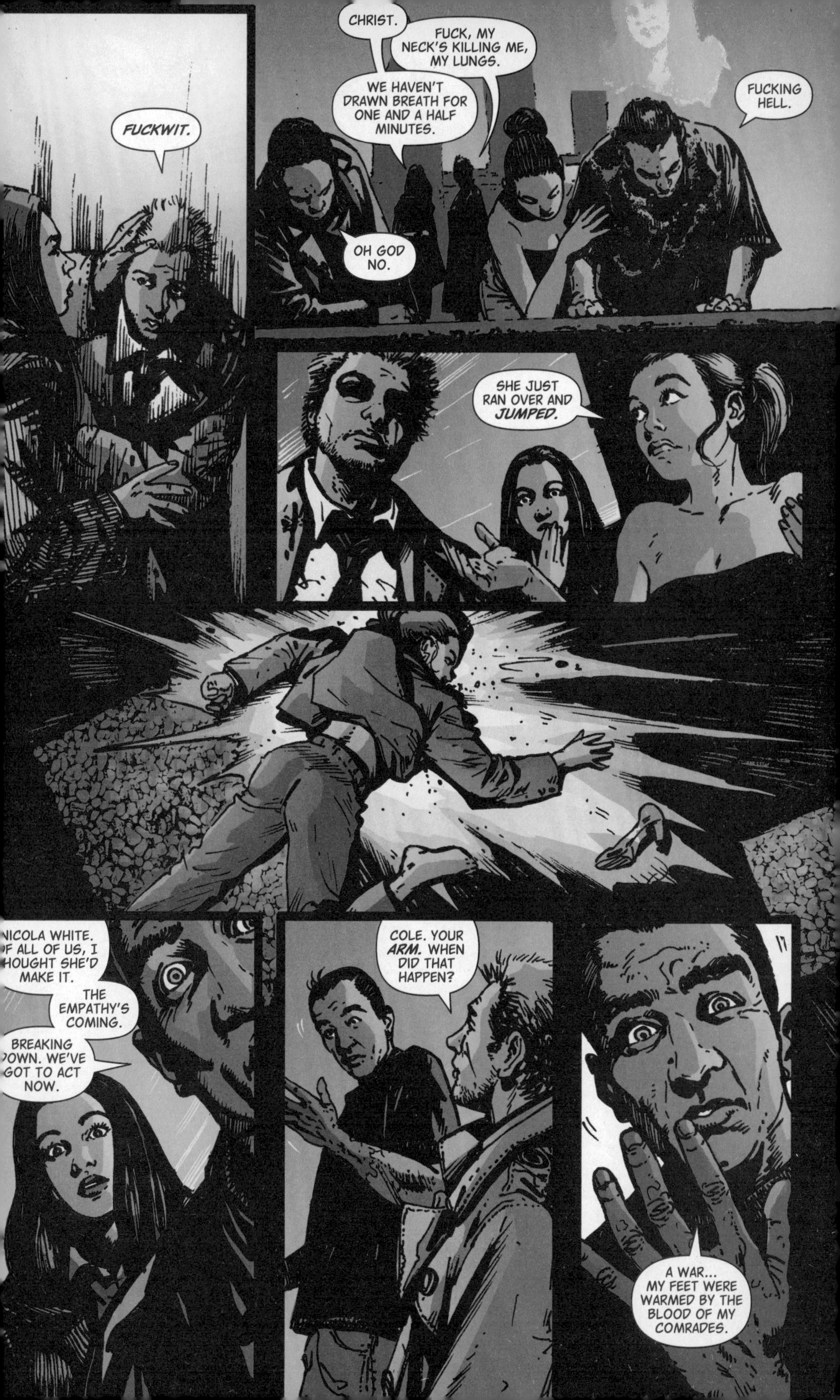
FUCKWIT.
CHRIST.
FUCK, MY NECK'S KILLING ME, MY LUNGS.
WE HAVEN'T DRAWN BREATH FOR ONE AND A HALF MINUTES.
FUCKING HELL.
OH GOD NO.
SHE JUST RAN OVER AND JUMPED.
NICOLA WHITE. F ALL OF US, I HOUGHT SHE'D MAKE IT.
THE EMPATHY'S COMING.
BREAKING OWN. WE'VE GOT TO ACT NOW.
COLE. YOUR ARM. WHEN DID THAT HAPPEN?
A WAR... MY FEET WERE WARMED BY THE BLOOD OF MY COMRADES.

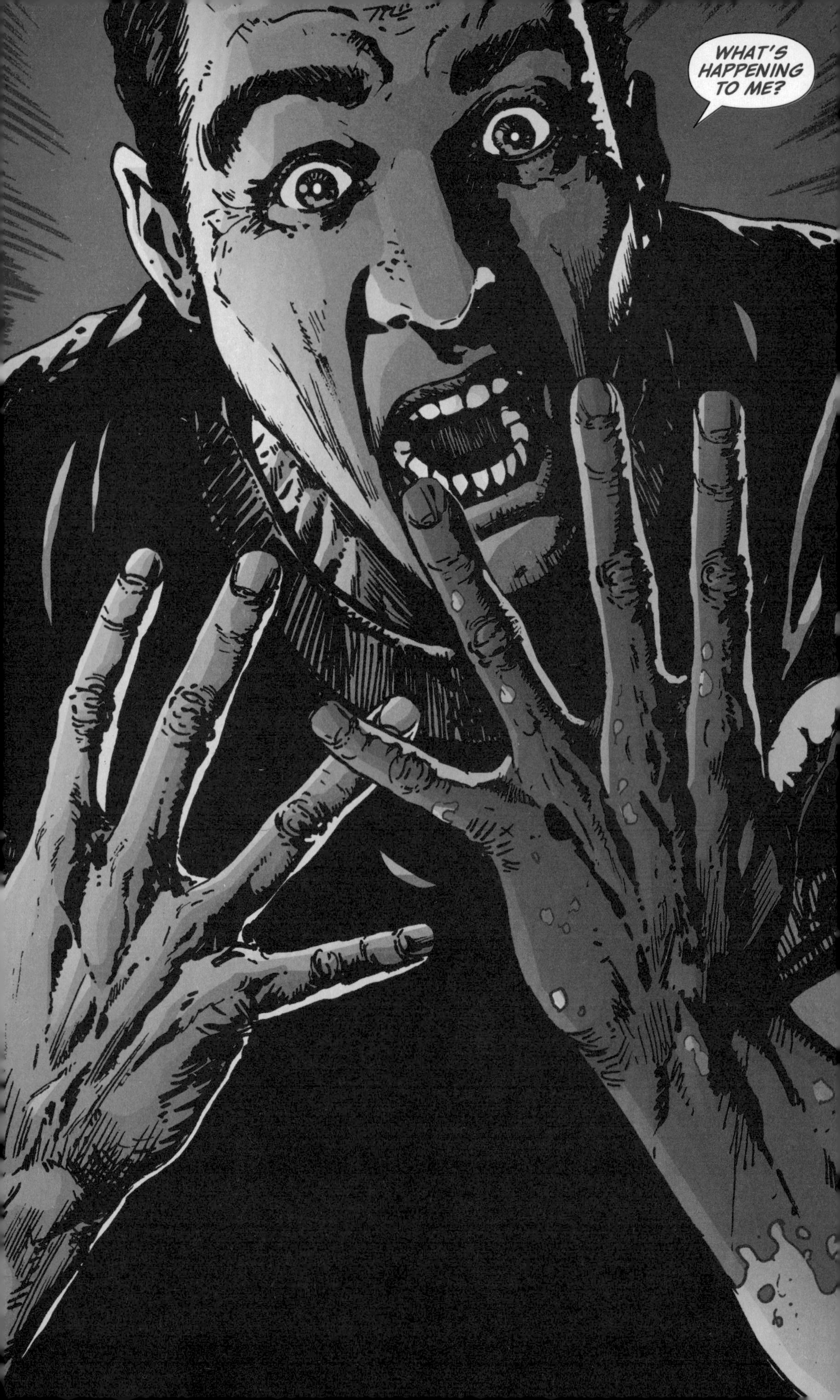
WHAT'S HAPPENING TO ME?

THE RED RIGHT HAND Chapter 4

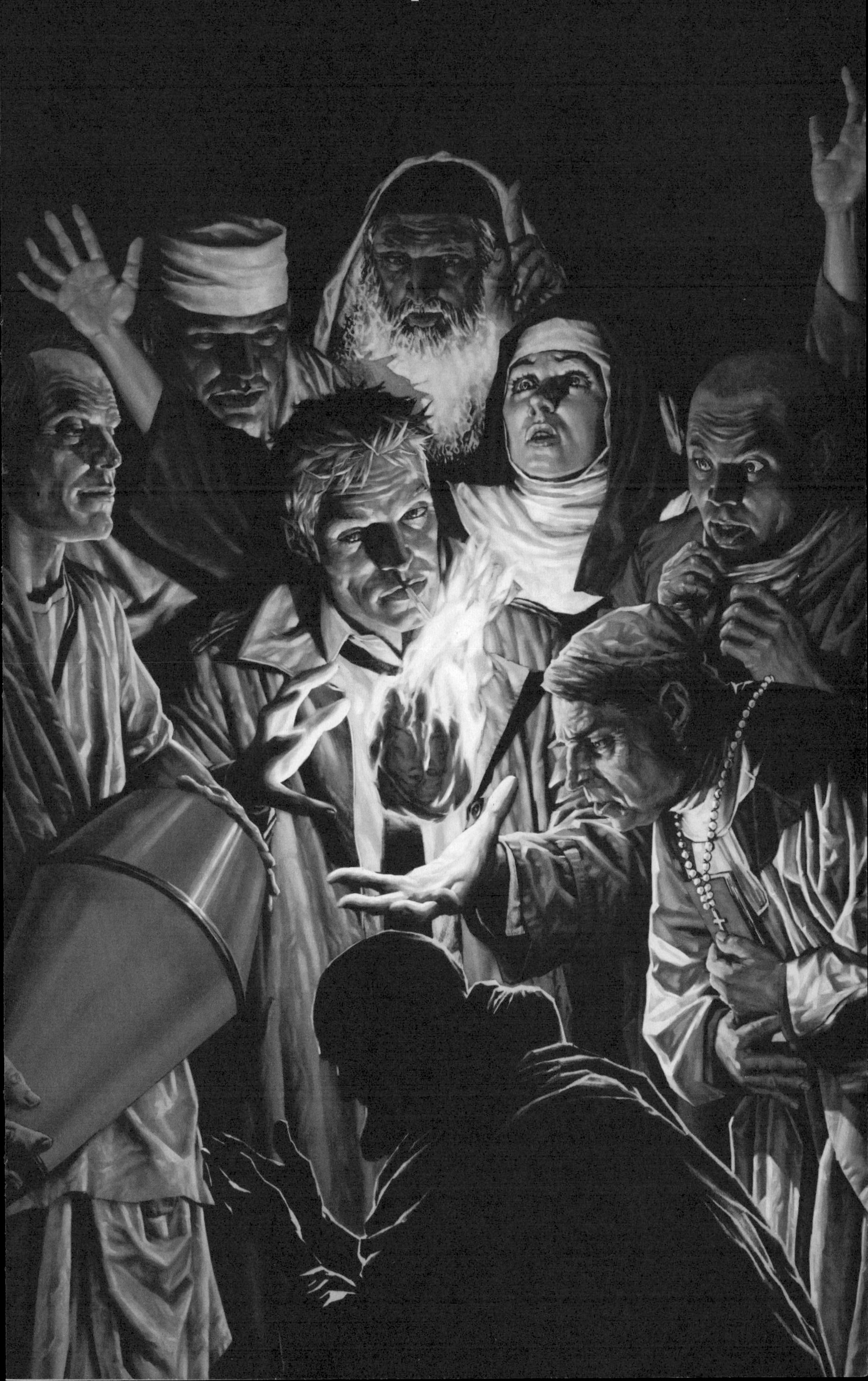

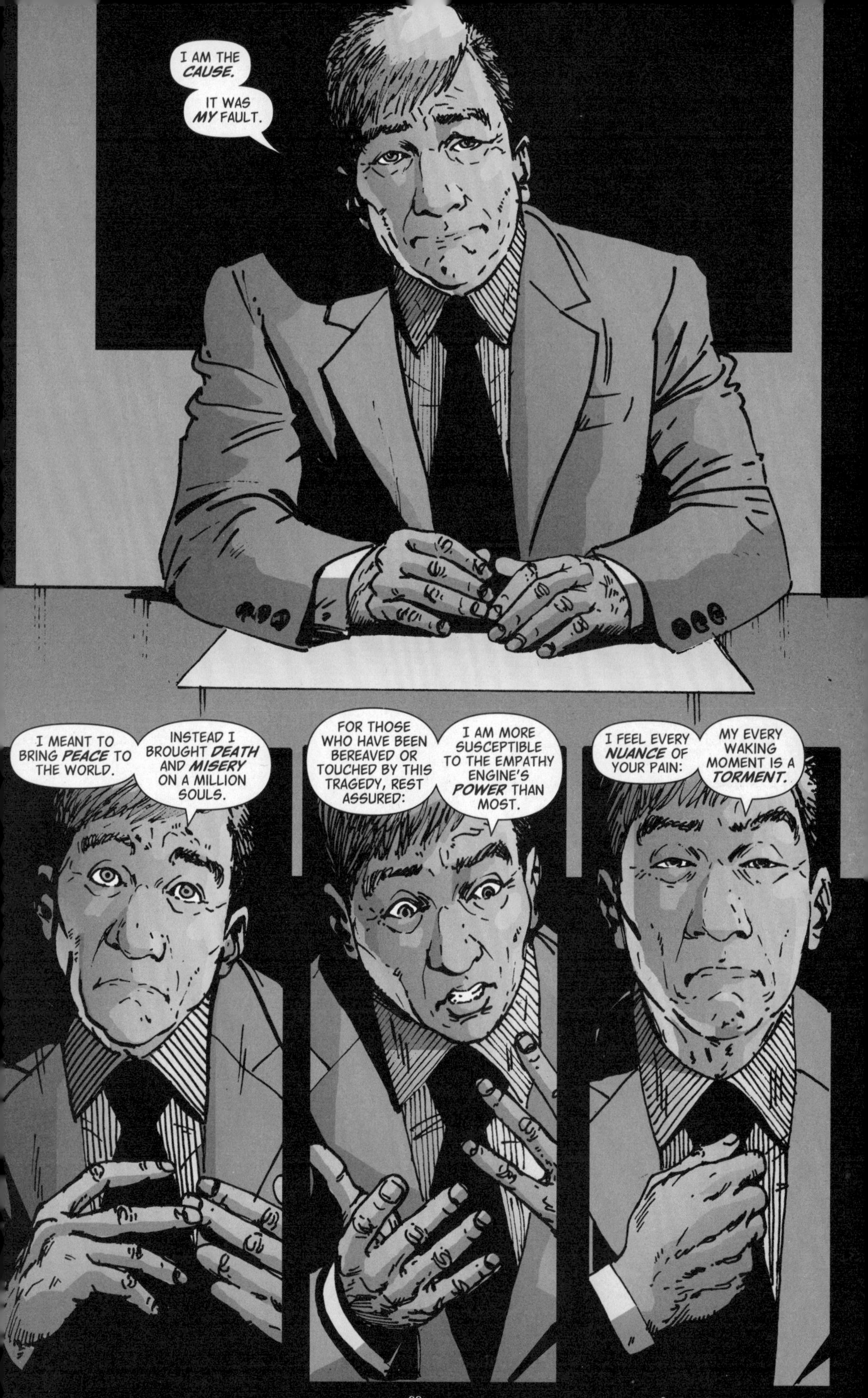
I AM THE CAUSE.
IT WAS MY FAULT.
I MEANT TO BRING PEACE TO THE WORLD.
INSTEAD I BROUGHT DEATH AND MISERY ON A MILLION SOULS.
FOR THOSE WHO HAVE BEEN BEREAVED OR TOUCHED BY THIS TRAGEDY, REST ASSURED:
I AM MORE SUSCEPTIBLE TO THE EMPATHY ENGINE'S POWER THAN MOST.
I FEEL EVERY NUANCE OF YOUR PAIN:
MY EVERY WAKING MOMENT IS A TORMENT.

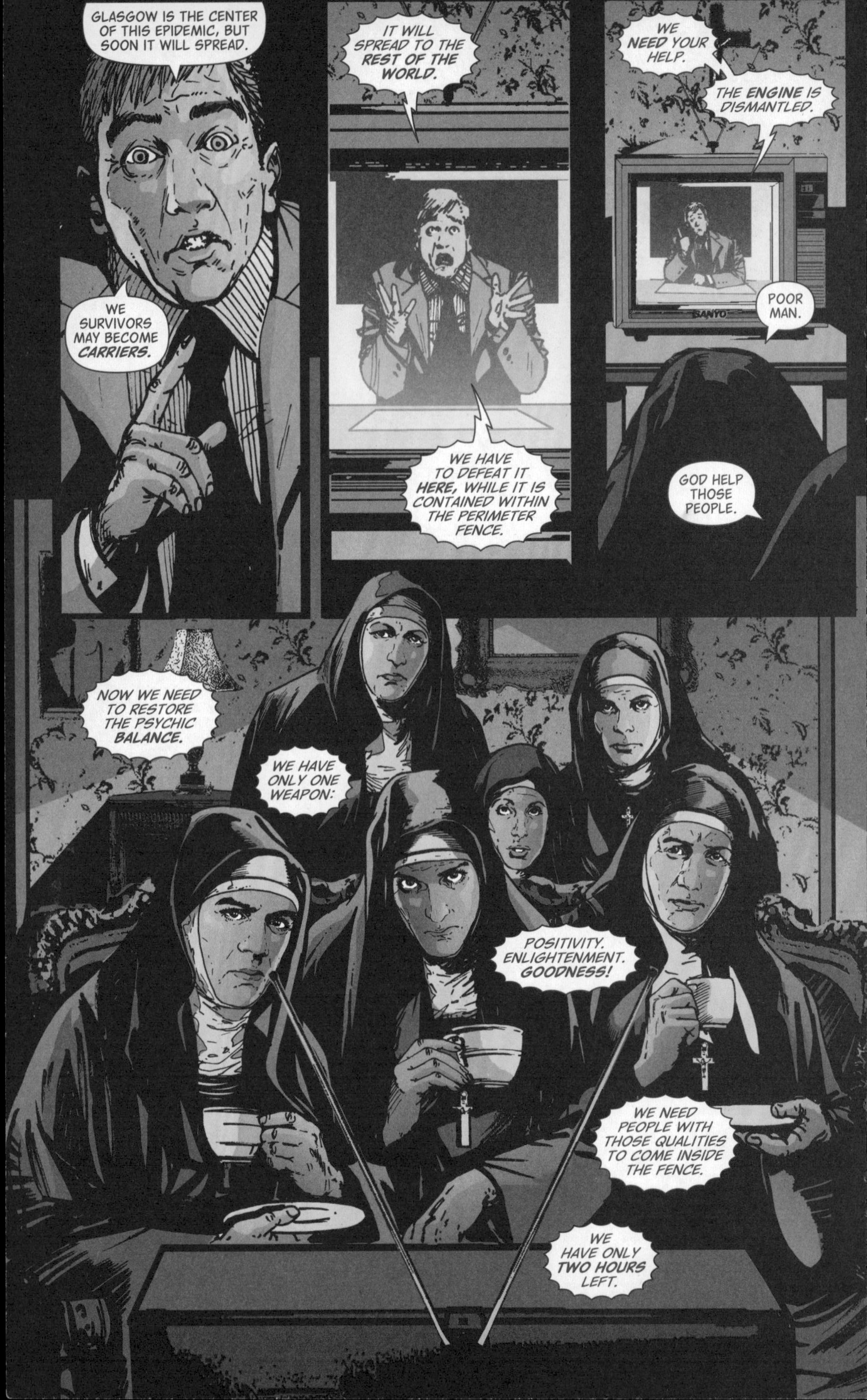
GLASGOW IS THE CENTER OF THIS EPIDEMIC, BUT SOON IT WILL SPREAD.
WE SURVIVORS MAY BECOME CARRIERS.
IT WILL SPREAD TO THE REST OF THE WORLD.
WE HAVE TO DEFEAT IT HERE, WHILE IT IS CONTAINED WITHIN THE PERIMETER FENCE.
WE NEED YOUR HELP.
THE ENGINE IS DISMANTLED.
SANYO
POOR MAN.
GOD HELP THOSE PEOPLE.
NOW WE NEED TO RESTORE THE PSYCHIC BALANCE.
WE HAVE ONLY ONE WEAPON:
POSITIVITY. ENLIGHTENMENT. GOODNESS!
WE NEED PEOPLE WITH THOSE QUALITIES TO COME INSIDE THE FENCE.
WE HAVE ONLY TWO HOURS LEFT.

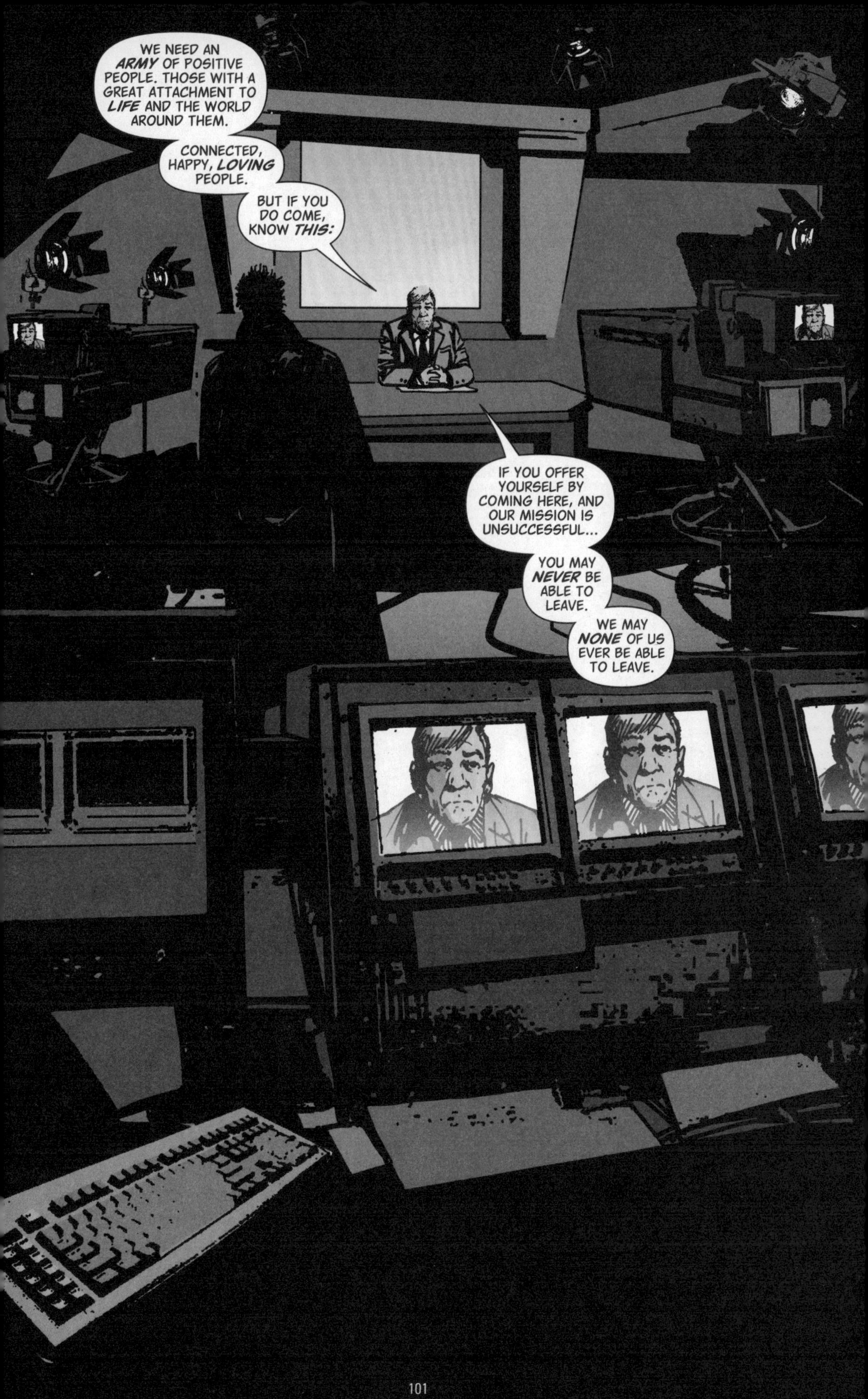
WE NEED AN ARMY OF POSITIVE PEOPLE. THOSE WITH A GREAT ATTACHMENT TO LIFE AND THE WORLD AROUND THEM.
CONNECTED, HAPPY, LOVING PEOPLE.
BUT IF YOU DO COME, KNOW THIS:
IF YOU OFFER YOURSELF BY COMING HERE, AND OUR MISSION IS UNSUCCESSFUL...
YOU MAY NEVER BE ABLE TO LEAVE.
WE MAY NONE OF US EVER BE ABLE TO LEAVE.

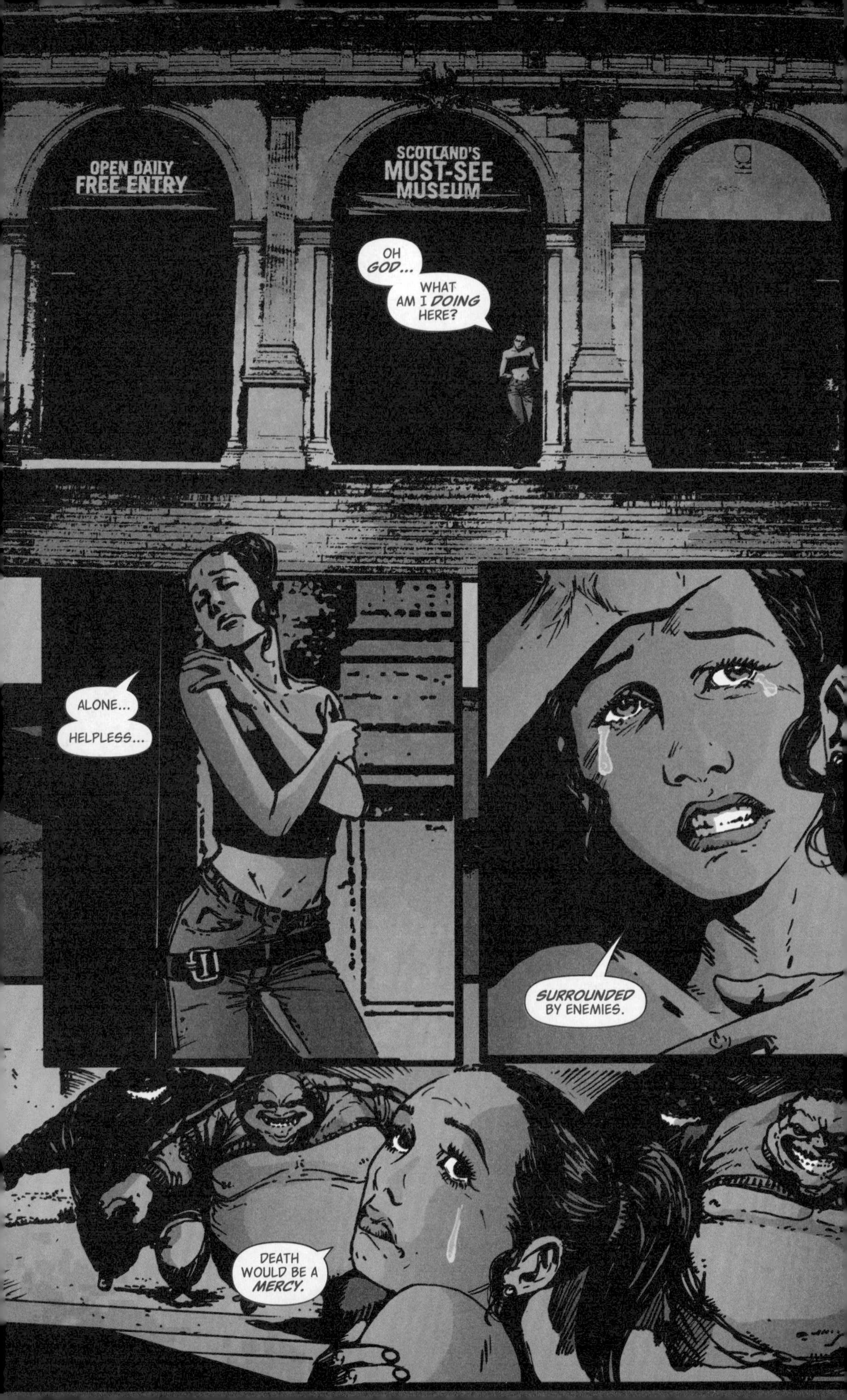
OPEN DAILY
FREE ENTRY
SCOTLAND'S
MUST-SEE
MUSEUM
OH GOD...
WHAT AM I DOING HERE?
ALONE...
HELPLESS...
SURROUNDED BY ENEMIES.
DEATH WOULD BE A MERCY.

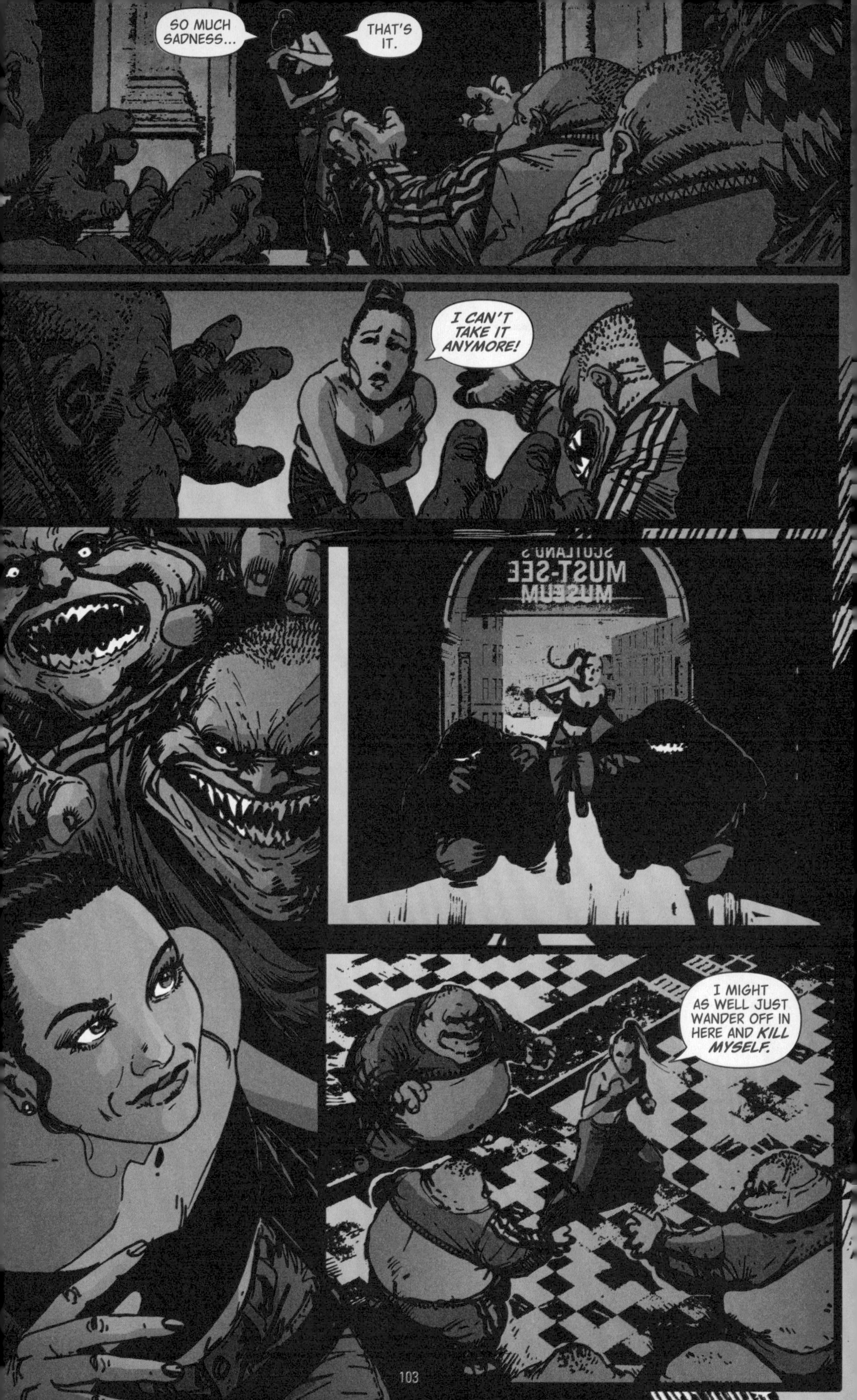
SO MUCH SADNESS...
THAT'S IT.
I CAN'T TAKE IT ANYMORE!
MUST-SEE MUSEUM
I MIGHT AS WELL JUST WANDER OFF IN HERE AND ***KILL MYSELF.***

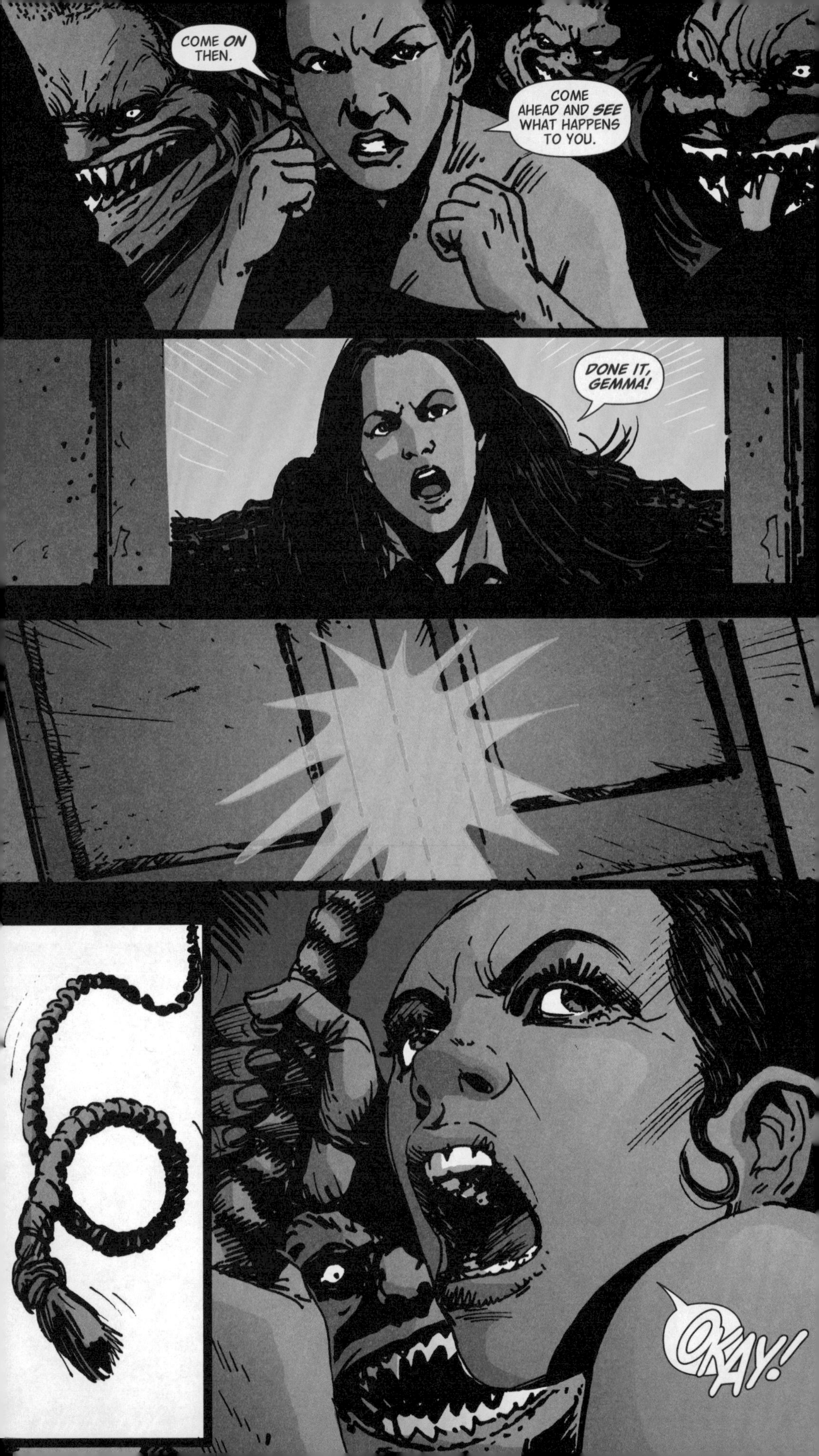
COME ON THEN.
COME AHEAD AND SEE WHAT HAPPENS TO YOU.
DONE IT, GEMMA!
OKAY!

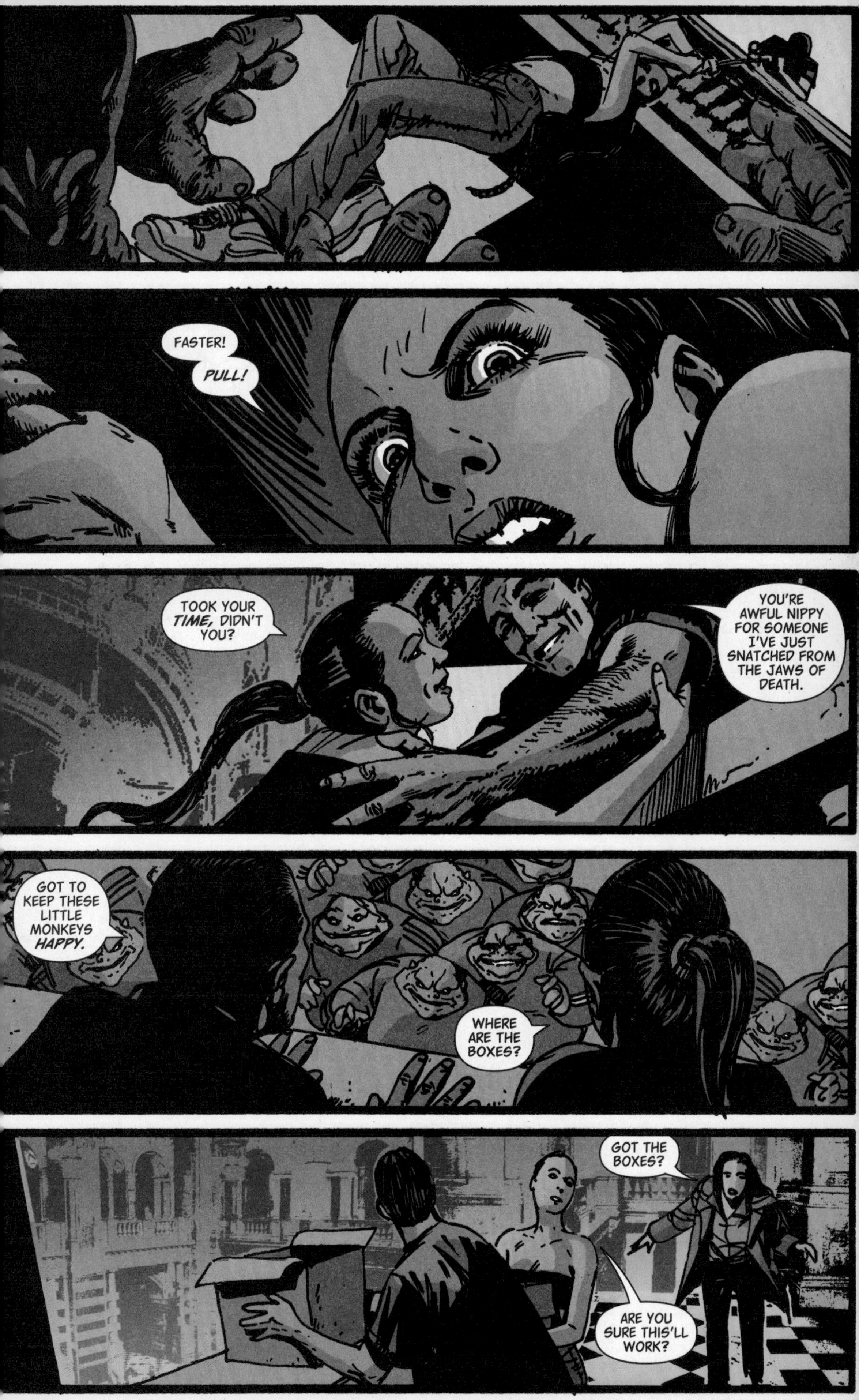
FASTER!
PULL!
TOOK YOUR TIME, DIDN'T YOU?
YOU'RE AWFUL NIPPY FOR SOMEONE I'VE JUST SNATCHED FROM THE JAWS OF DEATH.
GOT TO KEEP THESE LITTLE MONKEYS HAPPY.
WHERE ARE THE BOXES?
GOT THE BOXES?
ARE YOU SURE THIS'LL WORK?

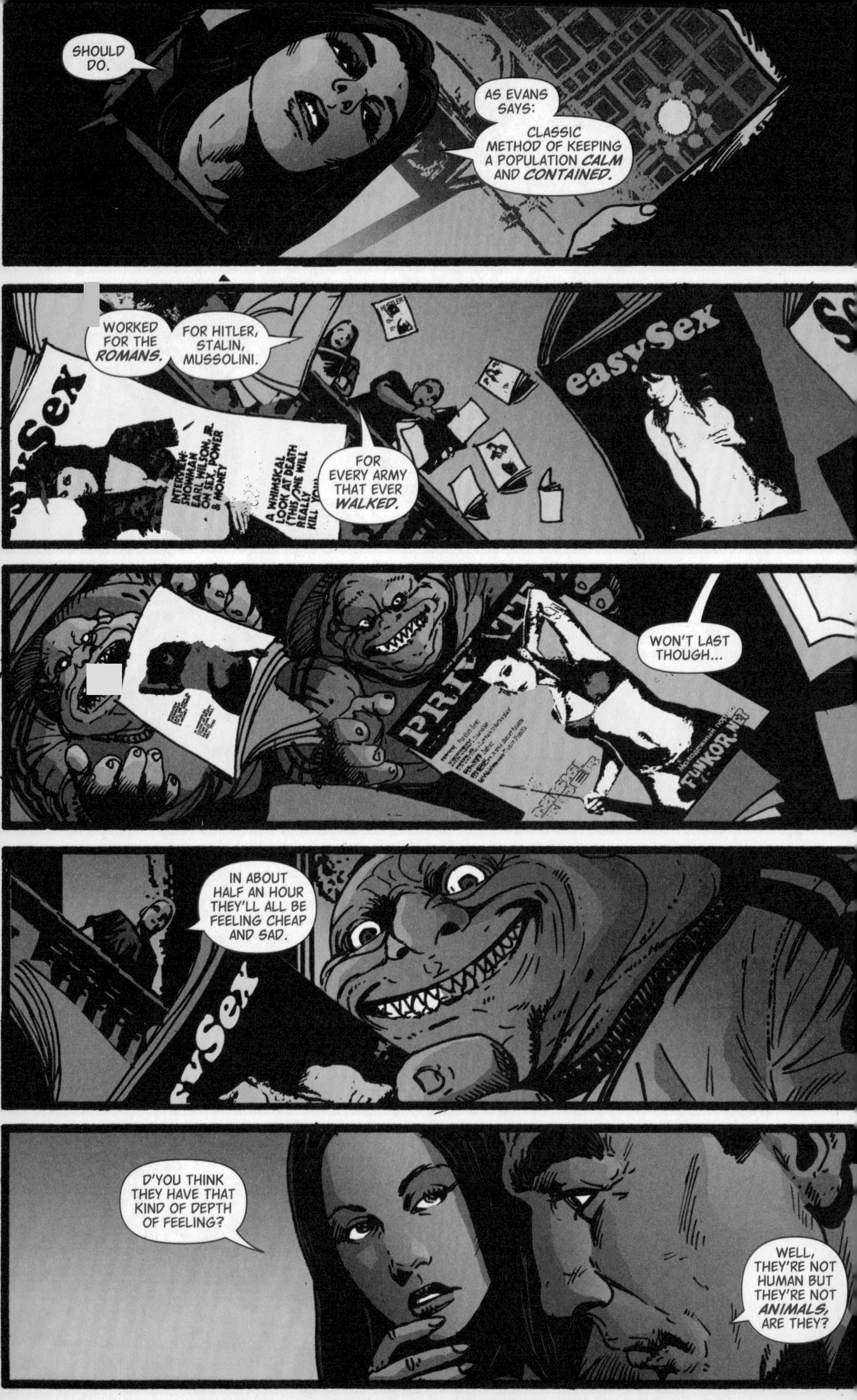

SHOULD DO.
AS EVANS SAYS:
CLASSIC METHOD OF KEEPING A POPULATION *CALM* AND *CONTAINED.*
WORKED FOR THE *ROMANS.*
FOR HITLER, STALIN, MUSSOLINI.
FOR EVERY ARMY THAT EVER *WALKED.*
easySex
WON'T LAST THOUGH...
IN ABOUT HALF AN HOUR THEY'LL ALL BE FEELING CHEAP AND SAD.
D'YOU THINK THEY HAVE THAT KIND OF DEPTH OF FEELING?
WELL, THEY'RE NOT HUMAN BUT THEY'RE NOT *ANIMALS,* ARE THEY?

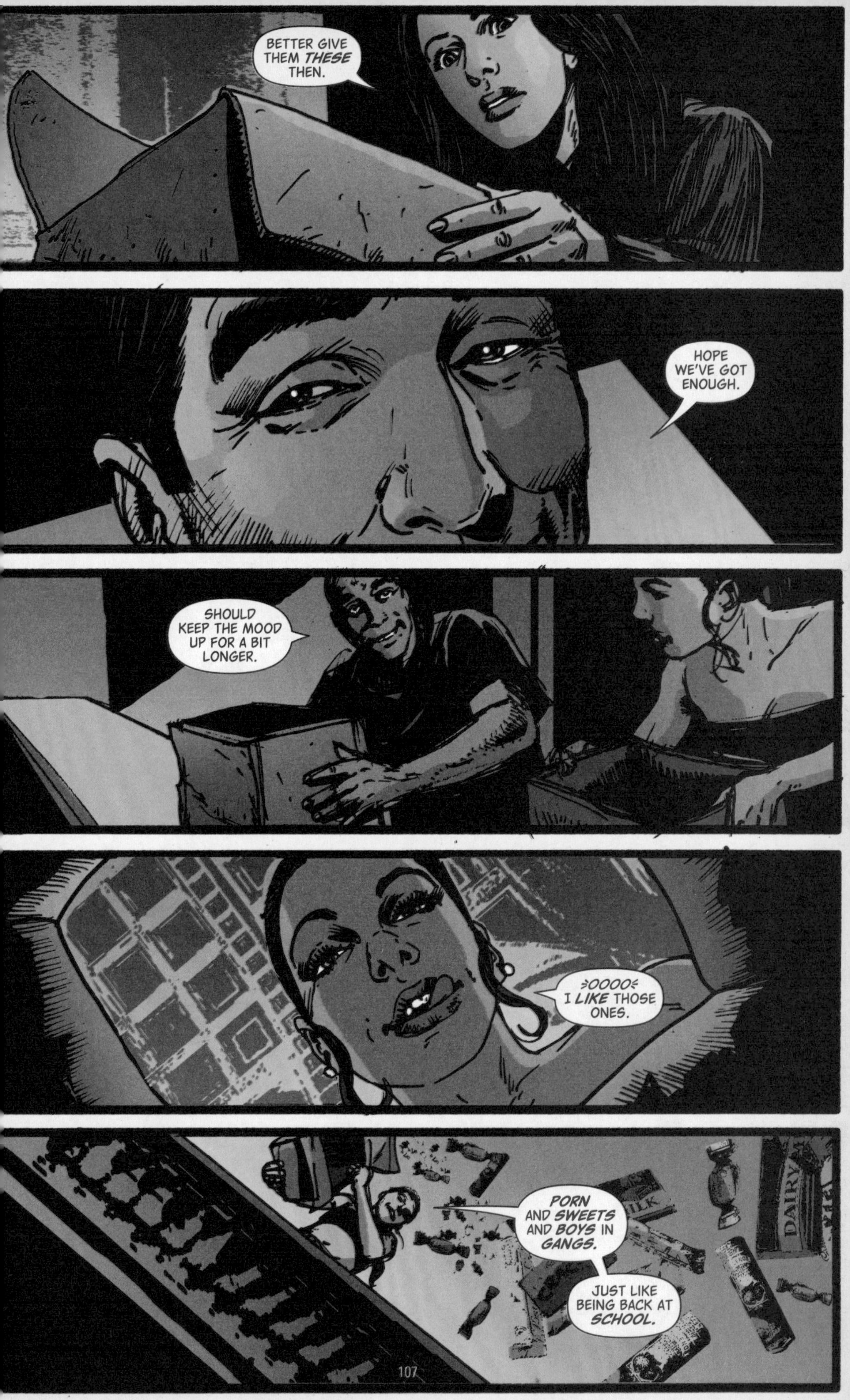

BETTER GIVE THEM *THESE* THEN.
HOPE WE'VE GOT ENOUGH.
SHOULD KEEP THE MOOD UP FOR A BIT LONGER.
OOOO
I *LIKE* THOSE ONES.
PORN AND *SWEETS* AND *BOYS* IN *GANGS*.
JUST LIKE BEING BACK AT *SCHOOL*.
DAIRY
MILK

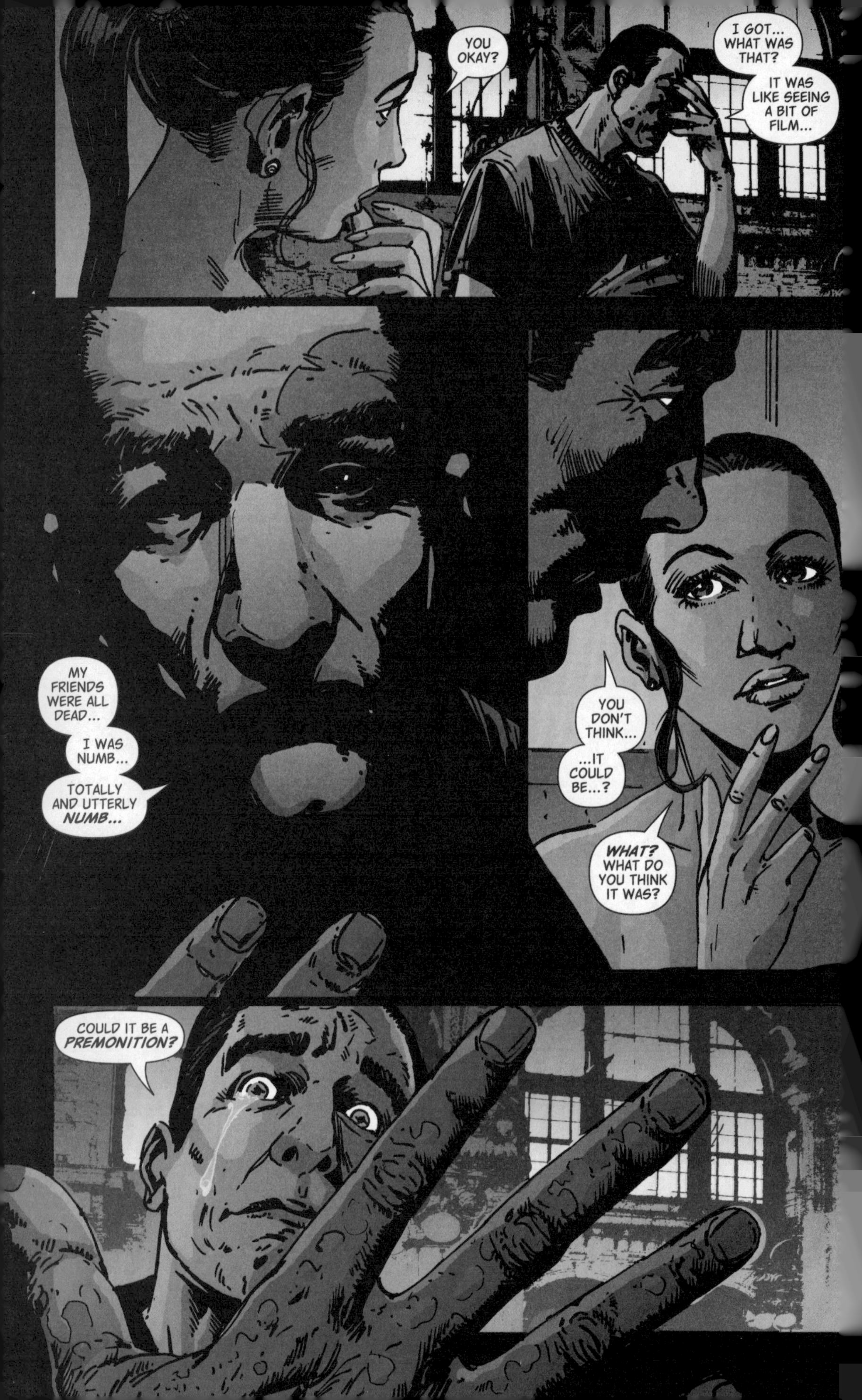
YOU OKAY?
I GOT... WHAT WAS THAT?
IT WAS LIKE SEEING A BIT OF FILM...
MY FRIENDS WERE ALL DEAD...
I WAS NUMB...
TOTALLY AND UTTERLY *NUMB...*
YOU DON'T THINK...
...IT COULD BE...?
WHAT? WHAT DO YOU THINK IT WAS?
COULD IT BE A *PREMONITION?*

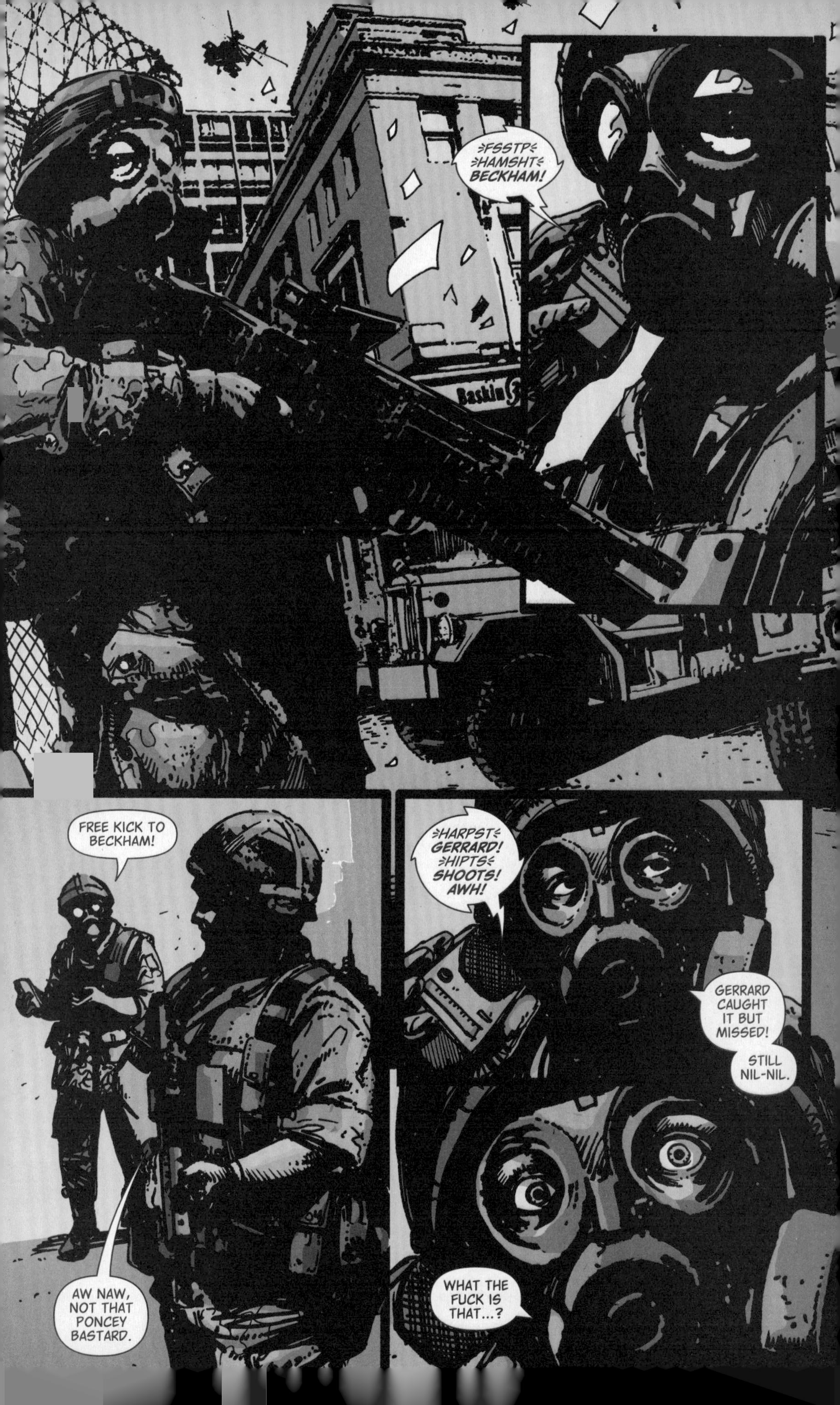

Bashin
FSSTP HAMSHT BECKHAM!
FREE KICK TO BECKHAM!
AW NAW, NOT THAT PONCEY BASTARD.
HARPST GERRARD! HIPTS SHOOTS! AWH!
GERRARD CAUGHT IT BUT MISSED!
STILL NIL-NIL.
WHAT THE FUCK IS THAT...?

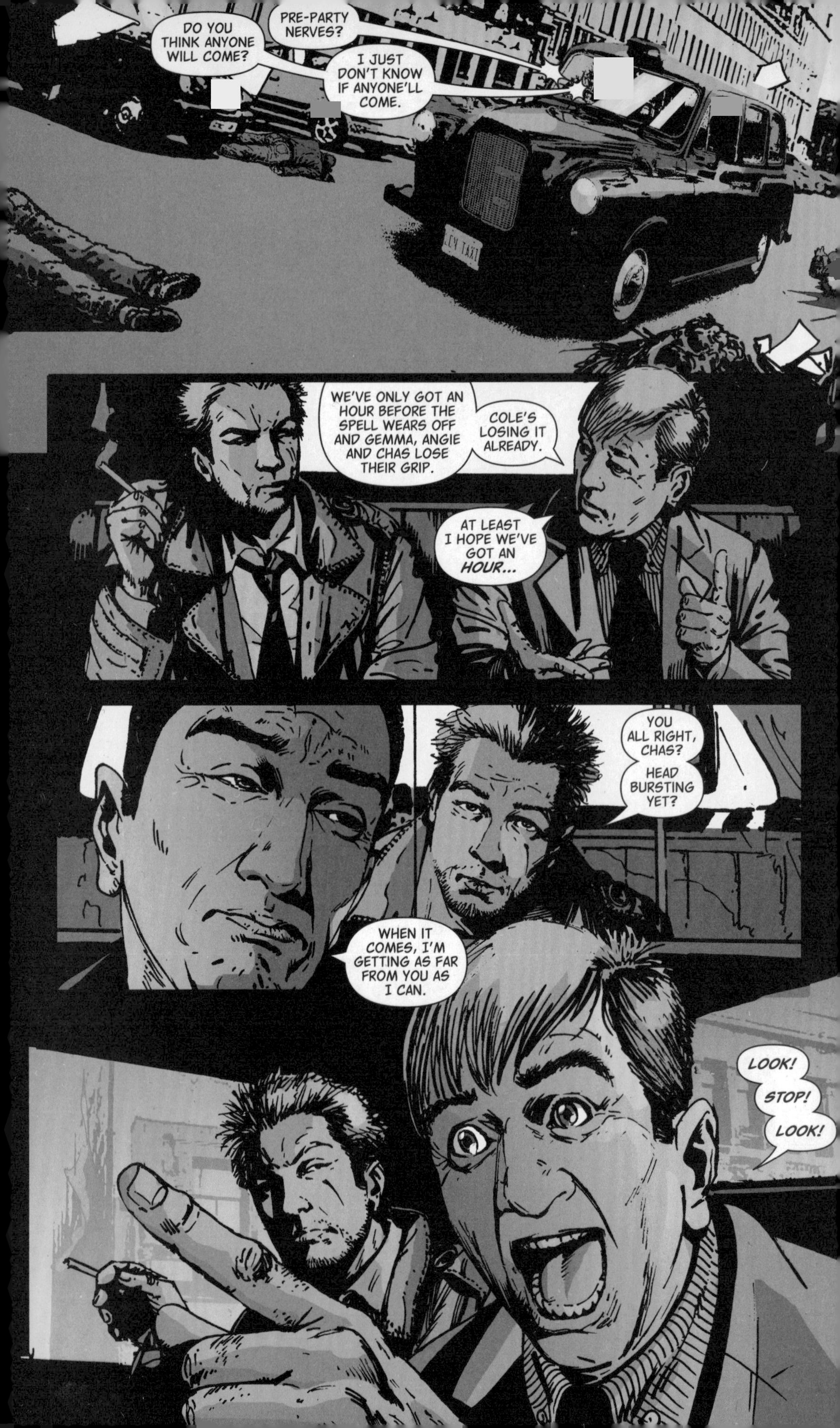
DO YOU THINK ANYONE WILL COME?
PRE-PARTY NERVES?
I JUST DON'T KNOW IF ANYONE'LL COME.
WE'VE ONLY GOT AN HOUR BEFORE THE SPELL WEARS OFF AND GEMMA, ANGIE AND CHAS LOSE THEIR GRIP.
COLE'S LOSING IT ALREADY.
AT LEAST I HOPE WE'VE GOT AN HOUR...
YOU ALL RIGHT, CHAS?
HEAD BURSTING YET?
WHEN IT COMES, I'M GETTING AS FAR FROM YOU AS I CAN.
LOOK!
STOP!
LOOK!

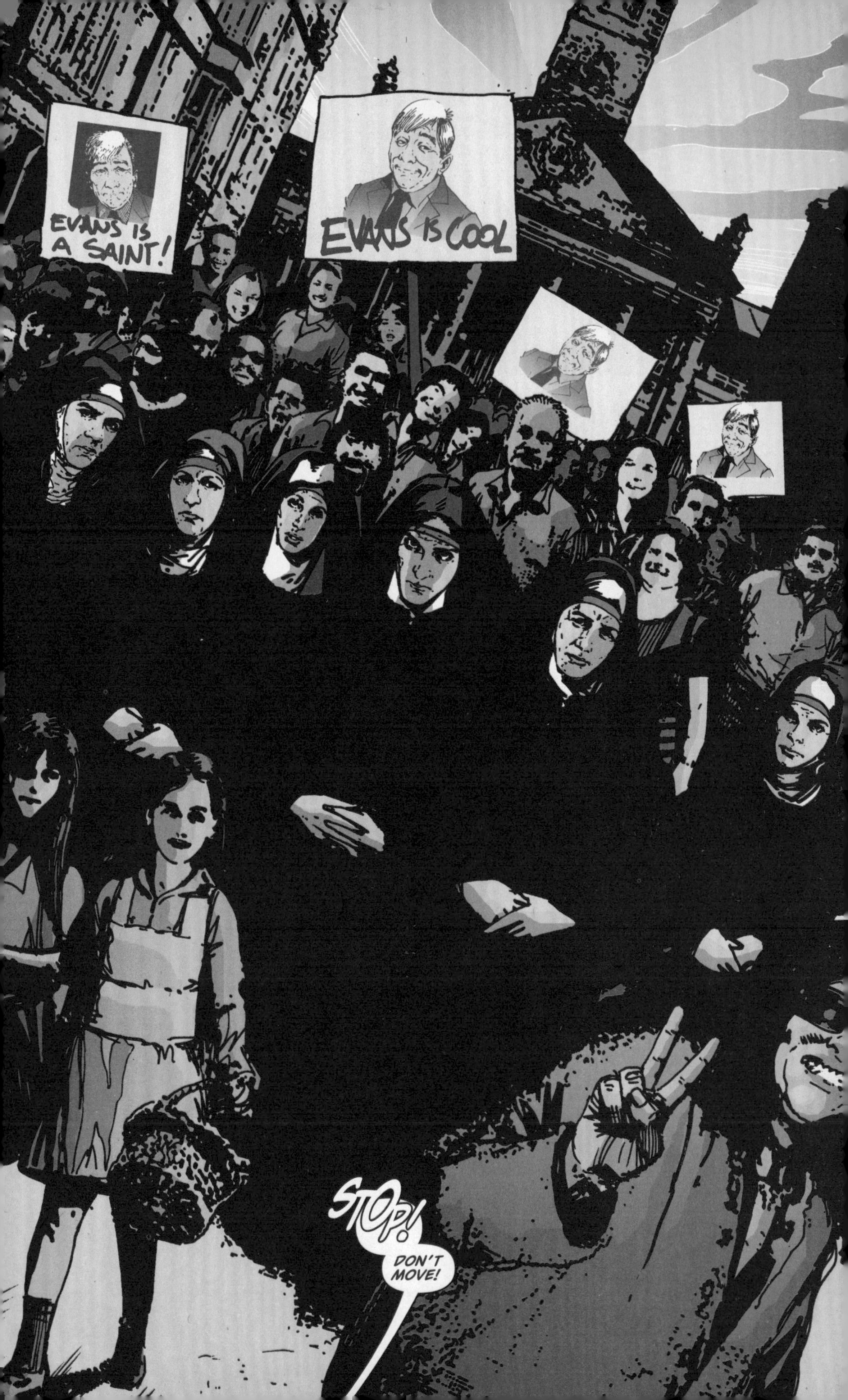
EVANS IS A SAINT!
EVANS IS COOL
STOP!
DON'T MOVE!

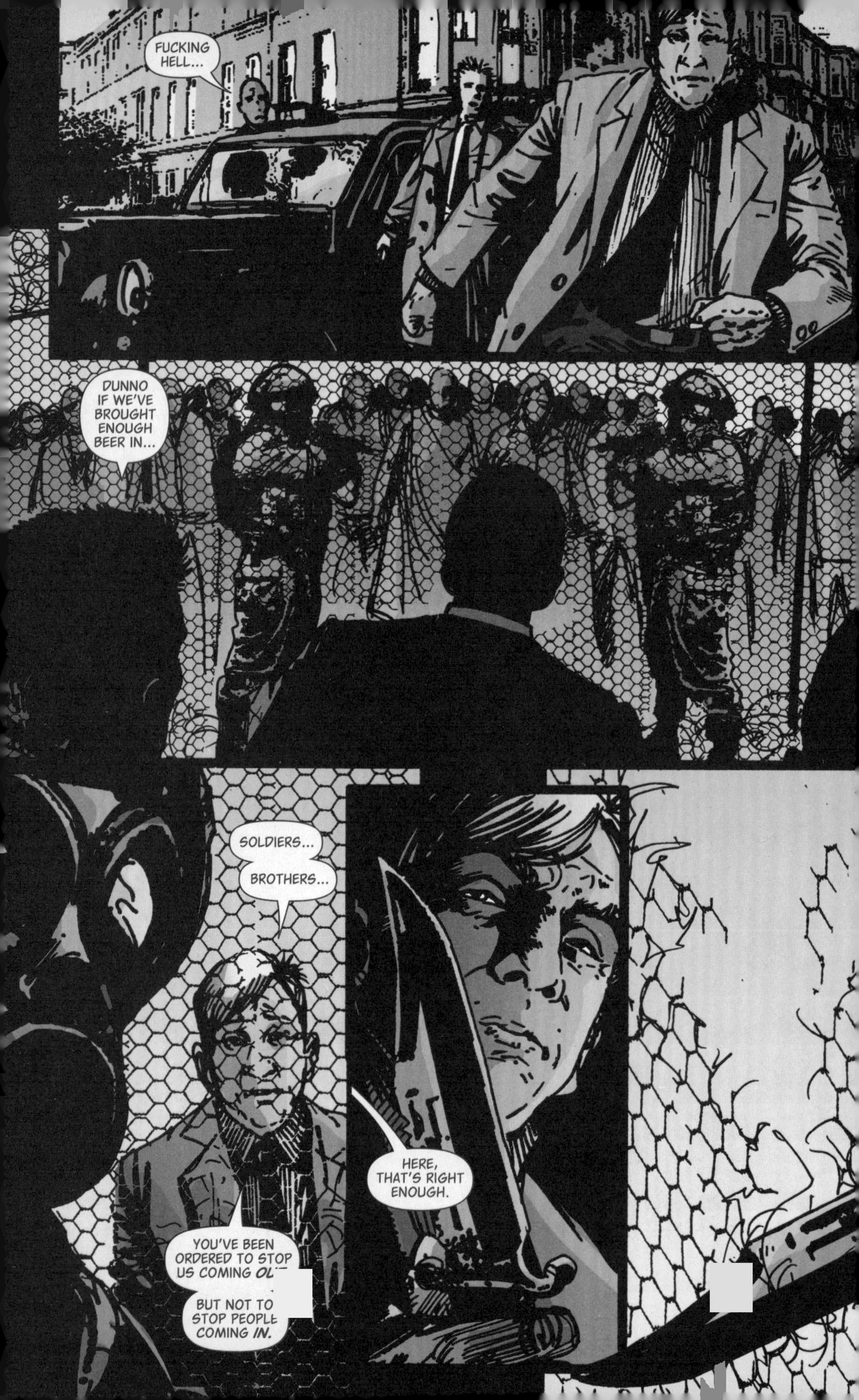
FUCKING HELL...
DUNNO IF WE'VE BROUGHT ENOUGH BEER IN...
SOLDIERS...
BROTHERS...
YOU'VE BEEN ORDERED TO STOP US COMING OU
BUT NOT TO STOP PEOPLE COMING IN.
HERE, THAT'S RIGHT ENOUGH.

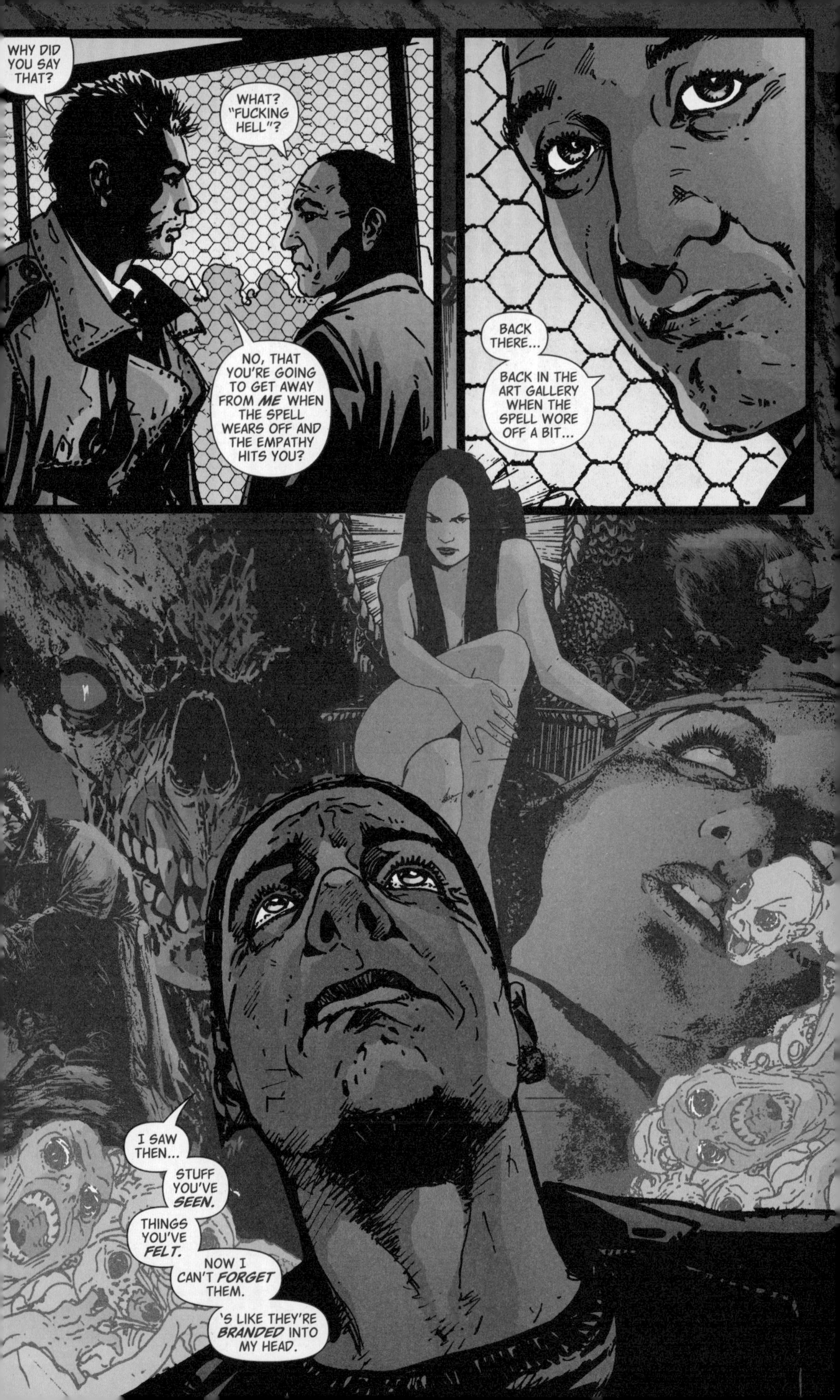
WHY DID YOU SAY THAT?
WHAT? "FUCKING HELL"?
NO, THAT YOU'RE GOING TO GET AWAY FROM *ME* WHEN THE SPELL WEARS OFF AND THE EMPATHY HITS YOU?
BACK THERE...
BACK IN THE ART GALLERY WHEN THE SPELL WORE OFF A BIT...
I SAW THEN...
STUFF YOU'VE *SEEN.*
THINGS YOU'VE *FELT.*
NOW I CAN'T *FORGET* THEM.
'S LIKE THEY'RE *BRANDED* INTO MY HEAD.

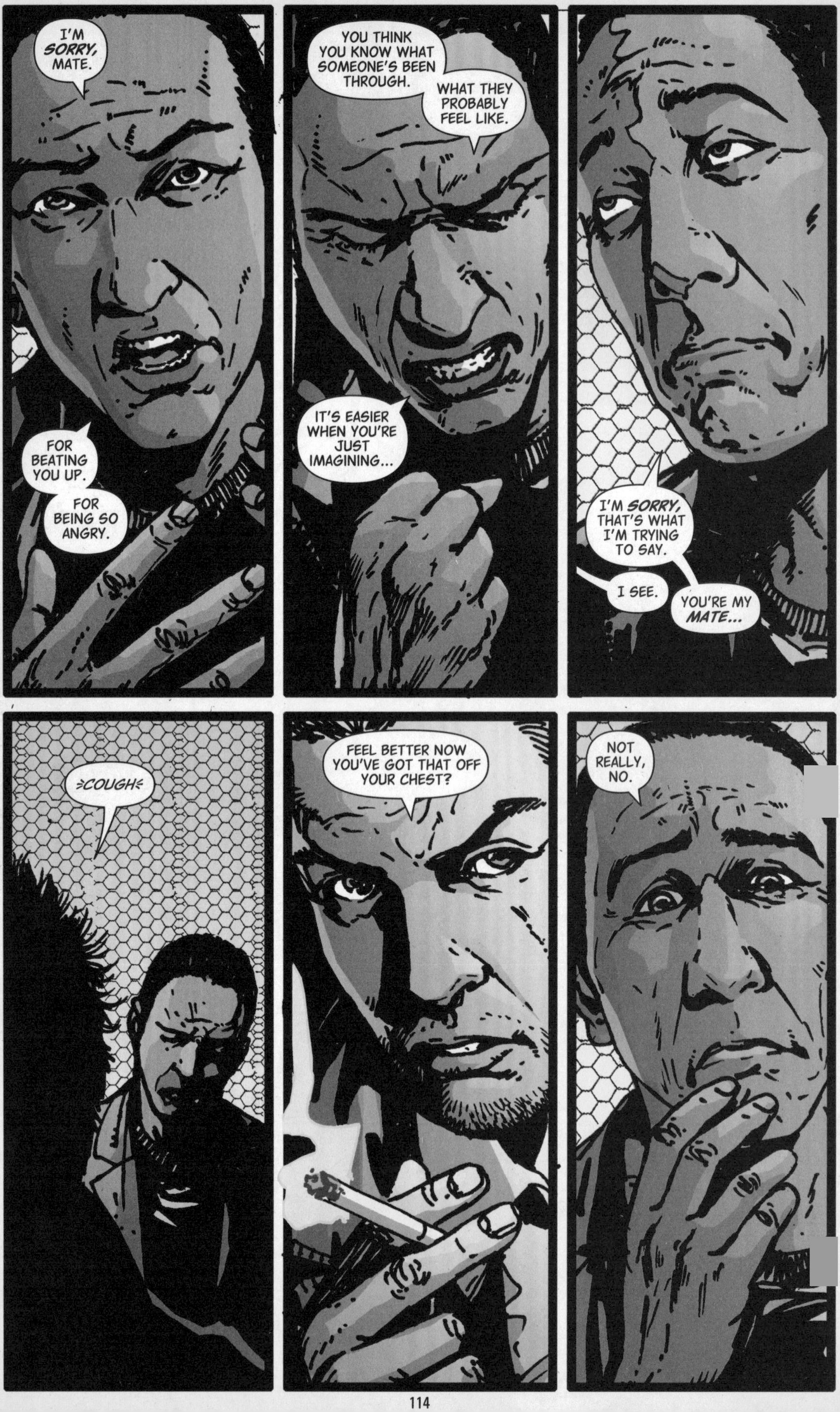
I'M SORRY, MATE.
FOR BEATING YOU UP.
FOR BEING SO ANGRY.
YOU THINK YOU KNOW WHAT SOMEONE'S BEEN THROUGH.
WHAT THEY PROBABLY FEEL LIKE.
IT'S EASIER WHEN YOU'RE JUST IMAGINING...
I'M SORRY, THAT'S WHAT I'M TRYING TO SAY.
I SEE.
YOU'RE MY MATE...
≈COUGH≈
FEEL BETTER NOW YOU'VE GOT THAT OFF YOUR CHEST?
NOT REALLY, NO.

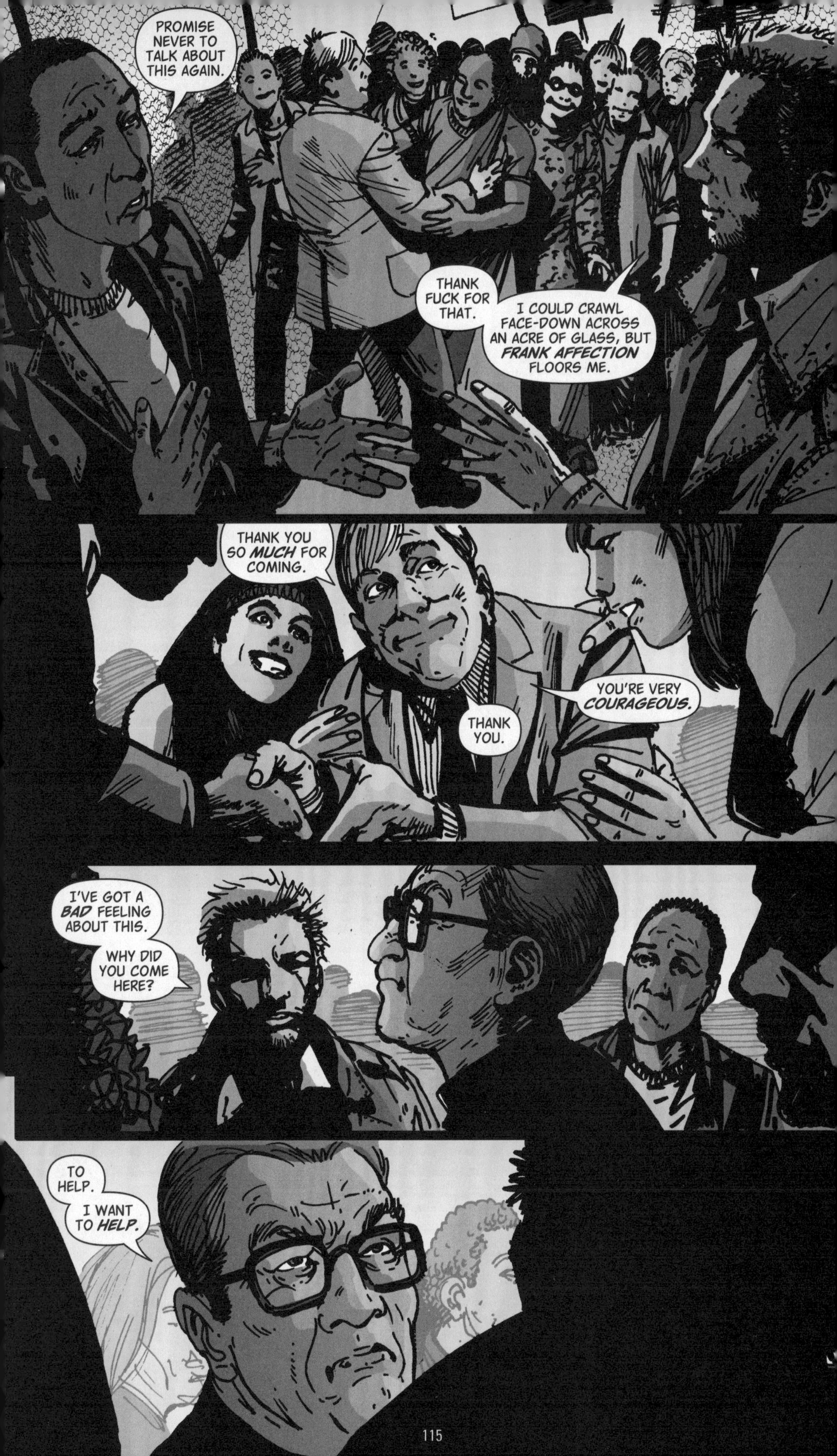
PROMISE NEVER TO TALK ABOUT THIS AGAIN.
THANK FUCK FOR THAT.
I COULD CRAWL FACE-DOWN ACROSS AN ACRE OF GLASS, BUT FRANK AFFECTION FLOORS ME.
THANK YOU SO MUCH FOR COMING.
THANK YOU.
YOU'RE VERY COURAGEOUS.
I'VE GOT A BAD FEELING ABOUT THIS.
WHY DID YOU COME HERE?
TO HELP.
I WANT TO HELP.

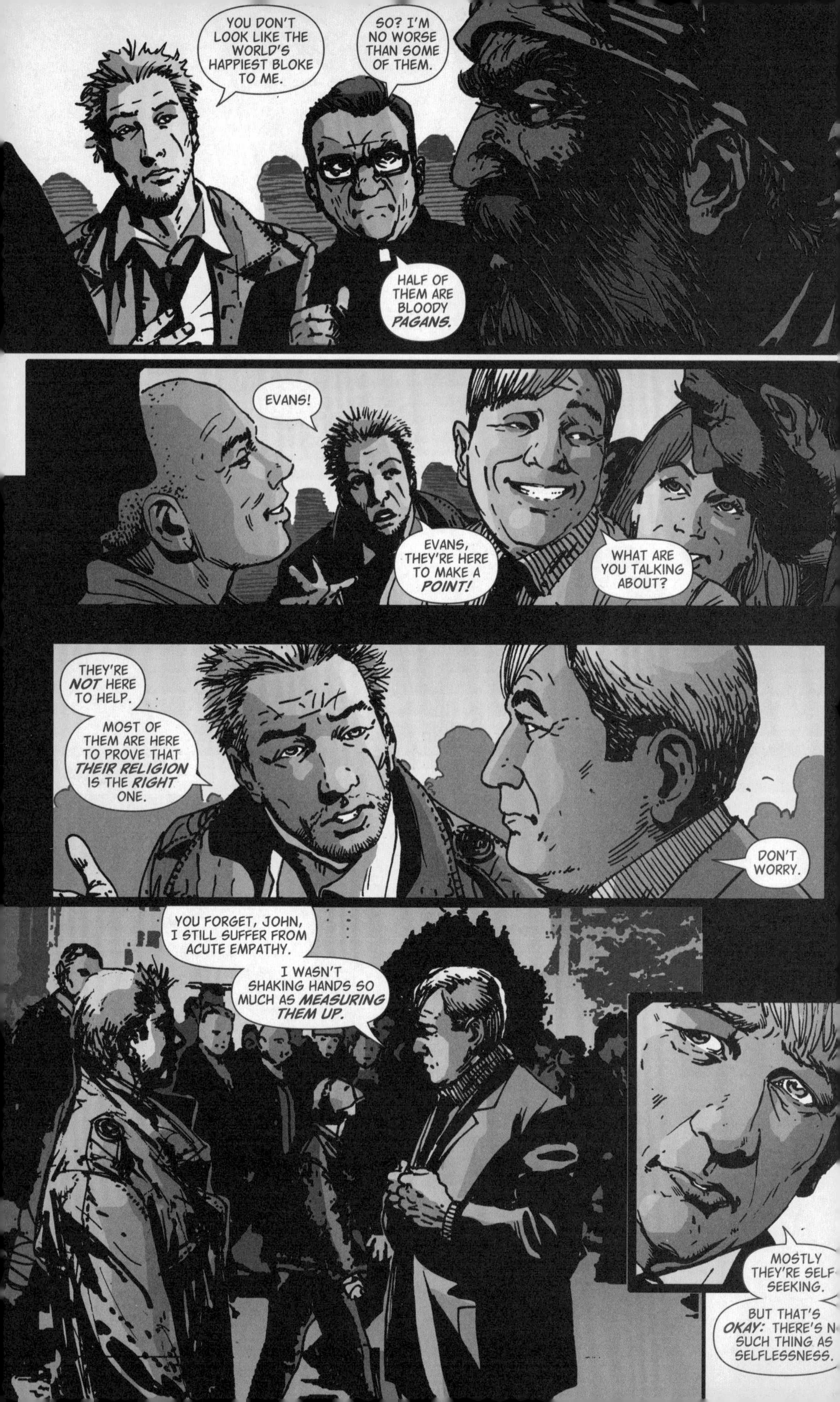
YOU DON'T LOOK LIKE THE WORLD'S HAPPIEST BLOKE TO ME.
SO? I'M NO WORSE THAN SOME OF THEM.
HALF OF THEM ARE BLOODY *PAGANS.*
EVANS!
EVANS, THEY'RE HERE TO MAKE A *POINT!*
WHAT ARE YOU TALKING ABOUT?
THEY'RE *NOT* HERE TO HELP.
MOST OF THEM ARE HERE TO PROVE THAT *THEIR RELIGION* IS THE *RIGHT* ONE.
DON'T WORRY.
YOU FORGET, JOHN, I STILL SUFFER FROM ACUTE EMPATHY.
I WASN'T SHAKING HANDS SO MUCH AS *MEASURING THEM UP.*
MOSTLY THEY'RE SELF SEEKING.
BUT THAT'S *OKAY:* THERE'S N SUCH THING AS SELFLESSNESS.

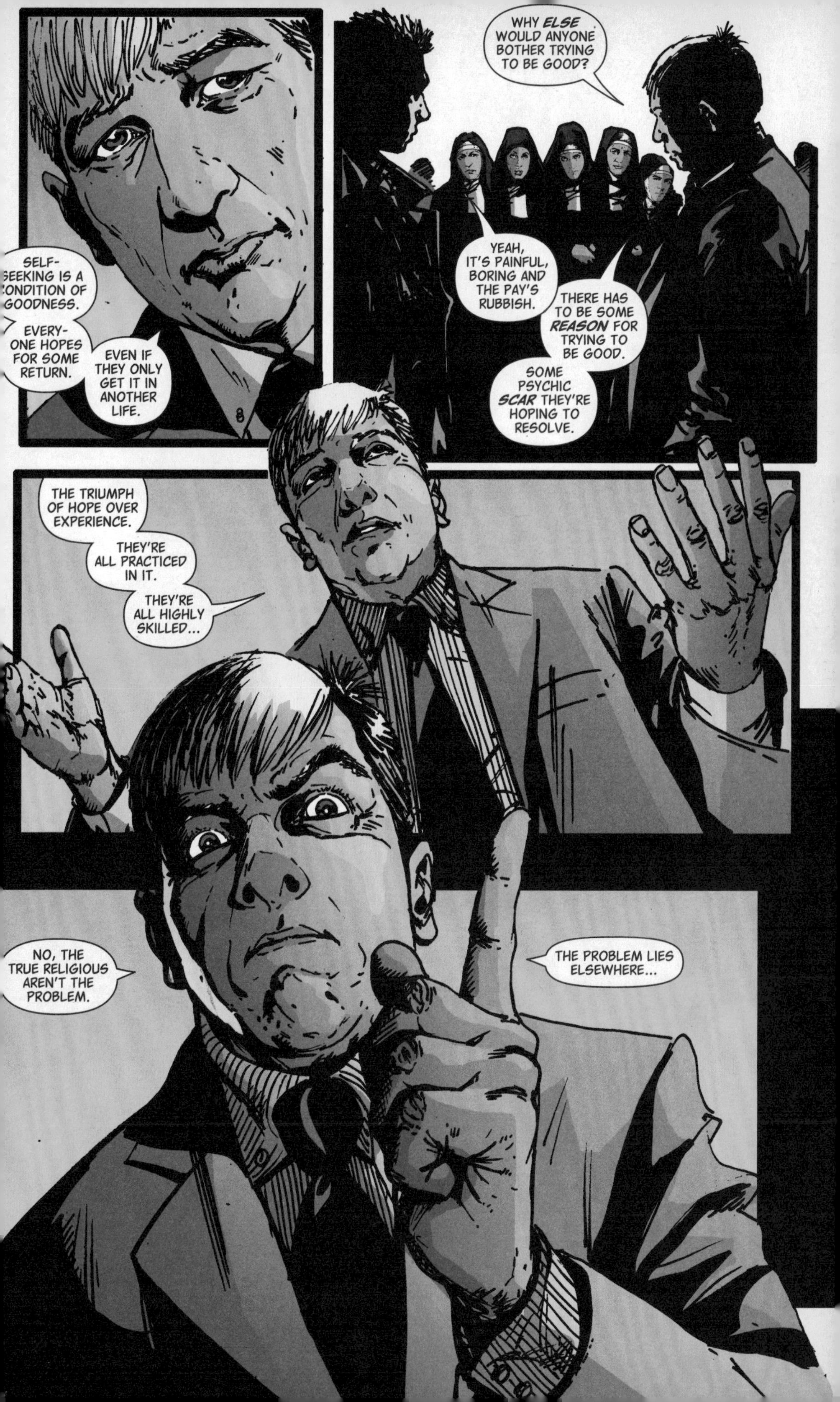
SELF-SEEKING IS A CONDITION OF GOODNESS.
EVERY-ONE HOPES FOR SOME RETURN.
EVEN IF THEY ONLY GET IT IN ANOTHER LIFE.
WHY ELSE WOULD ANYONE BOTHER TRYING TO BE GOOD?
YEAH, IT'S PAINFUL, BORING AND THE PAY'S RUBBISH.
THERE HAS TO BE SOME REASON FOR TRYING TO BE GOOD.
SOME PSYCHIC SCAR THEY'RE HOPING TO RESOLVE.
THE TRIUMPH OF HOPE OVER EXPERIENCE.
THEY'RE ALL PRACTICED IN IT.
THEY'RE ALL HIGHLY SKILLED...
NO, THE TRUE RELIGIOUS AREN'T THE PROBLEM.
THE PROBLEM LIES ELSEWHERE...

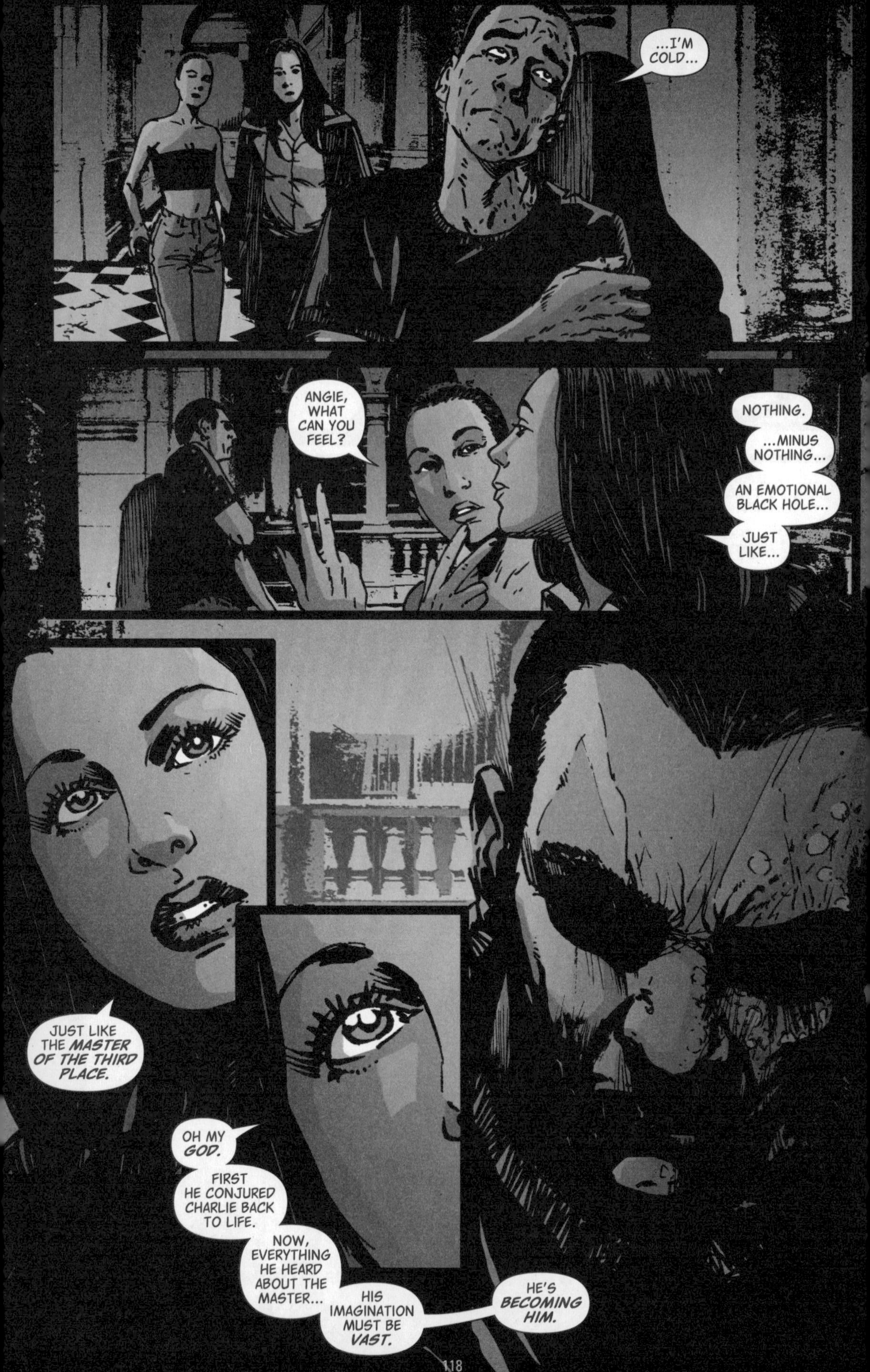
...I'M COLD...
ANGIE, WHAT CAN YOU FEEL?
NOTHING.
...MINUS NOTHING...
AN EMOTIONAL BLACK HOLE...
JUST LIKE...
JUST LIKE THE *MASTER OF THE THIRD PLACE.*
OH MY *GOD.*
FIRST HE CONJURED CHARLIE BACK TO LIFE.
NOW, EVERYTHING HE HEARD ABOUT THE MASTER...
HIS IMAGINATION MUST BE *VAST.*
HE'S *BECOMING HIM.*

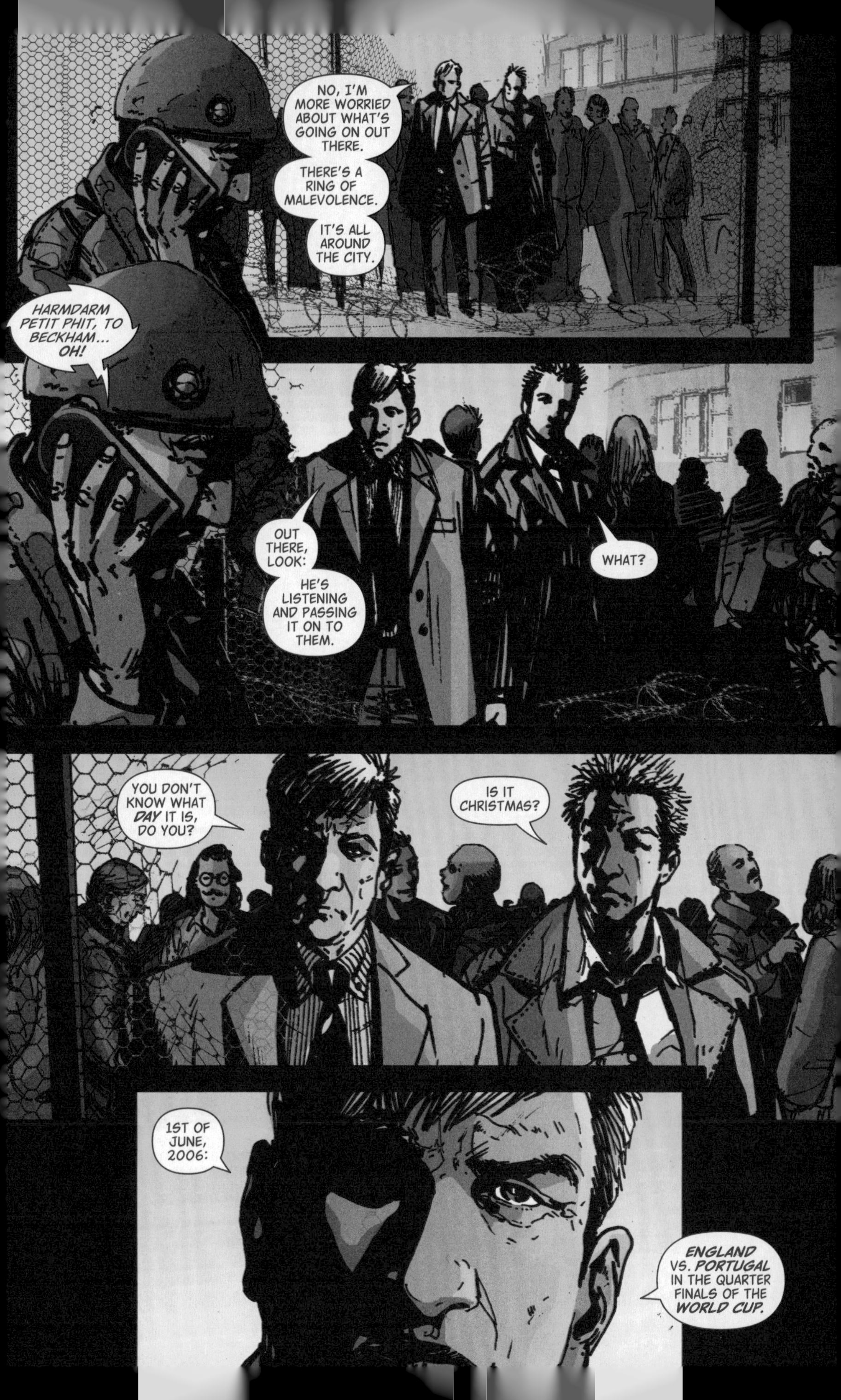
NO, I'M MORE WORRIED ABOUT WHAT'S GOING ON OUT THERE.
THERE'S A RING OF MALEVOLENCE.
IT'S ALL AROUND THE CITY.
HARMDARM PETIT PHIT, TO BECKHAM... OH!
OUT THERE, LOOK:
HE'S LISTENING AND PASSING IT ON TO THEM.
WHAT?
YOU DON'T KNOW WHAT DAY IT IS, DO YOU?
IS IT CHRISTMAS?
1ST OF JUNE, 2006:
ENGLAND VS. PORTUGAL IN THE QUARTER FINALS OF THE WORLD CUP.

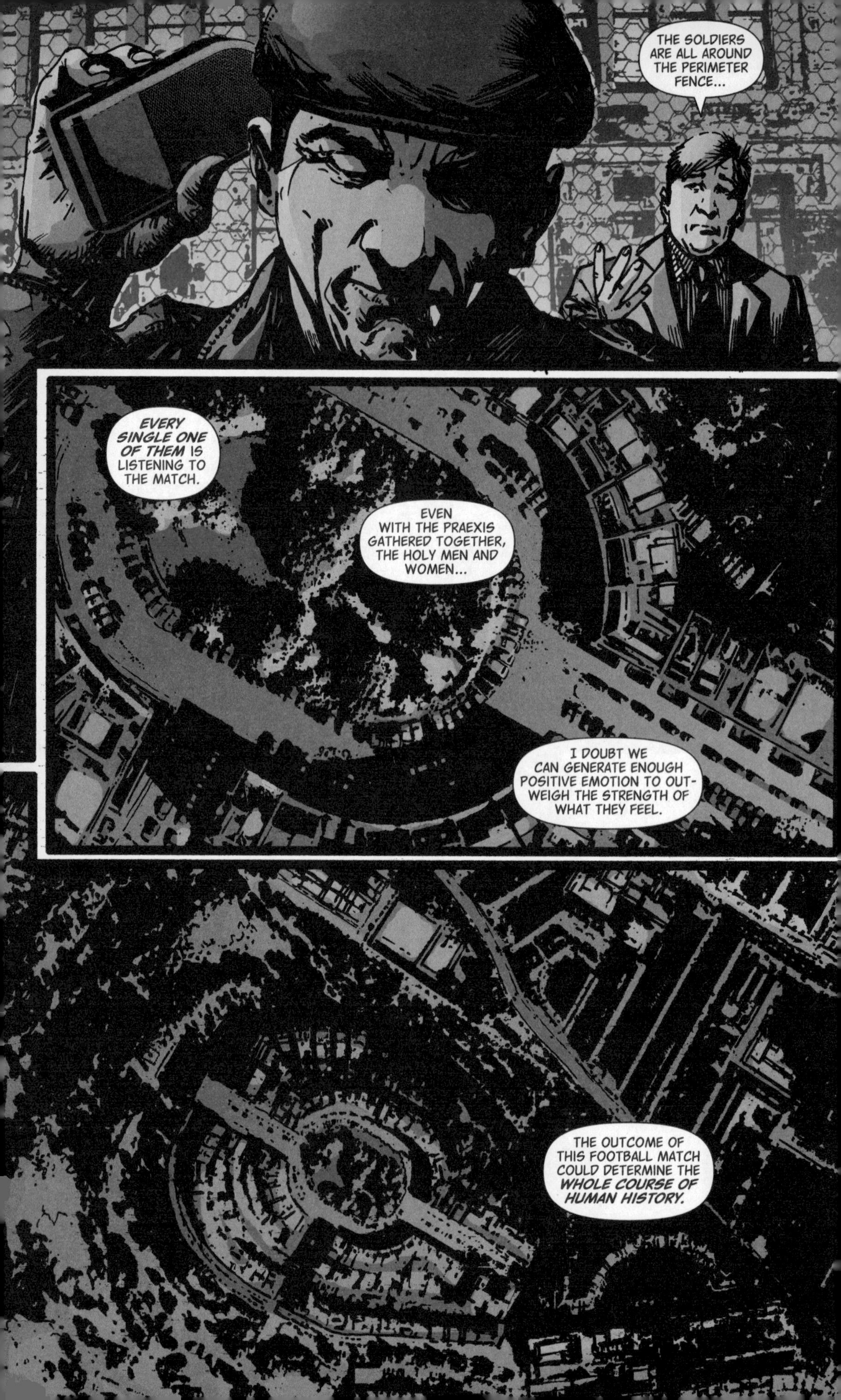
THE SOLDIERS ARE ALL AROUND THE PERIMETER FENCE...
EVERY SINGLE ONE OF THEM IS LISTENING TO THE MATCH.
EVEN WITH THE PRAEXIS GATHERED TOGETHER, THE HOLY MEN AND WOMEN...
I DOUBT WE CAN GENERATE ENOUGH POSITIVE EMOTION TO OUT-WEIGH THE STRENGTH OF WHAT THEY FEEL.
THE OUTCOME OF THIS FOOTBALL MATCH COULD DETERMINE THE WHOLE COURSE OF HUMAN HISTORY.

THE RED RIGHT HAND Chapter 5

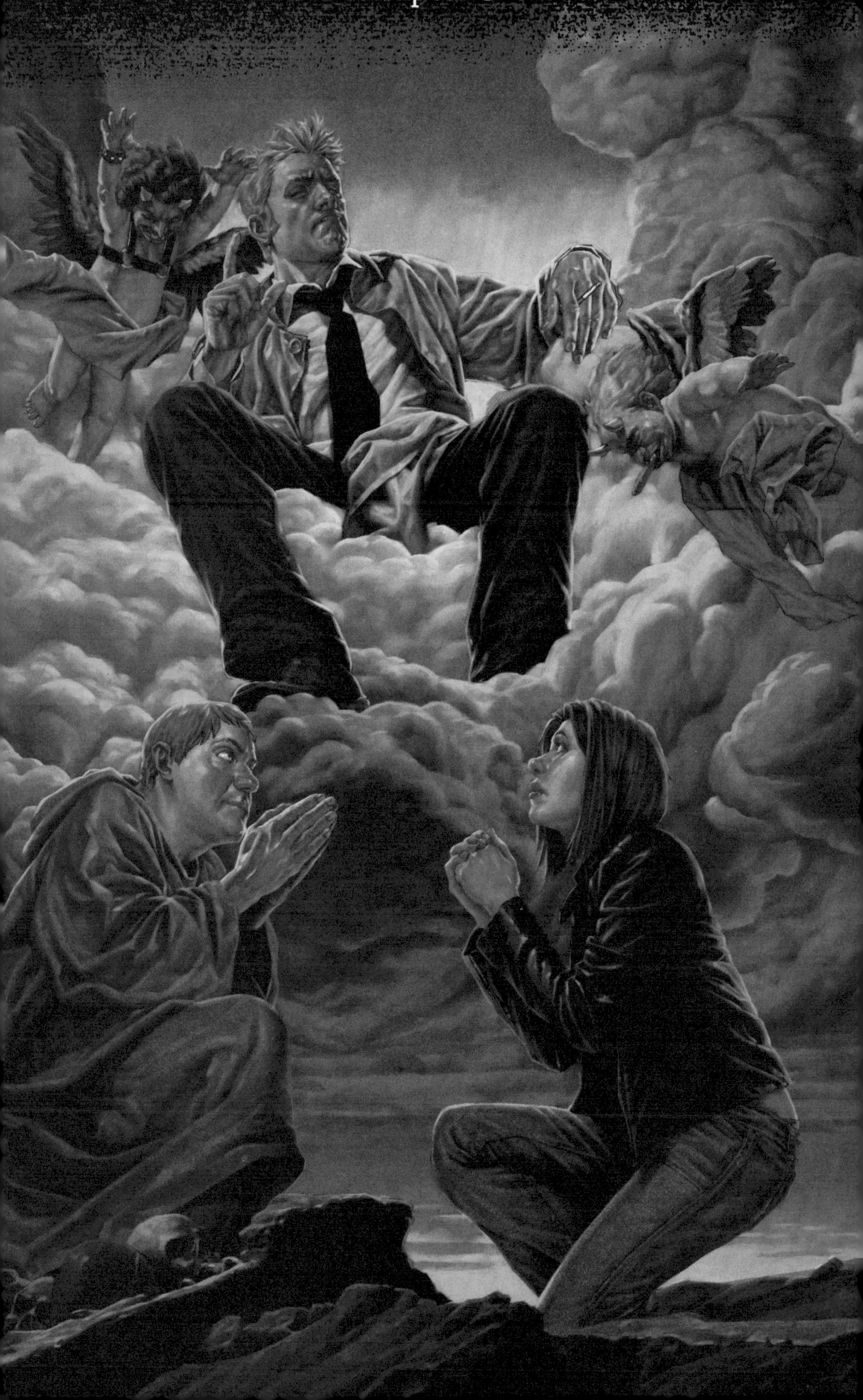

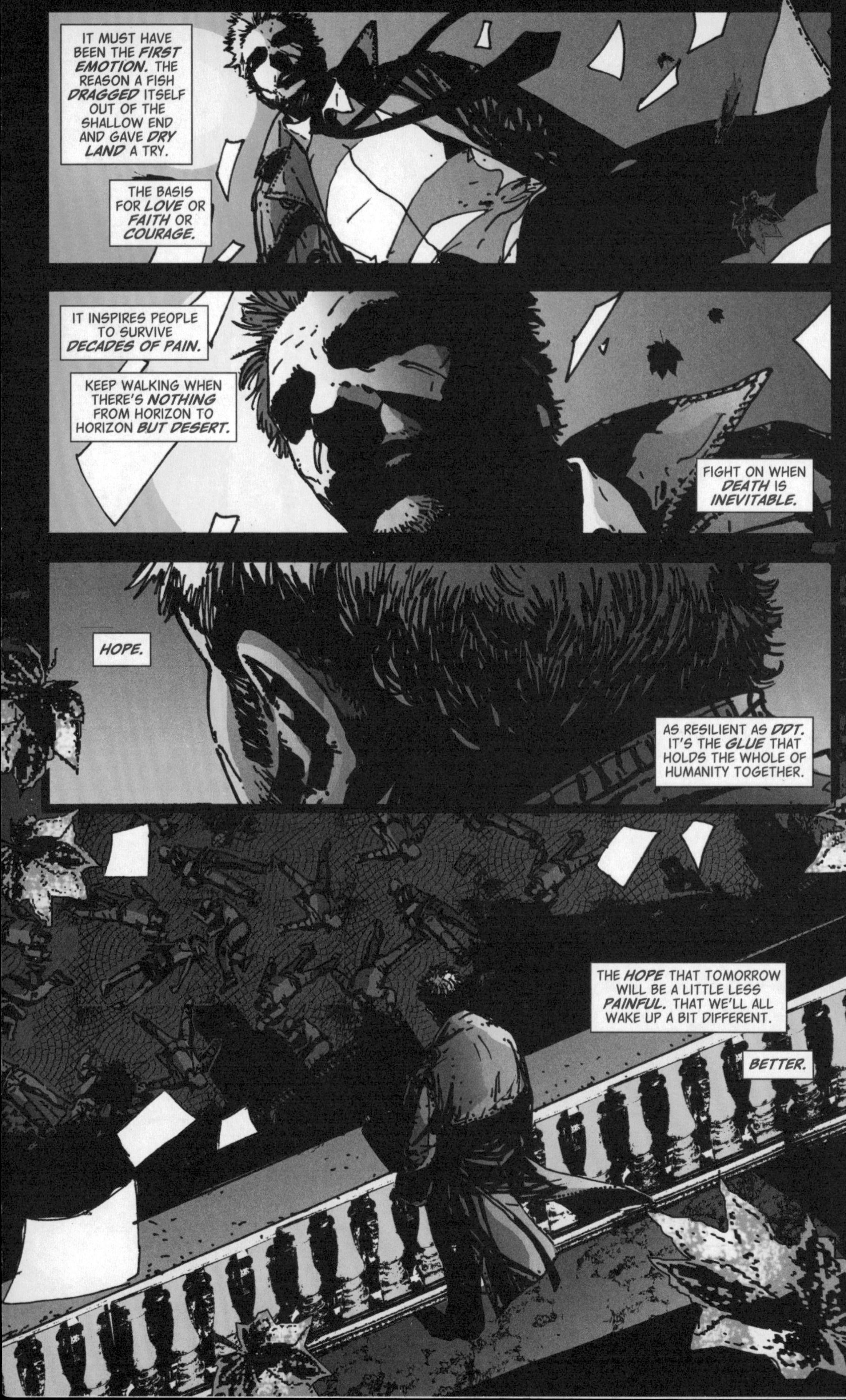
IT MUST HAVE BEEN THE FIRST EMOTION. THE REASON A FISH DRAGGED ITSELF OUT OF THE SHALLOW END AND GAVE DRY LAND A TRY.
THE BASIS FOR LOVE OR FAITH OR COURAGE.
IT INSPIRES PEOPLE TO SURVIVE DECADES OF PAIN.
KEEP WALKING WHEN THERE'S NOTHING FROM HORIZON TO HORIZON BUT DESERT.
FIGHT ON WHEN DEATH IS INEVITABLE.
HOPE.
AS RESILIENT AS DDT. IT'S THE GLUE THAT HOLDS THE WHOLE OF HUMANITY TOGETHER.
THE HOPE THAT TOMORROW WILL BE A LITTLE LESS PAINFUL. THAT WE'LL ALL WAKE UP A BIT DIFFERENT.
BETTER.

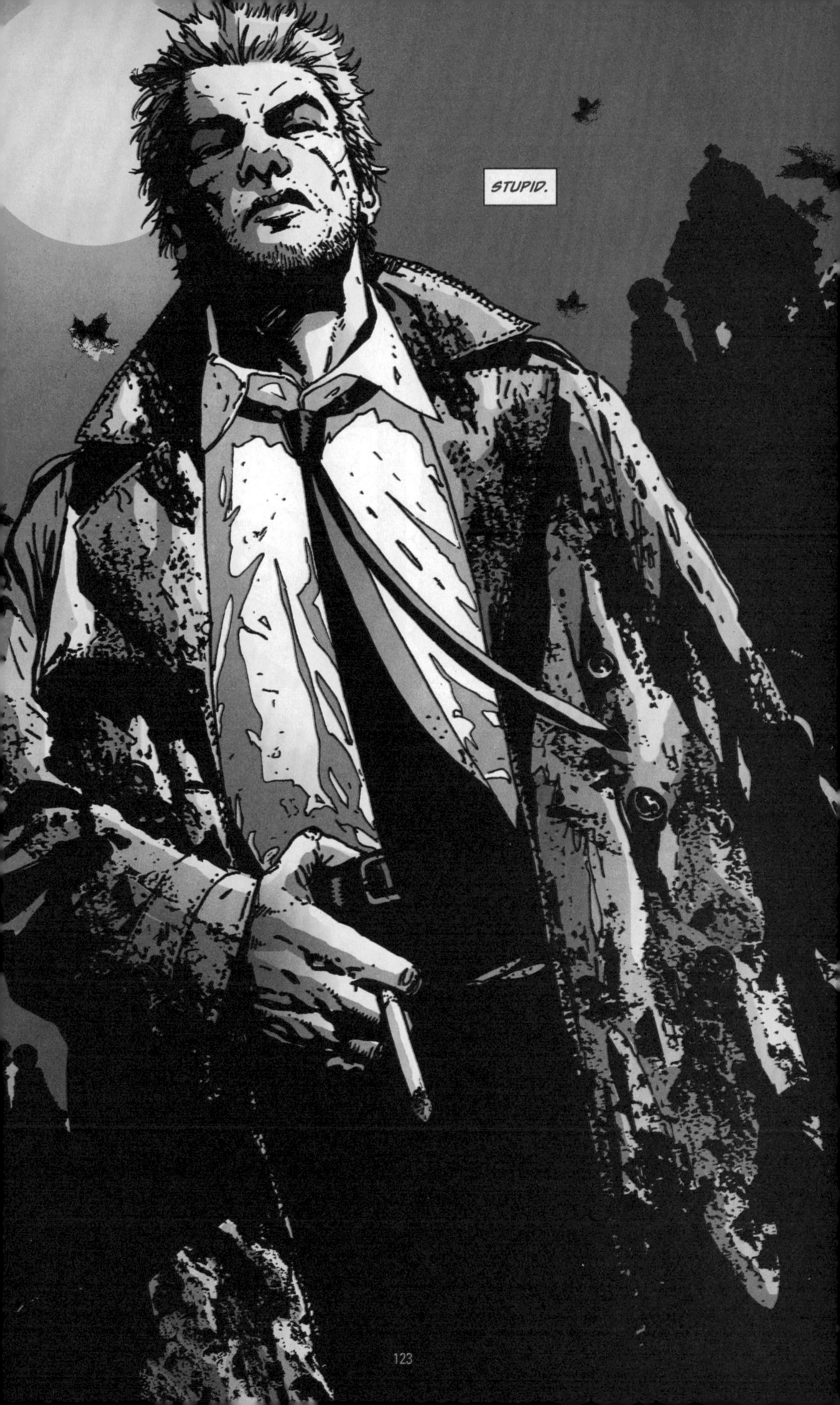
STUPID.

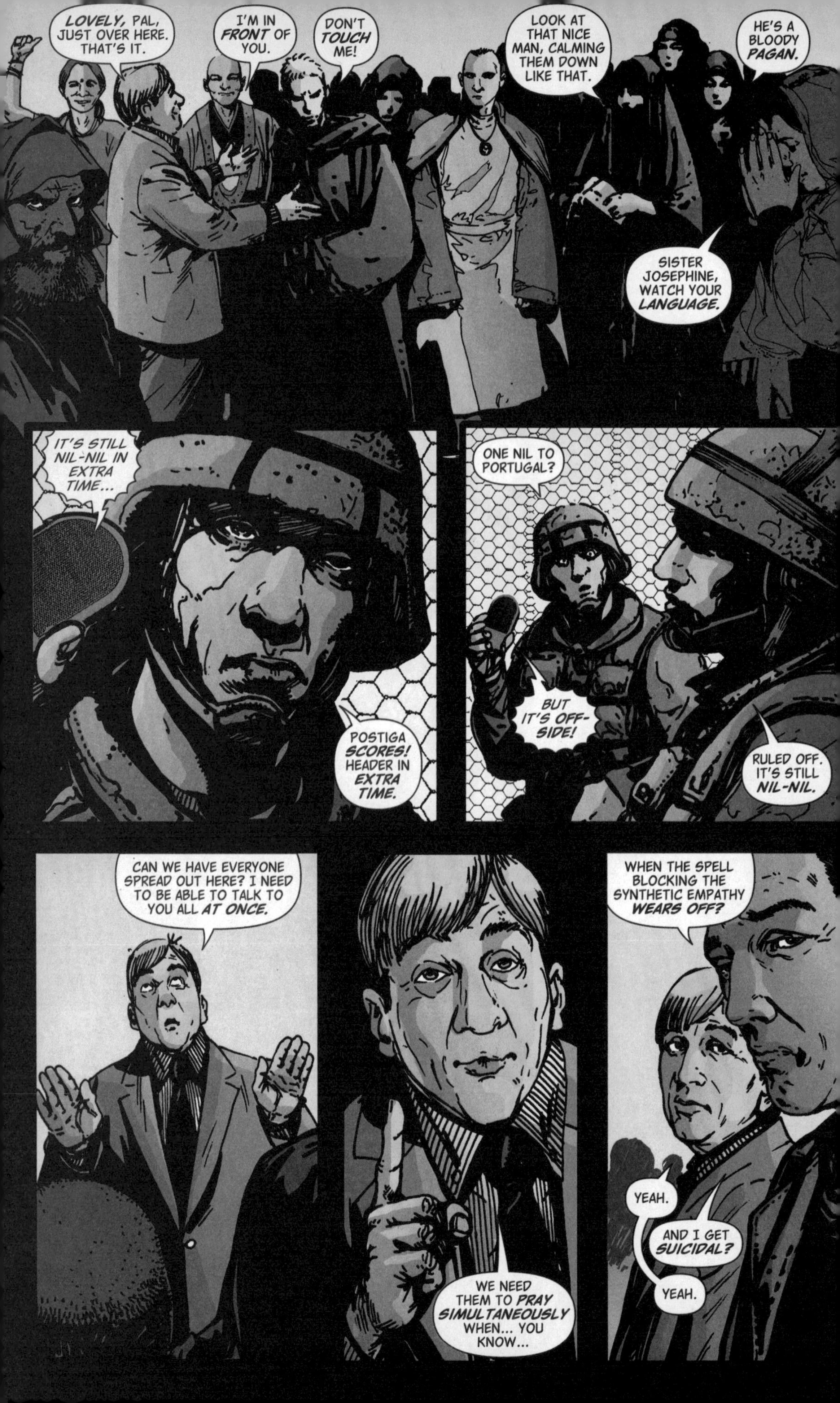
LOVELY, PAL, JUST OVER HERE. THAT'S IT.
I'M IN FRONT OF YOU.
DON'T TOUCH ME!
LOOK AT THAT NICE MAN, CALMING THEM DOWN LIKE THAT.
HE'S A BLOODY PAGAN.
SISTER JOSEPHINE, WATCH YOUR LANGUAGE.
IT'S STILL NIL-NIL IN EXTRA TIME...
POSTIGA SCORES! HEADER IN EXTRA TIME.
ONE NIL TO PORTUGAL?
BUT IT'S OFF-SIDE!
RULED OFF. IT'S STILL NIL-NIL.
CAN WE HAVE EVERYONE SPREAD OUT HERE? I NEED TO BE ABLE TO TALK TO YOU ALL AT ONCE.
WE NEED THEM TO PRAY SIMULTANEOUSLY WHEN... YOU KNOW...
WHEN THE SPELL BLOCKING THE SYNTHETIC EMPATHY WEARS OFF?
YEAH.
AND I GET SUICIDAL?
YEAH.

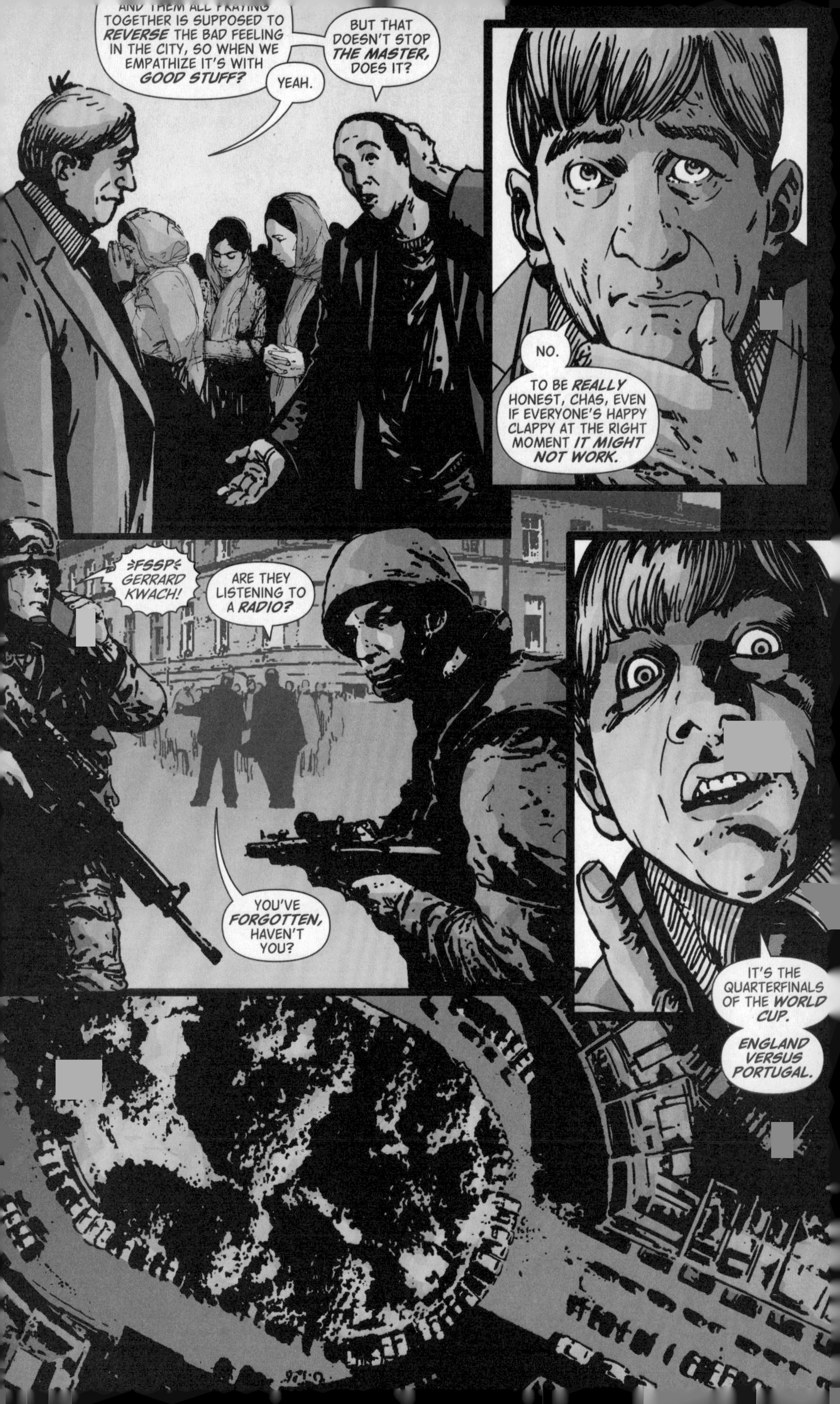
TOGETHER IS SUPPOSED TO REVERSE THE BAD FEELING IN THE CITY, SO WHEN WE EMPATHIZE IT'S WITH GOOD STUFF?
YEAH.
BUT THAT DOESN'T STOP THE MASTER, DOES IT?
NO.
TO BE REALLY HONEST, CHAS, EVEN IF EVERYONE'S HAPPY CLAPPY AT THE RIGHT MOMENT IT MIGHT NOT WORK.
FSSP GERRARD KWACH!
ARE THEY LISTENING TO A RADIO?
YOU'VE FORGOTTEN, HAVEN'T YOU?
IT'S THE QUARTERFINALS OF THE WORLD CUP.
ENGLAND VERSUS PORTUGAL.

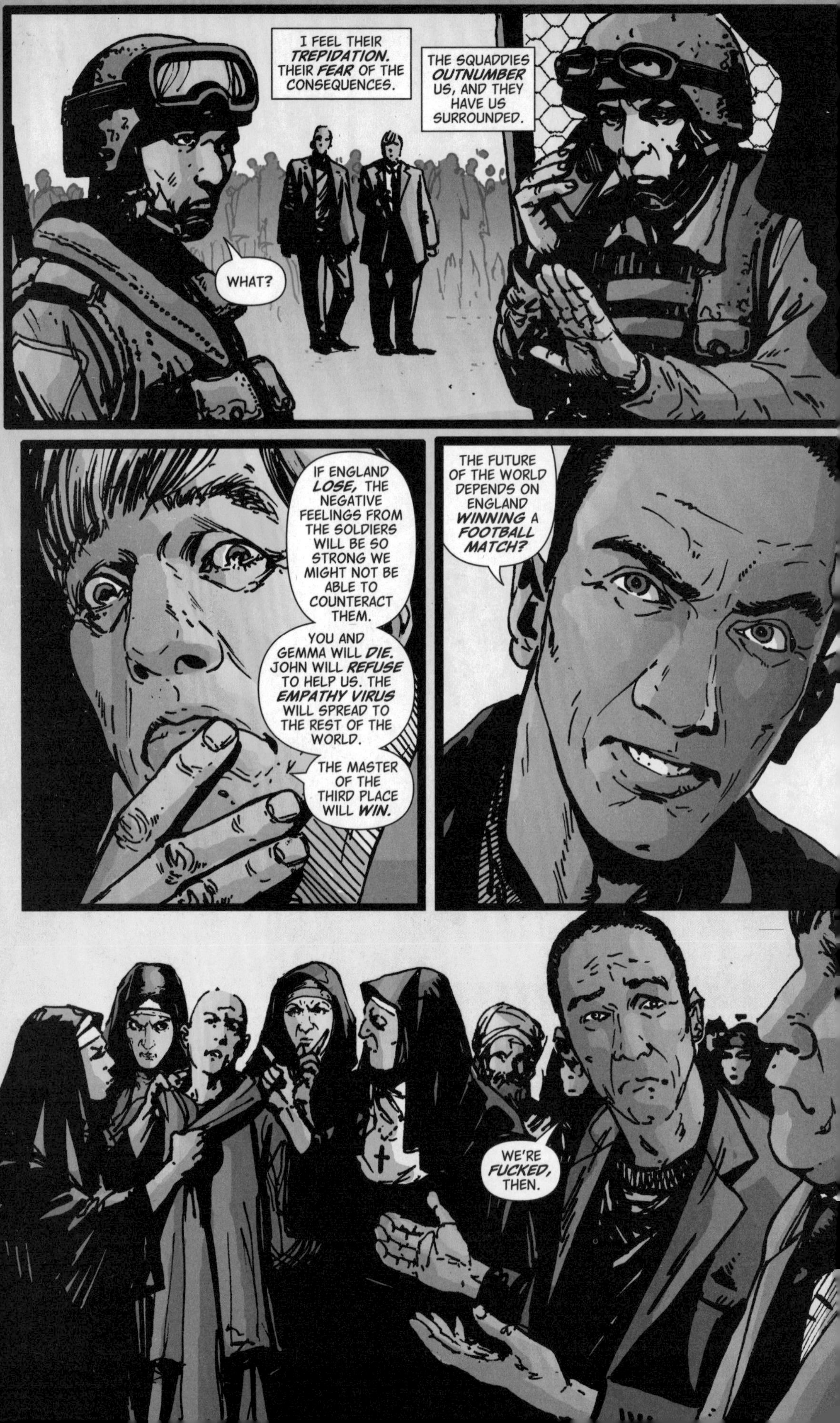

I FEEL THEIR TREPIDATION. THEIR FEAR OF THE CONSEQUENCES.
THE SQUADDIES OUTNUMBER US, AND THEY HAVE US SURROUNDED.
WHAT?
IF ENGLAND LOSE, THE NEGATIVE FEELINGS FROM THE SOLDIERS WILL BE SO STRONG WE MIGHT NOT BE ABLE TO COUNTERACT THEM.
YOU AND GEMMA WILL DIE. JOHN WILL REFUSE TO HELP US. THE EMPATHY VIRUS WILL SPREAD TO THE REST OF THE WORLD.
THE MASTER OF THE THIRD PLACE WILL WIN.
THE FUTURE OF THE WORLD DEPENDS ON ENGLAND WINNING A FOOTBALL MATCH?
WE'RE FUCKED, THEN.

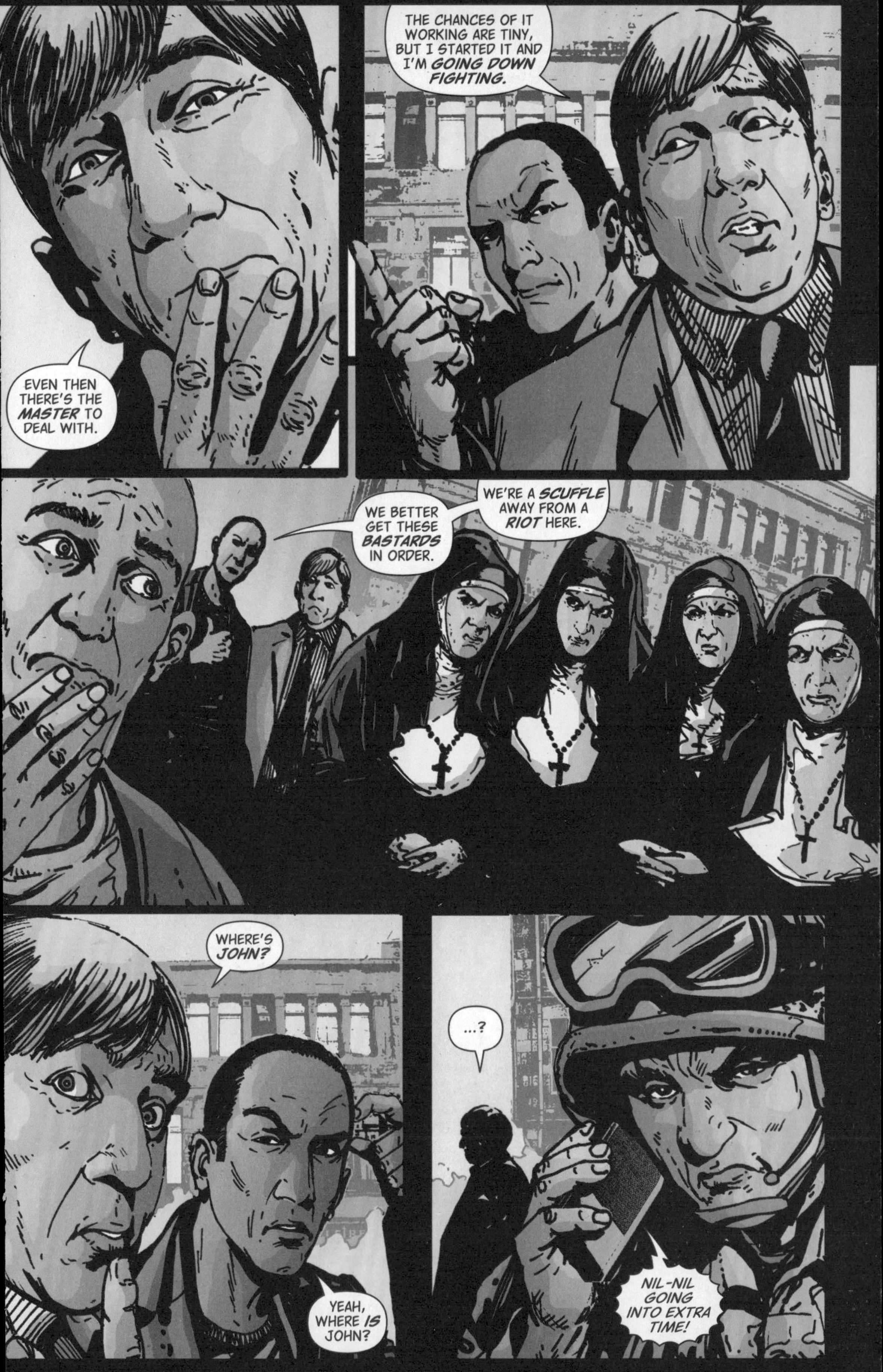
EVEN THEN THERE'S THE MASTER TO DEAL WITH.
THE CHANCES OF IT WORKING ARE TINY, BUT I STARTED IT AND I'M GOING DOWN FIGHTING.
WE BETTER GET THESE BASTARDS IN ORDER.
WE'RE A SCUFFLE AWAY FROM A RIOT HERE.
WHERE'S JOHN?
YEAH, WHERE IS JOHN?
...?
NIL-NIL GOING INTO EXTRA TIME!

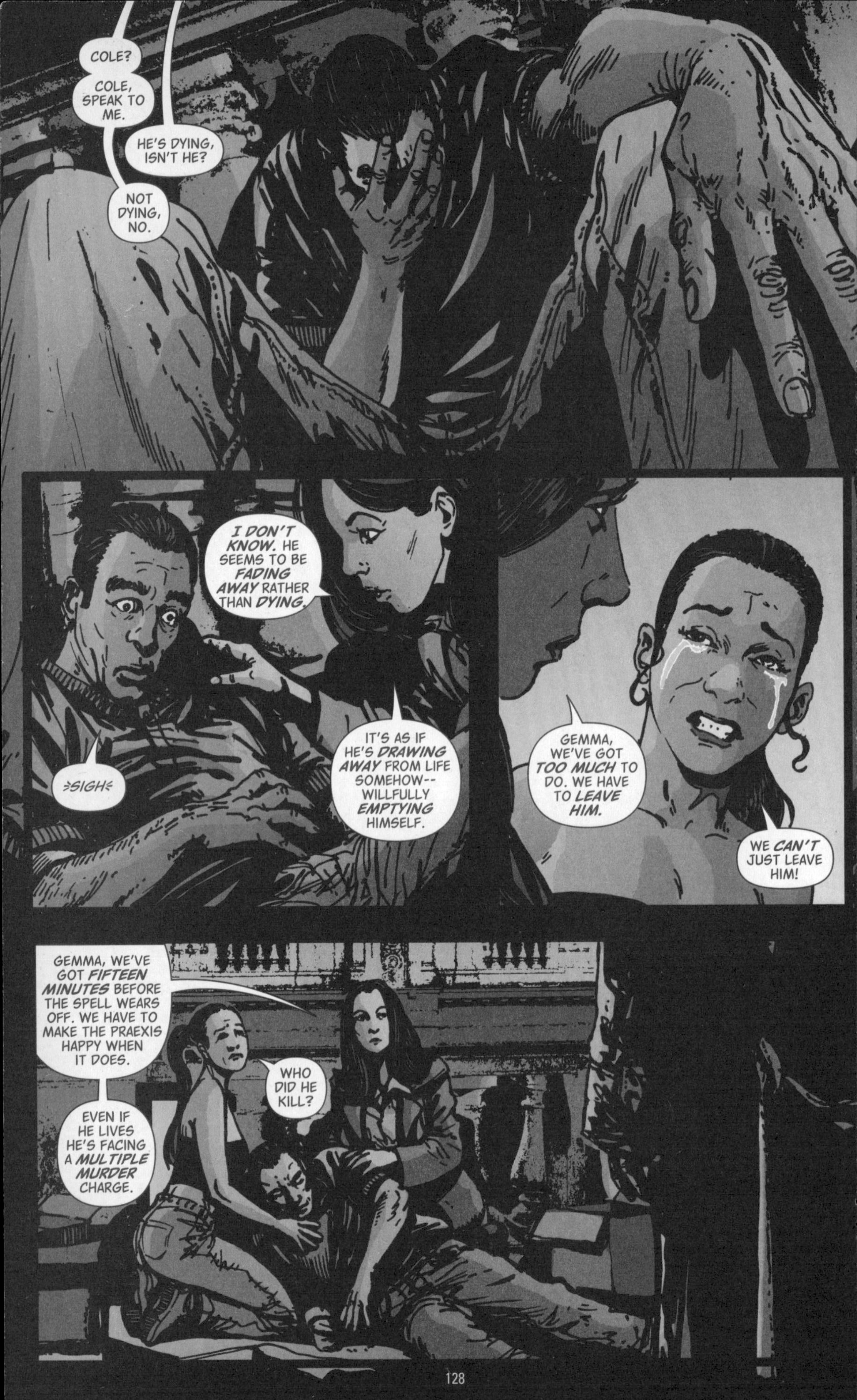
COLE?
COLE, SPEAK TO ME.
HE'S DYING, ISN'T HE?
NOT DYING, NO.
I DON'T KNOW. HE SEEMS TO BE FADING AWAY RATHER THAN DYING.
≥SIGH≤
IT'S AS IF HE'S DRAWING AWAY FROM LIFE SOMEHOW-- WILLFULLY EMPTYING HIMSELF.
GEMMA, WE'VE GOT TOO MUCH TO DO. WE HAVE TO LEAVE HIM.
WE CAN'T JUST LEAVE HIM!
GEMMA, WE'VE GOT FIFTEEN MINUTES BEFORE THE SPELL WEARS OFF. WE HAVE TO MAKE THE PRAEXIS HAPPY WHEN IT DOES.
WHO DID HE KILL?
EVEN IF HE LIVES HE'S FACING A MULTIPLE MURDER CHARGE.

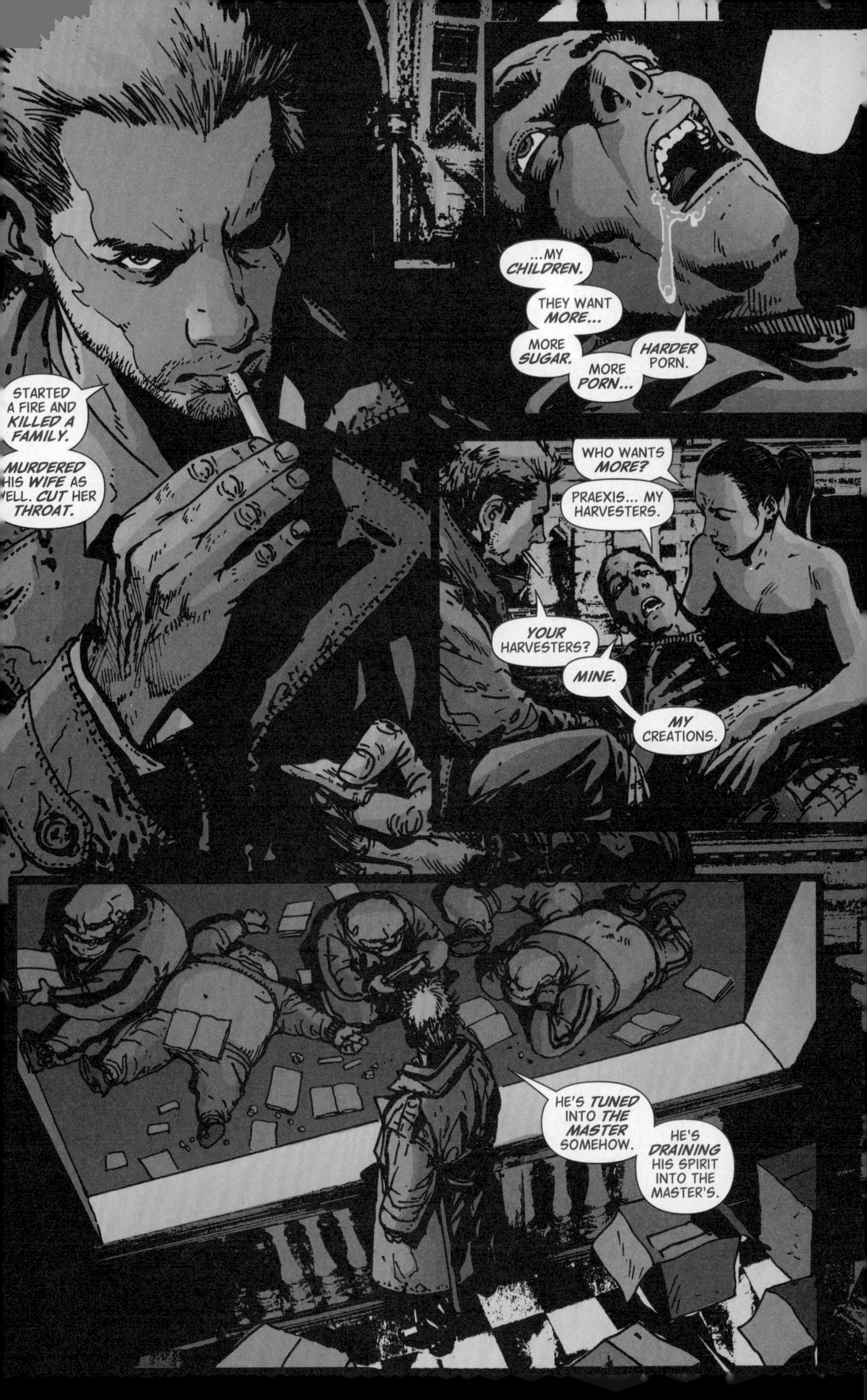
STARTED A FIRE AND KILLED A FAMILY.
MURDERED HIS WIFE AS WELL. CUT HER THROAT.
...MY CHILDREN.
THEY WANT MORE...
MORE SUGAR.
MORE PORN...
HARDER PORN.
WHO WANTS MORE?
PRAEXIS... MY HARVESTERS.
YOUR HARVESTERS?
MINE.
MY CREATIONS.
HE'S TUNED INTO THE MASTER SOMEHOW.
HE'S DRAINING HIS SPIRIT INTO THE MASTER'S.

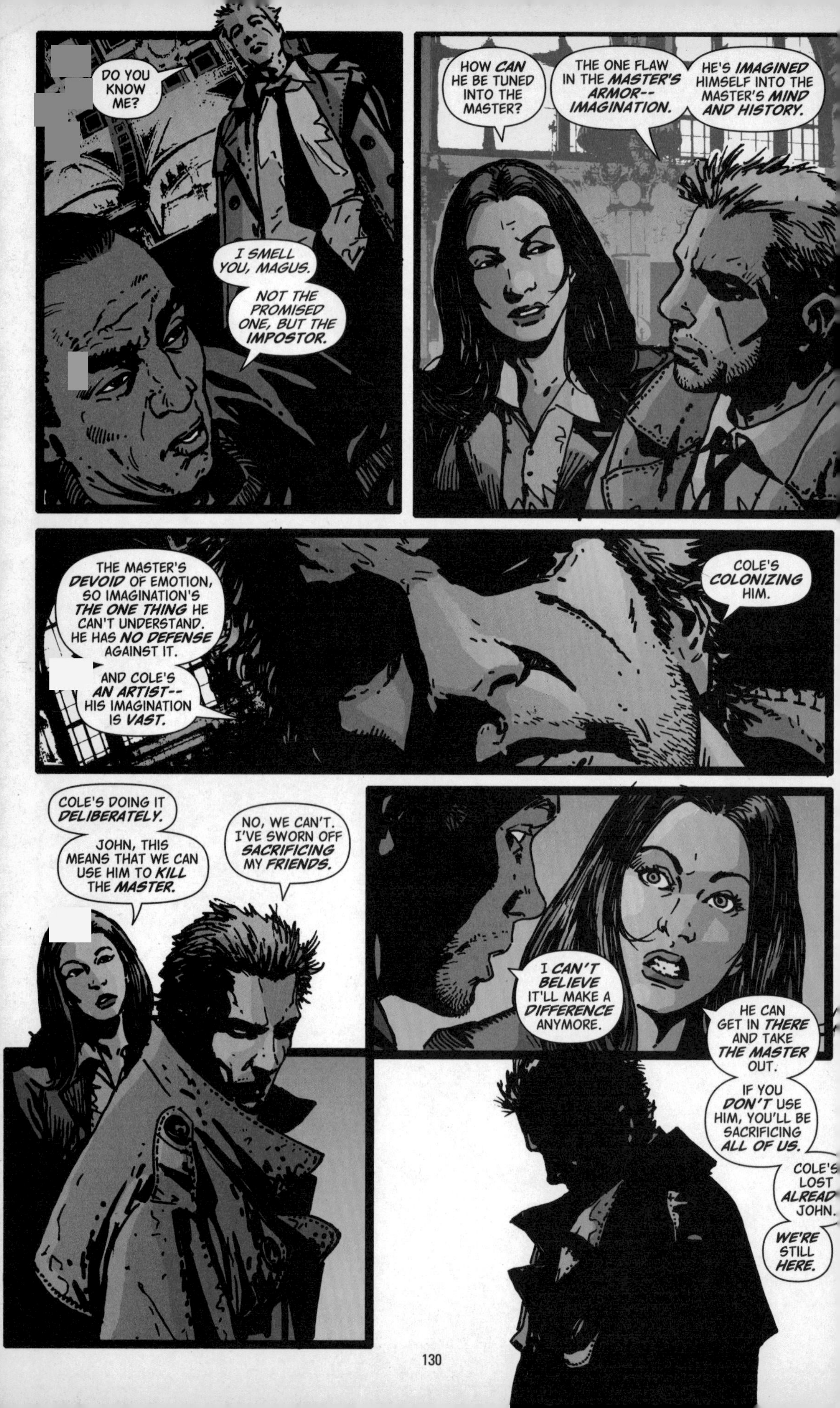

DO YOU KNOW ME?
I SMELL YOU, MAGUS.
NOT THE PROMISED ONE, BUT THE IMPOSTOR.
HOW CAN HE BE TUNED INTO THE MASTER?
THE ONE FLAW IN THE MASTER'S ARMOR-- IMAGINATION.
HE'S IMAGINED HIMSELF INTO THE MASTER'S MIND AND HISTORY.
THE MASTER'S DEVOID OF EMOTION, SO IMAGINATION'S THE ONE THING HE CAN'T UNDERSTAND. HE HAS NO DEFENSE AGAINST IT.
AND COLE'S AN ARTIST-- HIS IMAGINATION IS VAST.
COLE'S COLONIZING HIM.
COLE'S DOING IT DELIBERATELY.
JOHN, THIS MEANS THAT WE CAN USE HIM TO KILL THE MASTER.
NO, WE CAN'T. I'VE SWORN OFF SACRIFICING MY FRIENDS.
I CAN'T BELIEVE IT'LL MAKE A DIFFERENCE ANYMORE.
HE CAN GET IN THERE AND TAKE THE MASTER OUT.
IF YOU DON'T USE HIM, YOU'LL BE SACRIFICING ALL OF US.
COLE'S LOST ALREAD JOHN.
WE'RE STILL HERE.

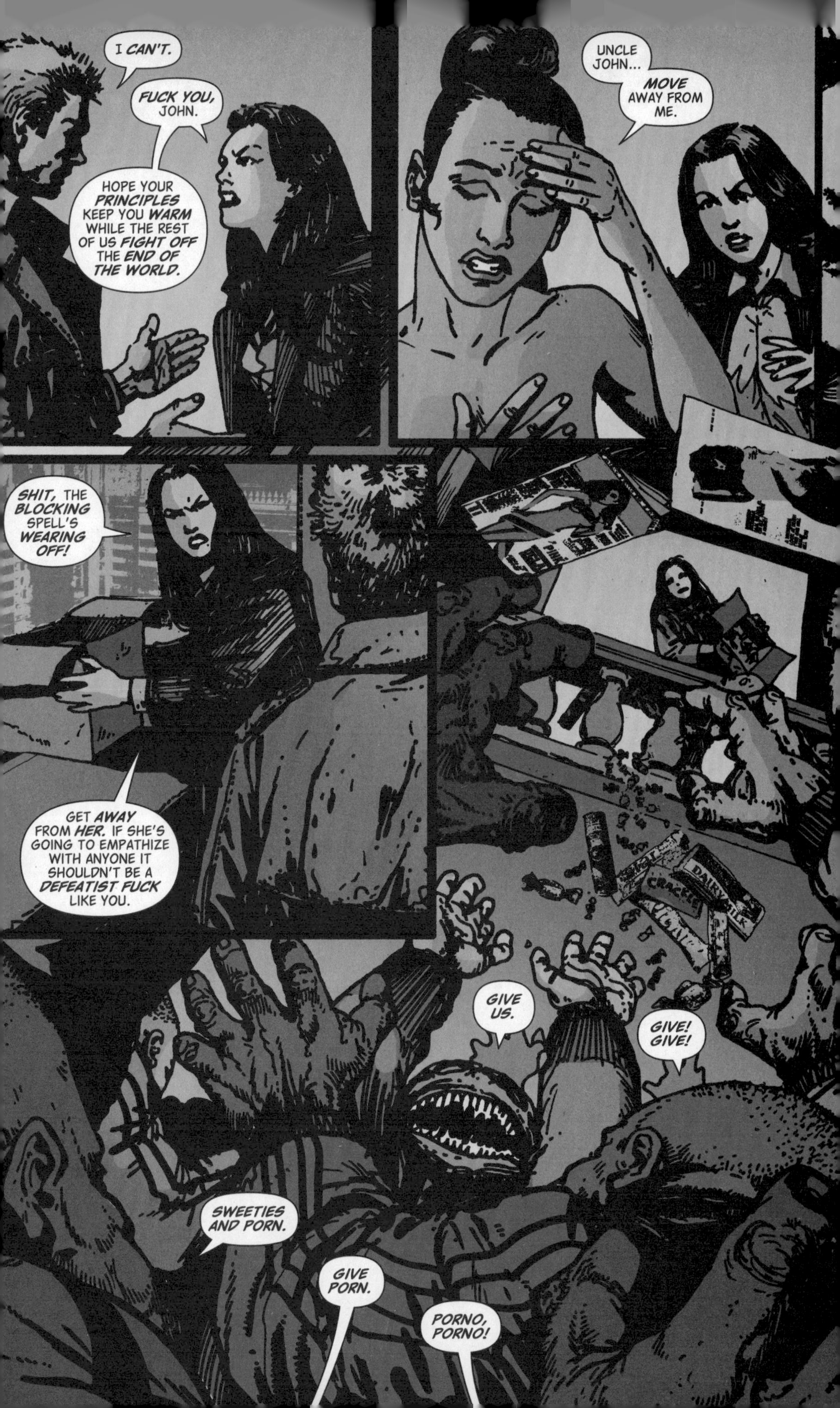

I CAN'T.
FUCK YOU, JOHN.
HOPE YOUR PRINCIPLES KEEP YOU WARM WHILE THE REST OF US FIGHT OFF THE END OF THE WORLD.
UNCLE JOHN...
MOVE AWAY FROM ME.
SHIT, THE BLOCKING SPELL'S WEARING OFF!
GET AWAY FROM HER. IF SHE'S GOING TO EMPATHIZE WITH ANYONE IT SHOULDN'T BE A DEFEATIST FUCK LIKE YOU.
GIVE US.
GIVE! GIVE!
SWEETIES AND PORN.
GIVE PORN.
PORNO, PORNO!

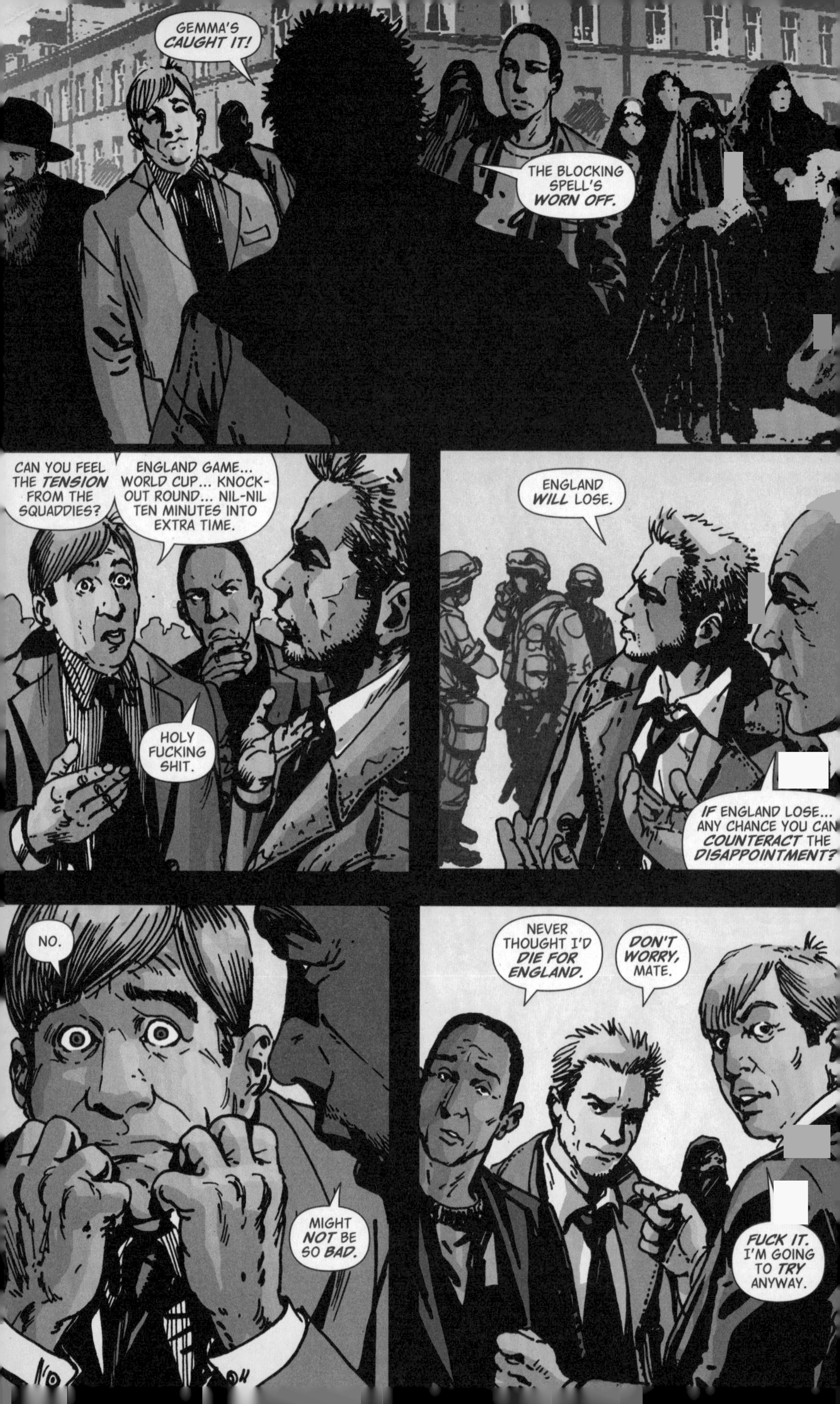
GEMMA'S CAUGHT IT!
THE BLOCKING SPELL'S WORN OFF.
CAN YOU FEEL THE TENSION FROM THE SQUADDIES?
ENGLAND GAME... WORLD CUP... KNOCK-OUT ROUND... NIL-NIL TEN MINUTES INTO EXTRA TIME.
HOLY FUCKING SHIT.
ENGLAND WILL LOSE.
IF ENGLAND LOSE... ANY CHANCE YOU CAN COUNTERACT THE DISAPPOINTMENT?
NO.
MIGHT NOT BE SO BAD.
NEVER THOUGHT I'D DIE FOR ENGLAND.
DON'T WORRY, MATE.
FUCK IT. I'M GOING TO TRY ANYWAY.

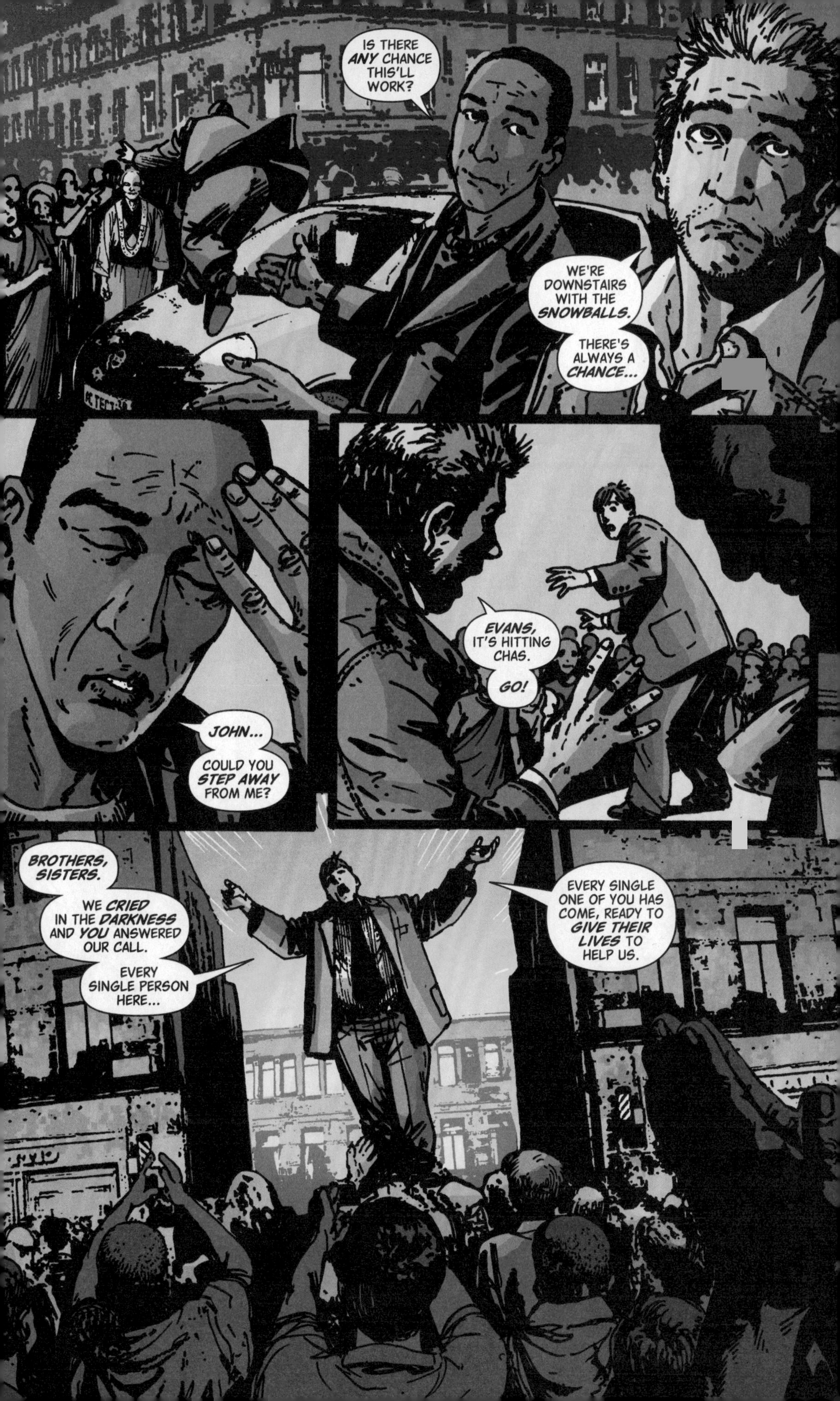
IS THERE ANY CHANCE THIS'LL WORK?
WE'RE DOWNSTAIRS WITH THE SNOWBALLS.
THERE'S ALWAYS A CHANCE...
JOHN...
COULD YOU STEP AWAY FROM ME?
EVANS, IT'S HITTING CHAS.
GO!
BROTHERS, SISTERS.
WE CRIED IN THE DARKNESS AND YOU ANSWERED OUR CALL.
EVERY SINGLE PERSON HERE...
EVERY SINGLE ONE OF YOU HAS COME, READY TO GIVE THEIR LIVES TO HELP US.

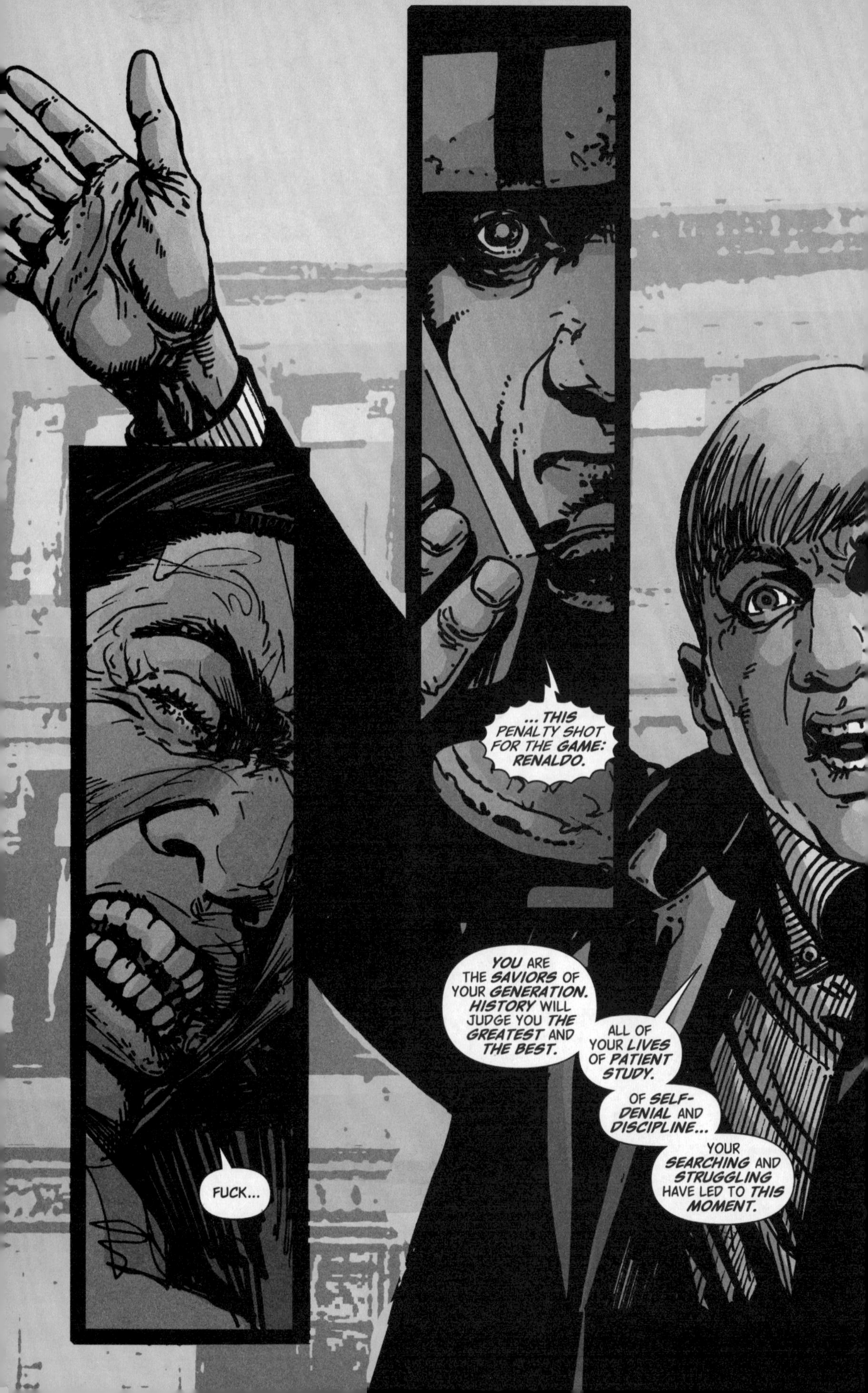
...THIS PENALTY SHOT FOR THE GAME: RENALDO.
YOU ARE THE SAVIORS OF YOUR GENERATION. HISTORY WILL JUDGE YOU THE GREATEST AND THE BEST.
ALL OF YOUR LIVES OF PATIENT STUDY.
OF SELF-DENIAL AND DISCIPLINE...
YOUR SEARCHING AND STRUGGLING HAVE LED TO THIS MOMENT.
FUCK...

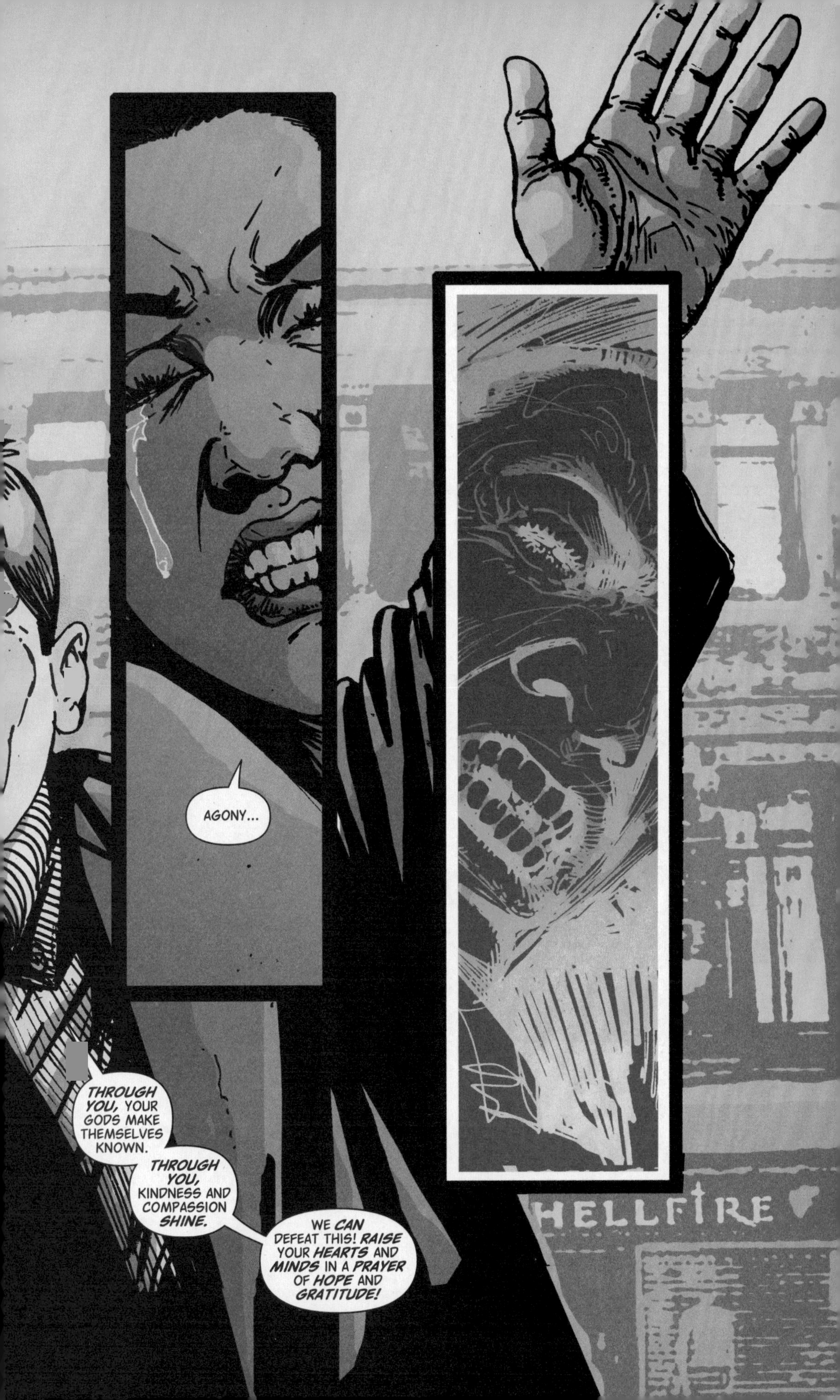
AGONY...
THROUGH YOU, YOUR GODS MAKE THEMSELVES KNOWN.
THROUGH YOU, KINDNESS AND COMPASSION SHINE.
WE CAN DEFEAT THIS! RAISE YOUR HEARTS AND MINDS IN A PRAYER OF HOPE AND GRATITUDE!
HELLFIRE

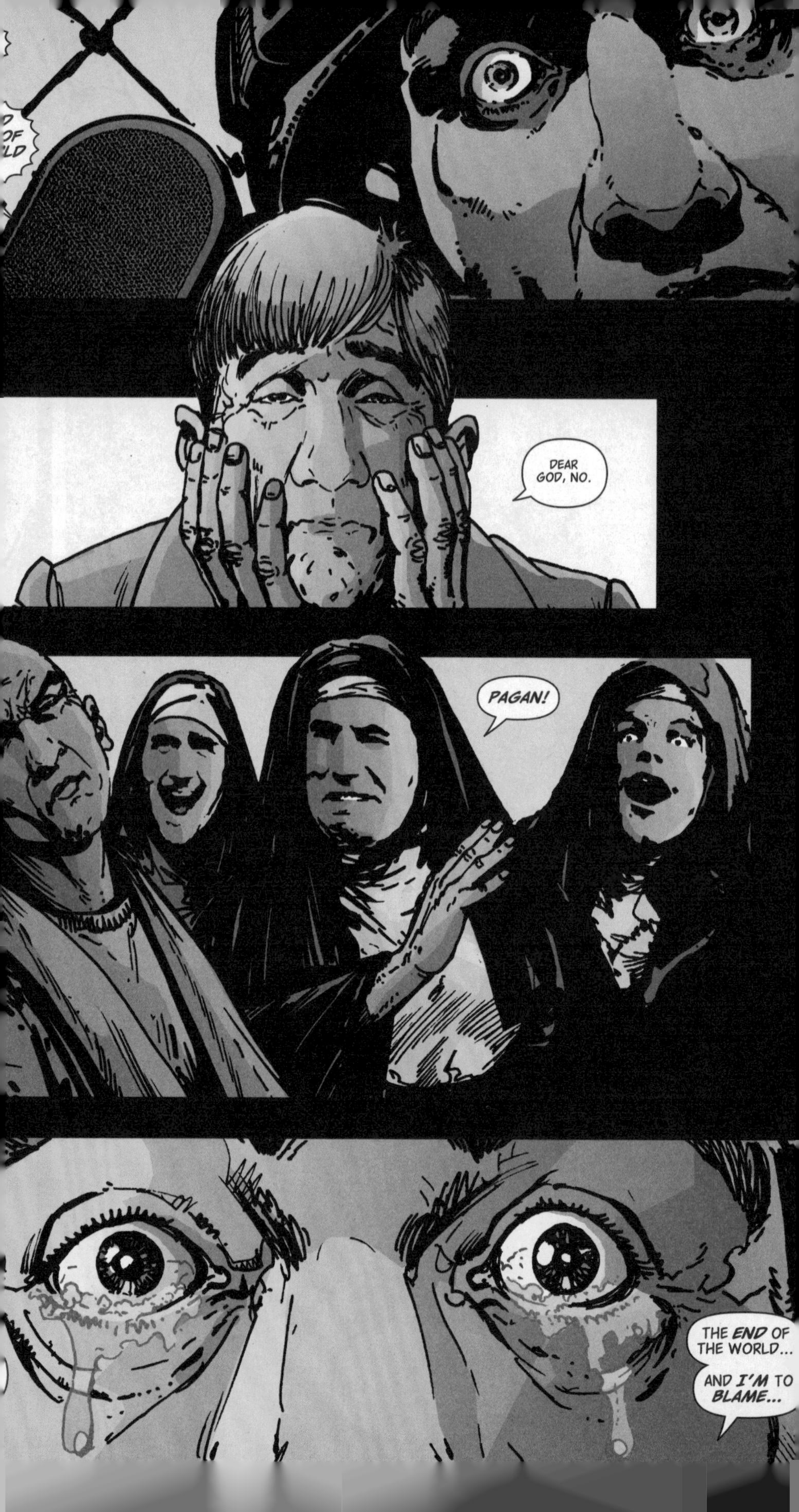
DEAR GOD, NO.
PAGAN!
THE *END* OF THE WORLD...
AND *I'M* TO *BLAME...*

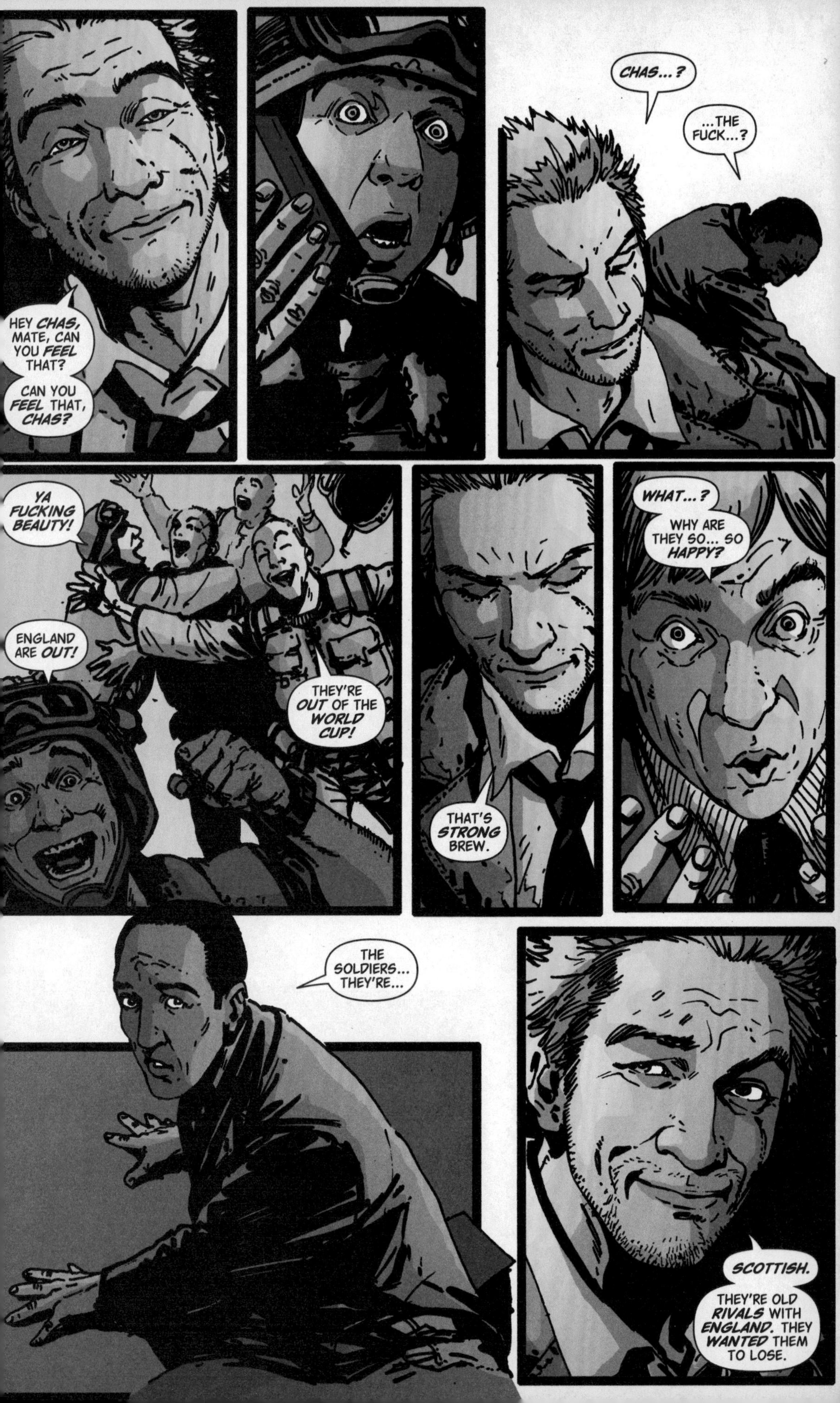
HEY CHAS, MATE, CAN YOU FEEL THAT?
CAN YOU FEEL THAT, CHAS?
CHAS...?
...THE FUCK...?
YA FUCKING BEAUTY!
ENGLAND ARE OUT!
THEY'RE OUT OF THE WORLD CUP!
THAT'S STRONG BREW.
WHAT...?
WHY ARE THEY SO... SO HAPPY?
THE SOLDIERS... THEY'RE...
SCOTTISH.
THEY'RE OLD RIVALS WITH ENGLAND. THEY WANTED THEM TO LOSE.

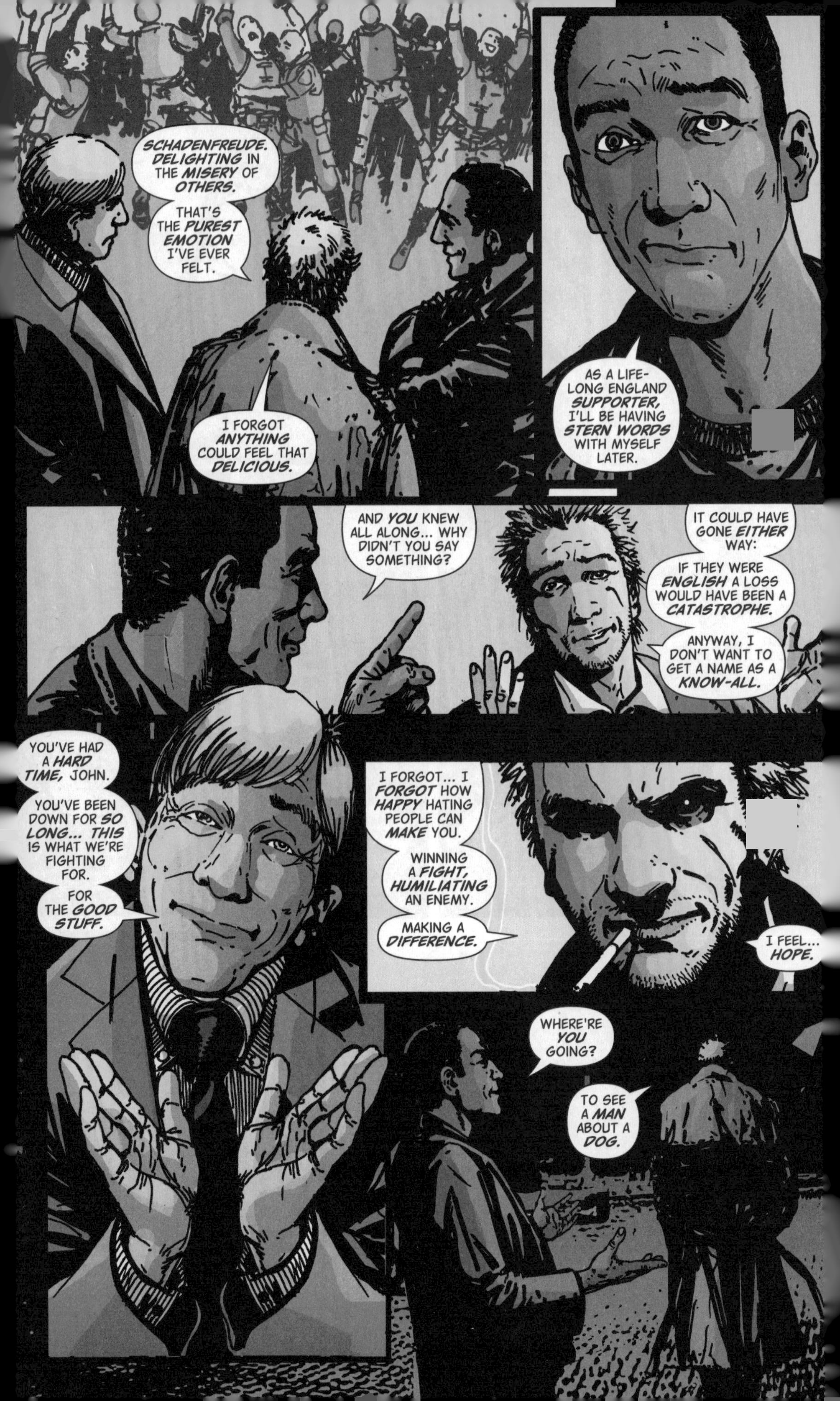

SCHADENFREUDE. DELIGHTING IN THE MISERY OF OTHERS.
THAT'S THE PUREST EMOTION I'VE EVER FELT.
I FORGOT ANYTHING COULD FEEL THAT DELICIOUS.
AS A LIFE-LONG ENGLAND SUPPORTER, I'LL BE HAVING STERN WORDS WITH MYSELF LATER.
AND YOU KNEW ALL ALONG... WHY DIDN'T YOU SAY SOMETHING?
IT COULD HAVE GONE EITHER WAY:
IF THEY WERE ENGLISH A LOSS WOULD HAVE BEEN A CATASTROPHE.
ANYWAY, I DON'T WANT TO GET A NAME AS A KNOW-ALL.
YOU'VE HAD A HARD TIME, JOHN.
YOU'VE BEEN DOWN FOR SO LONG... THIS IS WHAT WE'RE FIGHTING FOR.
FOR THE GOOD STUFF.
I FORGOT... I FORGOT HOW HAPPY HATING PEOPLE CAN MAKE YOU.
WINNING A FIGHT, HUMILIATING AN ENEMY.
MAKING A DIFFERENCE.
I FEEL... HOPE.
WHERE'RE YOU GOING?
TO SEE A MAN ABOUT A DOG.

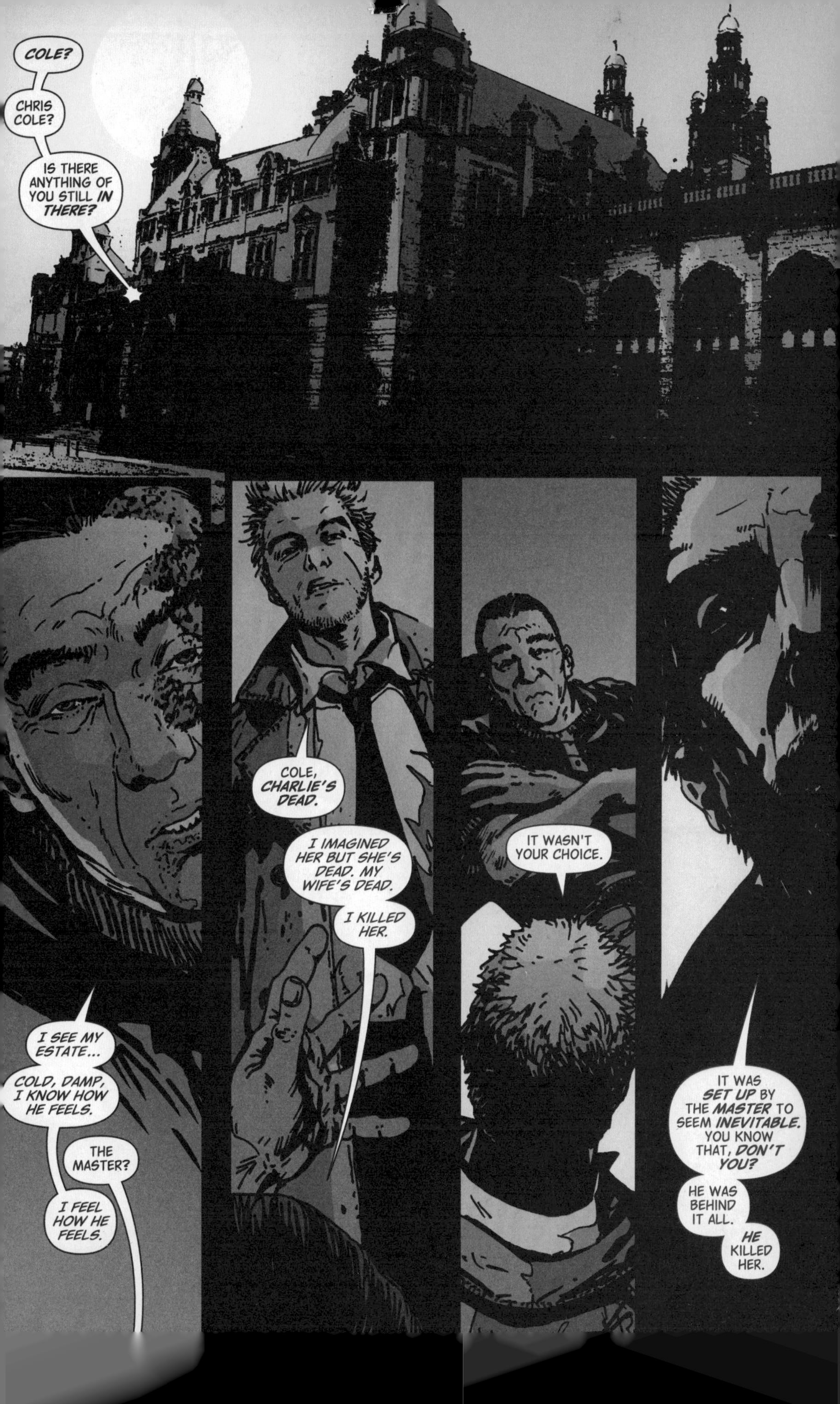
COLE?
CHRIS COLE?
IS THERE ANYTHING OF YOU STILL IN THERE?
I SEE MY ESTATE...
COLD, DAMP, I KNOW HOW HE FEELS.
THE MASTER?
I FEEL HOW HE FEELS.
COLE, CHARLIE'S DEAD.
I IMAGINED HER BUT SHE'S DEAD. MY WIFE'S DEAD.
I KILLED HER.
IT WASN'T YOUR CHOICE.
IT WAS SET UP BY THE MASTER TO SEEM INEVITABLE. YOU KNOW THAT, DON'T YOU?
HE WAS BEHIND IT ALL.
HE KILLED HER.

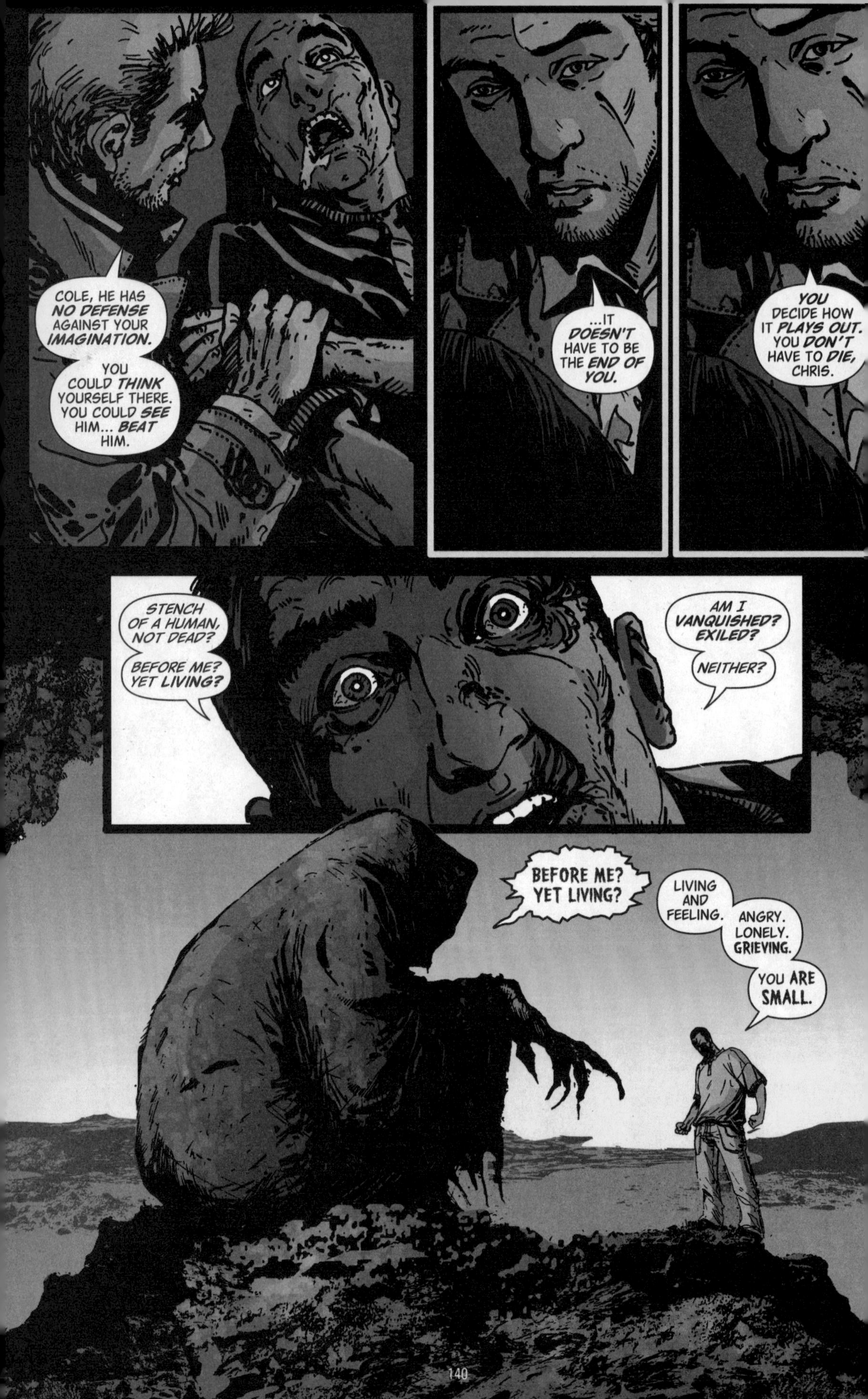
COLE, HE HAS NO DEFENSE AGAINST YOUR IMAGINATION.
YOU COULD THINK YOURSELF THERE. YOU COULD SEE HIM... BEAT HIM.
...IT DOESN'T HAVE TO BE THE END OF YOU.
YOU DECIDE HOW IT PLAYS OUT. YOU DON'T HAVE TO DIE, CHRIS.
STENCH OF A HUMAN, NOT DEAD?
BEFORE ME? YET LIVING?
AM I VANQUISHED? EXILED?
NEITHER?
BEFORE ME? YET LIVING?
LIVING AND FEELING.
ANGRY. LONELY. GRIEVING.
YOU ARE SMALL.

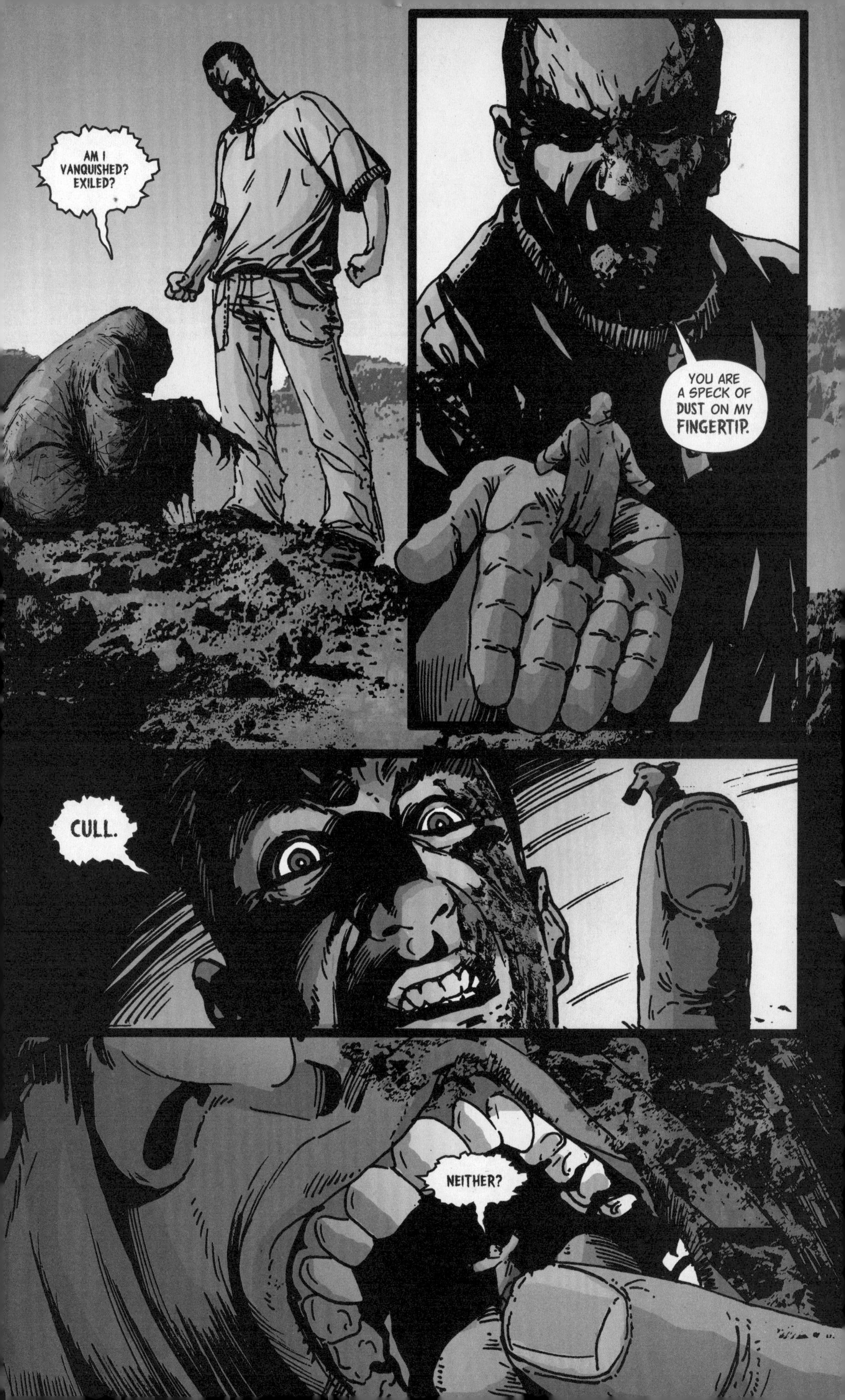
AM I VANQUISHED? EXILED?
YOU ARE A SPECK OF DUST ON MY FINGERTIP.
CULL.
NEITHER?

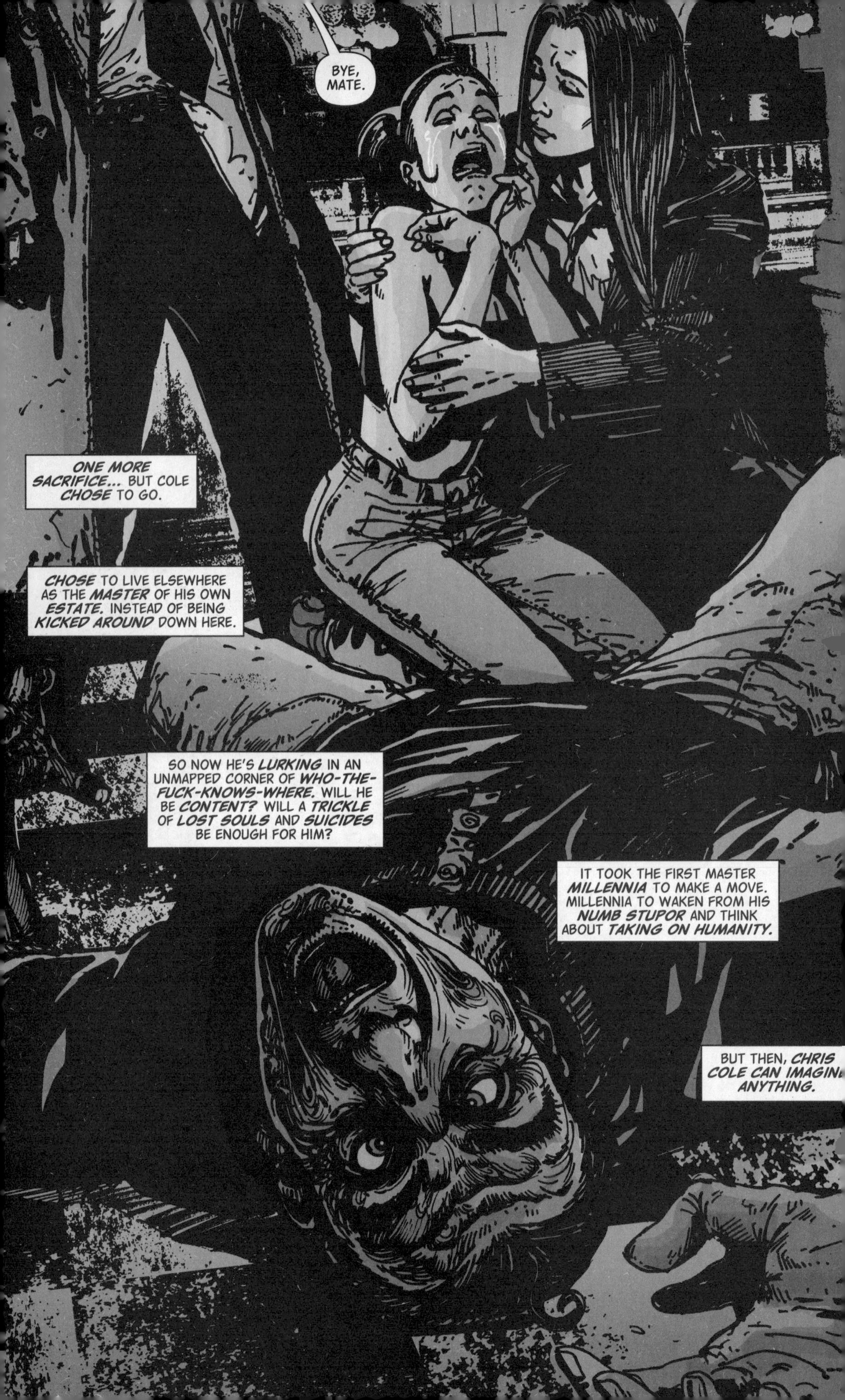
BYE, MATE.
ONE MORE SACRIFICE... BUT COLE *CHOSE* TO GO.
CHOSE TO LIVE ELSEWHERE AS THE *MASTER* OF HIS OWN *ESTATE*. INSTEAD OF BEING *KICKED AROUND* DOWN HERE.
SO NOW HE'S *LURKING* IN AN UNMAPPED CORNER OF *WHO-THE-FUCK-KNOWS-WHERE*. WILL HE BE *CONTENT?* WILL A *TRICKLE* OF *LOST SOULS* AND *SUICIDES* BE ENOUGH FOR HIM?
IT TOOK THE FIRST MASTER *MILLENNIA* TO MAKE A MOVE. MILLENNIA TO WAKEN FROM HIS *NUMB STUPOR* AND THINK ABOUT *TAKING ON HUMANITY*.
BUT THEN, *CHRIS COLE CAN IMAGINE ANYTHING.*

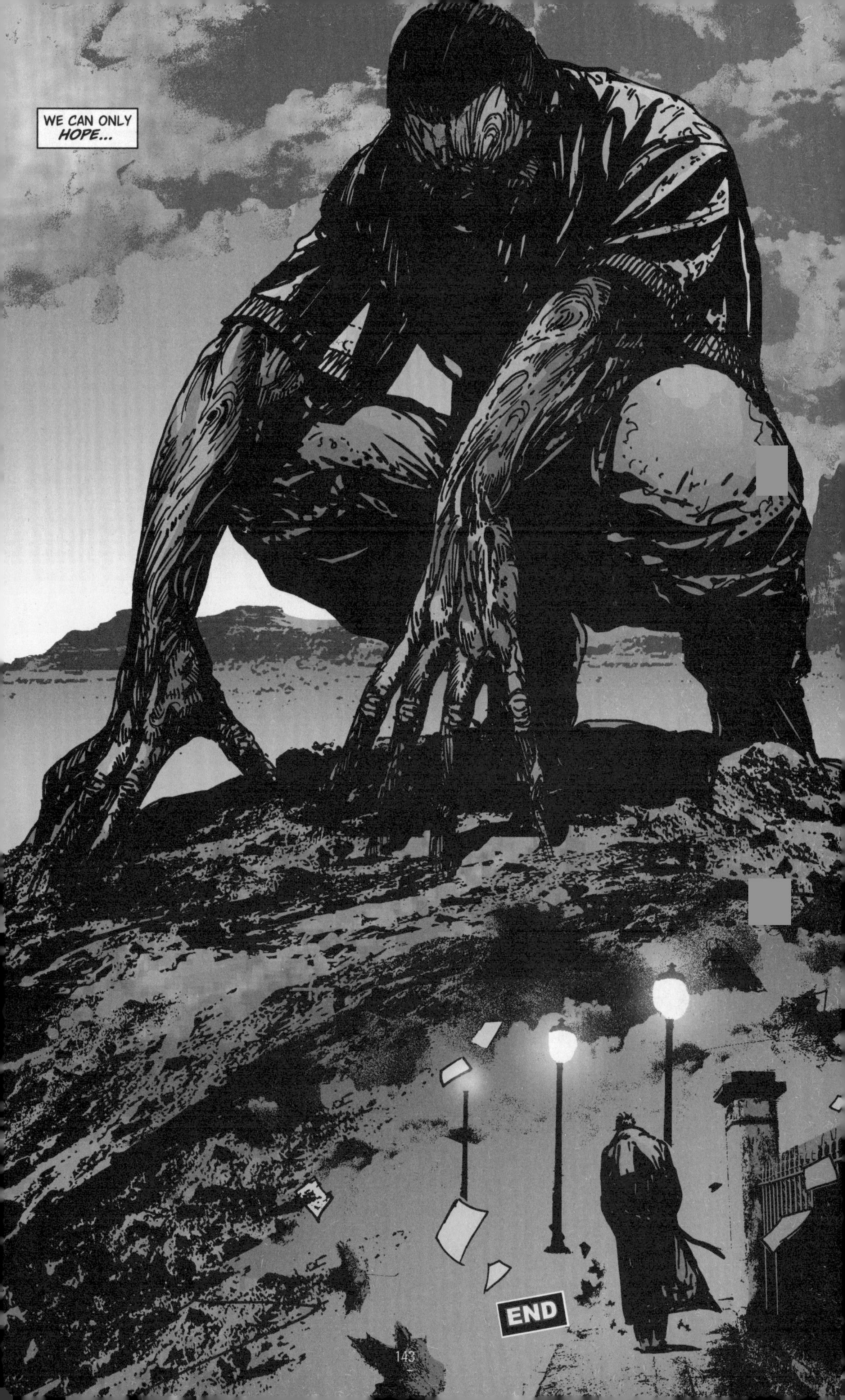
WE CAN ONLY HOPE...
END